Colección Támesis

SERIE A: MONOGRAFÍAS, 211

JUAN GOYTISOLO

THE AUTHOR AS DISSIDENT

Juan Goytisolo is one of the most prolific, controversial and engaging Spanish writers of the twentieth century.

Under the themes of authorship and dissidence, this book integrates his writing across several genres, providing a rounded assessment of his contribution to cultural debates in Spain since the sixties and arguing that resistance to repressive discourses characterizes his essays and autobiographies as much as his fiction.

It also revises the predominant critical interpretation of Goytisolo's fiction by building on four premises: that his novels are less clearly oppositional than prevailing interpretations imply; that, in order to engage with discourses of identity, he employs an idiom which, contrary to his own statements, is not a poststructuralist autonomous world of words; that a textual practice grounded in the recognizable experience of post-Civil War Spain, rather than one which seeks out the realm of pure textuality, is essential to Goytisolo's subversive political intentions; and that the autobiographical element of much of his work constitutes a more complex narrative aesthetic than has been appreciated.

The book argues that if Goytisolo's work is interpreted as an ethical engagement with postmodernist theory, rather than as an illustration of it, then certain contradictions for which he has been criticized are seen in a new and valuable light.

ALISON RIBEIRO DE MENEZES lectures in Spanish at University College Dublin.

JUAN GOYTISOLO

THE AUTHOR AS DISSIDENT

Alison Ribeiro de Menezes

TAMESIS

First published 2005 by Tamesis, Woodbridge

ISBN 1 85566 109 8

Tamesis is an imprint of Boydell & Brewer Ltd
PO Box 9, Woodbridge, Suffolk IP12 3DF, UK
and of Boydell & Brewer Inc.
668 Mt Hope Avenue, Rochester, NY 14620, USA
website: www.boydellandbrewer.com

A CIP catalogue record for this book is available
from the British Library

Library of Congress Cataloging-in-Publication Data
Ribeiro de Menezes, Alison, 1969–
    Juan Goytisolo : the author as dissident / Alison Ribeiro de Menezes.
      p. cm. – (Colección Támesis. Serie A, Monografías ; 211)
Includes bibliographical references and index.
    ISBN 1–85566–109–8 (hardback : alk. paper)
1. Goytisolo, Juan – Criticism and interpretation. I. Title.
PQ6513.O79Z838 2005
863'.64–dc22   2004022369

This publication is printed on acid-free paper

Typeset by Pru Harrison, Hacheston, Suffolk
Printed and bound in Great Britain by
Athenaeum Press Ltd., Gateshead, Tyne & Wear

CONTENTS

ACKNOWLEDGEMENTS

No book, as the case of Juan Goytisolo ably demonstrates, is ever written in isolation, and this one is no exception. Numerous people have helped and encouraged me in my research. Although this study is not a rewriting of my doctoral thesis, it does arise out of that original work, and I am grateful to my supervisors at Oxford, Robin Fiddian and Colin Thompson, for early and ongoing support. I should also like to thank Eric Southworth and Jo Labanyi, my examiners, for helpful comments so long ago, and Betty Rutson, my college tutor, for her unfailing encouragement over many years.

In University College Dublin, I owe a debt of gratitude to my colleagues in the Department of Spanish, who facilitated me with two periods of research leave to prepare the manuscript, and I am especially grateful to Don Cruickshank for his ever-enthusiastic interest in my work. I would also like thank UCD for authorizing that research leave, for awarding me a grant to visit the Goytisolo Archive in Boston University, and for providing a generous financial contribution to support the book's publication. The National University of Ireland likewise assisted with a publications grant, for which I am grateful. I am endebted to the Spanish Ministerio de Educación y Ciencia, and to the Spanish Embassy in Dublin, for a bursary to spend time at the Biblioteca Nacional in Madrid in June–July 2001. In the field of Goytisolo studies, I would like to thank Stanley Black and Stuart Davis for providing me with copies of their work, and the staff of Boston University Library and the Biblioteca de la Diputación Provincial de Almería for faciliting my research there. Material in chapters 6 and 7 previously appeared in the *Journal of Iberian and Latin American Studies*, 4 (1998), 109–19, and *Romance Studies*, 21 (2002), 105–14, and I am grateful to the editors for permission to reproduce it.

On a personal note, I should like to thank Catriona Clutterbuck, Charo Hernández, Kirstin Kennedy, and Catherine O'Leary for their friendship, advice, and encouragement. Finally, I owe the greatest debt of gratitude to my parents, for their unstinting support and example down the years, and to my husband, Filipe, for his cheery forbearance and enthusiastic encouragement. The book is dedicated to him and to our son, David, whose arrival interrupted its completion, but whose boundless energy and delightful antics provide the perfect antidote to work.

Dublin, June 2004

To
Filipe and David

The author and publishers are grateful to
University College Dublin and the National University of Ireland
for assistance with the production costs of this book.

The author is immensely grateful to Juan Goytisolo for
permission to cite from the following works:

Cogitus interruptus; © Juan Goytisolo, 1999
*Carajicomedia de Fray Bugeo Montesino y otros pájaros
de vario plumaje y pluma*; © Juan Goytisolo, 2000
Telón de boca; © Juan Goytisolo, 2003
Furgón de cola; © Juan Goytisolo, 1967
Obra inglesa de José María Blanco White; © Juan Goytisolo, 1973
Paisajes después de la batalla; © Juan Goytisolo, 1982
Reivindicación del Conde don Julián; © Juan Goytisolo, 1970
Coto vedado; © Juan Goytisolo, 1985
En los reinos de Taifa; © Juan Goytisolo, 1986
Señas de identidad; © Juan Goytisolo, 1966
Crónicas Sarracinas; © Juan Goytisolo, 1981
Las virtudes del pájaro solitario; © Juan Goytisolo, 1988
Aproximaciones a Gaudí en Capadocia; © Juan Goytisolo, 1990
La cuarentena; © Juan Goytisolo, 1991
Disidencias; © Juan Goytisolo, 1977
Cuaderno de Sarajevo; © Juan Goytisolo, 1993
La saga de los Marx; © Juan Goytisolo, 1993
Juan sin Tierra; © Juan Goytisolo, 1975
El sitio de los sitios; © Juan Goytisolo, 1995
Makbara; © Juan Goytisolo, 1979
Las semanas del jardín; © Juan Goytisolo, 1997

INTRODUCTION
AUTHORSHIP AND DISSIDENCE

*Com a mão firme [o revisor] segura a esferográfica e acrescenta
uma palavra à página, uma palavra que o historiador não
poderia ter escrito nunca, a palavra Não, agora o que o
livro passou a dizer é que os cruzados Não auxiliarão
os portugueses a conquistar Lisboa, assim está
escrito e portanto passou a ser verdade.*
José Saramago[1]

The humble proof-reader in José Saramago's *História do cerco de Lisboa*,
who inserts a negative in a text where the author had intended none, thus
changing retrospectively the course of historical events, raises some of the
most pressing questions preoccupying contemporary novelists: the issues of
truth and relativity, the possibility and implications of multiple authoring, and
the potency of authorship as narrative authority. Impersonalizing authorship,
by turning it into a process involving one or more agents and various stages,
does not, however, remove textual author-ity. As Cervantes magnificently
demonstrated in *Don Quixote* five centuries ago, it can also, paradoxically,
reinforce that which it seeks to obscure. The sovereign subject – the Cartesian
cogito – may have been pronounced dead by mid-twentieth-century literary
theory, but it would be premature to assume from this the demise of the
closely related concept of authorship – all the more so since we are currently
witnessing a 'return' or 'rebirth' of subjectivity, albeit in radically modified
form. Indeed, one of the consequences of recent radical interrogations of the
subject has been to decentre the notion of a unified and sovereign self in
favour of multiple subjectivities writing from a plurality of perspectives.
What has accompanied these changing views of the subject is a reconfigura-
tion of authorship, and not for the first time in the history of Western letters.

An author is conventionally agreed to be the originator, creator, or primary
source of something (*auctor*), whether text, act, or event; he or she bears
responsibility for and carries authority over his or her creation (*auctoritas*).
The origin of the word thus bears the traces of two fundamental ideas: genesis
and control. Yet, the relationship between these is not necessarily simple or

---

1   José Saramago, *História do cerco de Lisboa* (Lisboa: Caminho, 1989), p. 50.

direct. To the medieval mind, the human author derived his creativity and authority from God, and worked within the field of a complex critical apparatus that allowed for the interplay of multiple determinants in Scriptural exegesis. Authorship was, in this view, essentially public and collaborative, not private and individual. The medieval author is 'a privileged reader [. . .] an elect who inspirationally mimes the Divine discourse'.[2] With the onset of the Renaissance, such a view becomes problematic in at least two aspects. First, despite an evident celebration of genius, evident in such works as Vasari's *The Lives of the Artists*, which might be said to prefigure the much later shift to a Romantic eulogizing of individual consciousness, the Renaissance author retained a strong sense of tradition in the form of the theory of *imitatio*. Artistic originality was seen in terms of both an anxious desire to live up to the example of past masters and a confident belief in the capacities of the intellectuals of the present. As Thomas Greene notes, imitation 'assigned the Renaissance creator a convenient and flexible stance towards a past that threatened to overwhelm him'.[3] This past was, of course, the classical era, since the Renaissance conceived of itself in terms of a rebirth that relied upon the myth of a prior medieval death from which a sense of self-confident progress could be measured. Imitation as artistic practice was thus inherently connected with the question of identity, as Terence Cave argues: 'Rewriting [in the Renaissance] betrays its own anxiety by personifying itself as the product of an author; it imprints on itself – one might even say *forges* – an identity.'[4]

A second shift of emphasis in the Renaissance involved the problematization of reading as interpretation. If the medieval author had, through a series of complex heuristic procedures, securely interpreted the world as God's book, then the Renaissance author confronted the question of multiple meanings configured as a fissure between the text and its potential meanings. Erasmus' preoccupation with the notion of the *sensus germanus* of a text, for example, reflected his awareness of the need in biblical interpretation both for a categorical reading and the theoretical impossibility of achieving such a reading. So, according to Cave (p. 9), 'the voice which seeks to erase the arbitrary proliferation of readings (allegories, glosses) by the singularity of its enunciation cannot but assert its own freedom from formal constraints.' The notion of the isolated individual, whimsically directing his creation – until the middle of the twentieth century, the dominant conception

---

[2] Seán Burke, 'Reconstructing the Author', in *Authorship From Plato to the Postmodern: A Reader* (Edinburgh: Edinburgh University Press, 1995), pp. xv–xxx (pp. xxi–xxii).

[3] Thomas Greene, *The Light in Troy: Imitation and Discovery in Renaissance Poetry* (New Haven: Yale University Press, 1982), p. 2.

[4] Terence Cave, *The Cornucopian Text: Problems of Writing in the French Renaissance* (Oxford: Clarendon Press, 1979), p. 77.

of authorship – is thus of relatively recent origin, even if its source may lie with the Kantian transcendental ego. The Kantian revolution sees the author as shaping the world through *a priori* categories of space, time, and causality.[5] The author, previously an agent of God, became implicated in the act of creation itself. And the world, previously God's book (however problematic that concept may have become by the Renaissance) became man's book, a metaphor for life. Genesis and direction, creativity and control, thus became the exclusive preserve of the author.

It is the notion of the transcendental ego that contemporary theory, with its objection to totalization, universalization, and synthesis, has most vociferously rejected. If, in the words of Seán Burke, 'the war on totalities must be a war waged on the transcendental/impersonal subject through whose putative construction totalities emerge',[6] then it would seem that contemporary rejection of authorship may be dependent upon a vision of the author as all-controlling ego, presiding over his fiction in a god-like manner. From this perspective, the rejection of authorship becomes a rejection of authority, orthodoxy, and universally imposed values. Nevertheless, the libertarian impulse that lies behind such a move comes into conflict with the lack of accepted standards and values that a pendulum swing to the opposite pole necessarily involves. The postmodernist rebuttal of humanism in the name of freedom thus becomes problematic. On the one hand, the desire for freedom becomes an overarching value to replace whatever is previously rejected; on the other, absolute relativity denies the possibility of action driven by political imperative.

Charles Taylor expresses this difficulty as moral impoverishment, proposing that ethical frameworks are unavoidable for a rich and fulfilling sense of self. 'Living within [. . .] strongly qualified horizons is constitutive of human agency,' he argues, while 'stepping outside these limits would be tantamount to stepping outside what we would recognize as integral, that is, undamaged human personhood.'[7] Taylor's emphasis on the need for recognition of the Good as a basis for ordinary life would be refuted by the postmodern, or neo-Nietzschean, thinkers who he criticizes in his study. They, however, fall into a trap of their own making, as he here explains:

> The point of view from which we might constate that all orders are equally arbitrary, in particular that all moral views are equally so, is just not available to us humans. It is a form of self-delusion to think that we do not speak from a moral orientation which we take to be right. [. . .] Oddly enough – or ironically – the neo-Nietzschean theory is open to the same kind of

---

5 Brian Morris, *Western Conceptions of the Individual* (Oxford: Berg, 1991), p. 49.
6 'Reconstructing the Author', p. xxix.
7 Charles Taylor, *Sources of the Self: The Making of the Modern Identity* (Cambridge: Cambridge University Press, 1989), p. 27.

criticism as that which we both, it and I, level against mainstream moral philosophy: that of not coming clean about its own moral motivations. Only here the problem is not that it denies having any [. . .], but that it accords them a false status. It claims a kind of distance from its own value commitments, which consists in the fact that it alone is lucid about their status as fruits of a constructed order, which lucidity sets it apart from other views and confers the advantage on itself of being free from delusion in a way that others aren't. (pp. 99–100)

The consequence, in Taylor's view, would seem to be a need to confess both our moral motivations and our need for them to exist – in short, to admit to needing and using shared moral frameworks in our daily lives. It is this dilemma that Juan Goytisolo's work, in its treatment of the tricky relationship between authorship and dissidence, illustrates comprehensively.

It might seem paradoxical, in our postmodern era, to suggest that Juan Goytisolo, as author and dissident, is the central focus of his extensive *obra*, yet the constant overlaps and the persistent interest in a small number of central themes, all of which relate to the articulation of marginality, in opposition to canonicity and orthodoxy, reveal the extent to which his literary project, despite its apparent emphasis on such issues as diversity, pluralism, and linguistic ambiguity, is in fact a unified one. Moreover, the self-conscious blurring of generic boundaries – between autobiography and fiction, criticism and fabulation – has the effect of both deflecting critical interest from Goytisolo and flamboyantly fomenting precisely that. His oft-stated rejection of canonical status, in the form of personal research institutes, statues, and so on,[8] is thus subverted by his own insistent presence within his texts, which constitute a literary monument to their creator, and by his ubiquitous presence on university syllabi, a point comprehensively demonstrated recently by Stuart Davis.[9] I do not want to suggest here that Goytisolo is represented directly by particular personages in each and every piece of writing, but it remains a fact that certain strategies seemingly intended to break his texts free from authorial intention are counterbalanced by other, intertextual practices which tantalizingly relate those texts to their flesh-and-blood author's openly expressed socio-political and ideological preoccupations. The tension in this pull between authorial responsibility and its abnegation is the focus of the present study.

This book is divided into four parts, although these should not be viewed as corresponding to rigidly defined phases in Goytisolo's writing. Rather, they are intended as complementary explorations of the themes of authorship

[8]   Most recently, in interview with Javier Valenzuela, 'La belleza del mundo es más duradera que el dolor humano', *El País*, 15 February 2003, Goytisolo commented: 'homenajes y fundaciones no tienen el menor sentido. No creo en nada de esto.'
[9]   Stuart Davis, 'Juan Goytisolo and the Institution of the Hispanic Canon', unpublished doctoral dissertation, University of Birmingham, 2003.

and dissidence across a career that spans five decades. Part One begins with a consideration of Goytisolo's autobiographies as an expression of a dissident identity, and then demonstrates how similar concerns shape his large body of literary criticism. Part Two addresses issues of identity and alterity in four key novels, which are often taken to form a reasonably homogeneous body of writing from the 1960s to the 1980s, though to fence them off entirely from the author's other works would be arbitrary, as their recurrence in discussions of later novels in this book shows. The truly overlapping nature of Goytisolo's work is brought home in Part Three, where a series of novels that seem to move in contrary directions – resorting to parody, a play with voyeurism, and an interest in mysticism – in fact coalesce around the author's preoccupation with articulating marginality and solidarity in a postmodern epoch. Finally, Part Four highlights the increasingly introverted nature of Goytisolo's late writing, which spirals back to reconsider key aspects of earlier works with the benefit of hindsight. The circular and reiterative nature of his work is thus witnessed by the very novels which, Goytisolo himself has suggested, represent the sunset of his fictional career. Whether or not this turns out to be the case, the present study is intended, first, as a comprehensive view of authorship and dissidence in the work of one of the most important Spanish intellectuals of the contemporary era, and, second, a contribution to the debate that the human orientation of the work of Charles Taylor has opened up in theoretical circles.

PART I

THE DISSIDENT VOICE

1

AUTHORING THE SELF:
COTO VEDADO AND *EN LOS REINOS DE TAIFA*

> *We have passed from a pleasure to be recounted*
> *and heard, centring on the heroic or marvellous*
> *narration of 'trials' of bravery or sainthood,*
> *to a literature ordered according to the infinite task*
> *of extracting from the depths of oneself, in between*
> *the words, a truth which the very form of the*
> *confession holds out like a shimmering mirage.*
> Michel Foucault[1]

Theories of Autobiography

If, for twentieth-century writers, the question of authorship and its relationship to the authority of a 'writing subject' has posed considerable problems, then writing the life of the self – encapsulated perfectly, if in reverse order, in the very term auto-bio-graphy – makes these issues even more acute. The practice of autobiography necessarily confers on the autobiographical text an implied truth value upon which the weight of contemporary theory since existentialism and structuralism has cast considerable doubt. Unmoored from the Cartesian certainties of consciousness, contemporary autobiography stages an interplay between facts and imaginative creativity, replacing the original 'confessional' status of autobiographical discourse – the revelation of some personal truth to a judging listener – with a process less of self-revelation than of self-creation.[2] Following the pattern of art since modern-

---

1 *History of Sexuality: The Will to Knowledge*, trans. Robert Hurley (Harmondsworth: Penguin, 1990), p. 59.
2 The link between autobiographical writing and confession was forged, famously, by St Augustine and then Rousseau. Both, in their different ways, required some element of truth in their practice of self-revelation – Augustine's was a confession directed to God and made in the name of grace, which left no space for self-deception; Rousseau's was shaped as a cult of truthfulness directed at his fellow man. For a discussion of each, see Karl Joachim Weintraub, *The Value of the Individual: Self and Circumstance in Autobiography* (Chicago: University of Chicago Press, 1978), chapters 2 and 12 respectively. Georges Gusdorf details the appearance of the term 'autobiography' in or around 1800 – interestingly, the date that Foucault accords to the birth of the subject. On this, and for a useful survey of pre-structuralist notions of autobiography, see Manuela Ledesma Pedraz,

ism, a movement that sought to turn the medium in on itself in order to examine its own premises, twentieth-century autobiography tends to focus on the *act* of writing, and shapes the past 'by memory and imagination to serve the needs of the present consciousness'.[3] Fiction is thus not necessarily a threat to the contemporary autobiographical project, but an inherent part of its creation.

For post-structuralist theory, the self is a fleeting, contingent, situated construct of language, a view that leaves autobiography as either impossible, or only provisionally possible insofar as it accepts and exploits this. Paul de Man, for example, starting from the structuralist rejection of a coherent subject, views autobiography's aspiration to knowledge as an illusion generated by the rhetorical structure of language. The 'confessional' gesture, the postulation of some truth about the self, is to his mind impossible. The self, rather than being the cause of language, is its effect.[4]

Nevertheless, this is not the only possible approach to the autobiographical dilemma, as the pervasiveness of the genre, despite post-structuralist theoretical pessimism, demonstrates. Unlike fiction, autobiography does not have at its disposal the option of a hermetically sealed text, devoid of connection with an external reality – if such a thing can even be said to exist. It *must* move beyond itself, in a gesture of representation, to posit some knowledge of the world and of the self.[5] As a genre, therefore, it strikes right to the heart of such questions as selfhood and identity, and their expression, inscription, or creation within discourse.[6] In a sense, autobiography marks an especially urgent point of connection between life and literature and, as such, should not be rejected as an impossibility. On the contrary, it serves to highlight the complex nature of the dialogue between these two. For James Olney, autobiography is a metaphorical discourse that draws attention to the process by which man gives shape to his life; it is a 'monument to the self at the summary moment of composition'.[7] For Paul John Eakin, this metaphorical

---

'Cuestiones preliminares sobre el género autobiográfico y presentación', in her *Escritura autobiográfica y géneros literarios* (Jaén: Universidad de Jaén, 1999), pp. 9–20.

[3] Paul John Eakin, *Fictions in Autobiography: Studies in the Art of Self-Invention* (Princeton: Princeton University Press, 1985), p. 5.

[4] Paul de Man, 'Autobiography as Defacement', in *The Rhetoric of Romanticism* (New York: Columbia University Press, 1984), pp. 67–81.

[5] In this regard, James Olney argues, in *Metaphors of Self: The Meaning of Autobiography* (Princeton: Princeton University Press, 1972), that 'it is the great virtue of autobiography [. . .] to offer us an understanding that is finally not of someone else but of ourselves' (p. x).

[6] Both Kristeva's notion of the writing subject as constructed through an *interaction* between language and world, in *Revolution in Poetic Language*, trans. Margaret Waller (New York: Columbia University Press, 1984), and Foucault's reintroduction of subjectivity in *The History of Sexuality: The Care of Self*, trans. Robert Hurley (Harmondsworth: Penguin, 1990), move beyond de Man's nihilism. The return of the subject – or of subjectivity – in contemporary literary theory might prove to be autobiography's redemption.

[7] Olney, p. 35.

basis is cause for celebration rather than alarm: 'If [autobiography as a] meta-phor of self can be said finally to be only a metaphor,' he asks, 'should we then cast off autobiography as an exercise in self-deception?' He proposes, instead, to see it as 'a symbolic analogue of the initial coming together of the individual and language that marks the origin of self-awareness'.[8] The dead-end idea of language as a 'prison-house'[9] of the self is thus rejected in favour of the affirmation that autobiography is a privileged moment in the construc-tion not of self, but of self-awareness. This does not mean that problems of truthfulness, of the reliability of memory, and of authorial distortion – whether intentional or not – are set aside; on the contrary, they are refracted through a writing process which, seemingly yearning for some sense of fixity of self in the autobiographical text, nevertheless accepts that it is part of the drama of self-invention. 'Even through no one can ever confirm the existence of the self as an ultimate fact,' Eakin writes, 'autobiographies attest by their very existence to the reality of the autobiographical imperative.' Alluding to the strange attractiveness of autobiography, despite the objections made by contemporary theory, he concludes, 'readers in their turn reciprocate, for it is hard to undo the art of self-invention once it has been ably performed, hard to unhear the voice of presence in the text.'[10]

Authoring a Dissident Perspective

Juan Goytisolo's autobiographies illustrate well the drama of self-invention central to contemporary writing in the genre.[11] Although self-conscious and fragmented, they remain clearly identifiable as a narrative of

---

8   Eakin, pp. 191 and 213 respectively.

9   The phrase is, of course, Fredric Jameson's, from *The Prison-House of Language: A Critical Account of Structuralism and Russian Formalism* (Princeton: Princeton Univer-sity Press, 1972).

10   Eakin, p. 277. In echo of Burke's protests in *The Death and Return of the Author* that contemporary theory has parted company with literary reality, Eakin notes that (post-)structuralist objections to selfhood and the possibility of autobiography as a genre have not prevented authors from producing autobiographies (p. 26): 'The impulse to take the fiction of the self and its acts as facts persists, a more than willing suspension of disbe-lief in which the behaviour of writer and reader refuses to coincide with theory.' Likewise, Ledesma Pedraz hints at some possible sources for the current fever for autobiography, all ironically conflicting with prevailing theoretical tendencies: a predominant individualism resulting from the questioning of grand narratives and/or the impotence of the individual in the face of contemporary life, the curiosity of the reader about the life of someone written by themselves, and the desire for introspection aroused by psychoanalysis. It may be that autobiography and, indeed, biography, which is also popular at present, offer a defence of the personal and individual in the face of globalization and universalism.

11   It seems almost *de rigueur* to question the validity of Goytisolo's autobiographies as life-writing. Sixto Plaza, 'Coto vedado, ¿autobiografía o novela?', in *Actas del IX Congreso de la Asociación Internacional de Hispanistas* (Frankfurt: Verlag, 1989), pp.

the emergence of Goytisolo as homosexual and his metaphorical rebirth as a politically, socially, and culturally subversive writer. Although, towards the end of *En los reinos de Taifa*, Goytisolo refers to his 'renacimiento a los treinta y cuatro años sin identidad precisa',[12] his emergence as a dissident writer is, in fact, enacted ambiguously in texts that pivot between a performative notion of identity and an essentialist one. On the one hand, they offer an awareness of the self as contingent and in flux; on the other, they seek to anchor this in an underlying coherence predicated upon a position of dissidence, a tension that belies the autobiographical dilemma that has faced many twentieth-century practitioners of the genre. Despite the apparent formal innovation of his texts, Goytisolo's motive for writing is a surprisingly traditional self-analysis and self-justification, arising not from the perspective of someone reflecting back at the end of a life lived, but someone reflecting from a place of achievement on how that point was reached. His texts do not imply closure, since their author, in his mid-sixties and at the peak of his literary career at the time of their writing, assumes that the battle enjoined in his fiction and recounted in his autobiographies will continue. There is little evidence that Goytisolo is engaged in a post-structuralist refutation of the very possibility of selfhood. On the contrary, the tension he establishes between an essentialist conception of the (homosexual) self and a constructivist view of an ethics of dissidence predicated upon the arrogation of the fragmentary voices of other writers reflects an existentialist *choice* of a life project to be performed through writing. Goytisolo will thus attempt to transform momentarily the contingency of existence into the book of his life, understood in two senses: the book is both the two-volume autobiography discussed in the present chapter, and the project of his *obra* as a whole, the focus of the present study.[13]

345–50; Gonzalo Navajas, 'Confession and Ethics in Juan Goytisolo's Fictive Autobiographies', *Letras Peninsulares*, 3 (1990), 259–78; and Cristina Moreiras-Menor, 'Ficción y autobiografía en Juan Goytisolo: algunos apuntes', *Anthropos*, 125 (1991), 71–6, all adopt this approach. However, like Brad Epps in his studies of Goytisolo – 'Thievish Subjectivity: Self-Writing in Jean Genet and Juan Goytisolo', *Revista de Estudios Hispánicos*, 26 (1992), 163–81; 'Estados de deseo: homosexualidad y nacionalidad (Juan Goytisolo y Reinaldo Arenas a vuelapluma)', *Revista Iberoamericana*, 62 (1996), 799–820; and *Significant Violence: Oppression and Resistance in the Narratives of Juan Goytisolo, 1970–1990* (Oxford: Clarendon Press, 1996) – I take it for granted that *Coto vedado* and *En los reinos de Taifa* are autobiographies. It is undoubtedly true that in his last works Goytisolo sought to blur the boundary between fiction and life, but this interplay depends in the first place on recognizable genre distinctions. Furthermore, both autobiographical volumes were initially presented to the reading public as just that – autobiographies. That their strength as examples of this genre derives from their play upon the problematics of narrative truth and memory that characterize twentieth-century autobiography does not mean that they should be classed as fiction.

   [12] *En los reinos de Taifa* (Barcelona: Seix Barral, 1986), p. 248.

   [13] Eakin (p. 129) emphasizes how Sartre, in *Les Mots*, regards literature as a means of transforming the contingency of existence into the permanence of a book. Sartre, however,

The writing of his autobiography is, for Goytisolo, a serious inquiry into the establishment of a dissident, homosexual identity. While he is aware of the pitfalls of the enterprise, his aim remains the structuring of a message – a particular narrative or metaphorical 'frame' that will painfully but beneficially enlighten his life – and its communication to a readership with whom he adopts a quasi-confessional relationship.[14] This structuring of the past as narrative provides the key to unlock the view of selfhood that Goytisolo offers in his autobiographies. We are presented with a two-part plot: first, recognition of having masked the true (homosexual, dissident) self and, therefore, lived inauthentically; and, second, realization of the authentic self through action and, more importantly, writing. Life, restructured with hindsight as narrative, will meet narrative fiction when Goytisolo declares at the close of *En los reinos de Taifa*, 'Don Julián *c'est moi*' (p. 309). This represents a trend towards an existentialist construction of self as an identity chosen on the basis of authenticity and action – the self is a possibility that must be created, even performed, through deliberate choice in the face of and against others in the world. Writing, which for Goytisolo is to be equated with subversive political action, will become the activity by which he gives meaning to his life as a dissident; that is to say, Goytisolo will consciously choose to write himself into a position of dissidence both through the metaphorical discourses that structure his autobiography and, as we shall see in the next chapter, through the construction of a canon of dissident writers whose voice he arrogates.

Although he employs flamboyantly self-conscious narrative techniques, dividing his texts into blocks of Roman and italic type which engage the reader in a debate about the difficulties of writing autobiography, and adopting a series of fluid voices represented by shifting pronouns, which seem to destabilize identity, Goytisolo's autobiographies contain a residual essentialism that derives from the adoption of dissidence as an authentic life project. Although Labanyi is correct to suggest that, by refracting the autobiographical self through a double intertextual reference to *Madame Bovary* and *Don Julián* in the comment, 'Don Julián *c'est moi*', Goytisolo denies the

---

rejects the 'before–after' structure of conventional autobiography by narrating a loss of conviction, whereas Goytisolo, as we shall see, recounts the acquisition of the ethical convictions that drive his mature writing. David Vilaseca makes this point in concluding, in 'Juan Goytisolo's Queer (Be)hindsight: Homosexuality, Epistemology, and the "Extimacy" of the Subject in *Coto vedado* and *En los reinos de Taifa*', *Modern Language Review*, 94 (1999), 426–37, that 'the crucial point is that "Goytisolo", as "outside" agency, still remains he who performatively constitutes "himself": he who [. . .] determines which history and which biographical necessity will, through hindsight, become his own (hence determining "him")' (p. 137).

14 This is evident in the epigraph to *Coto vedado* from René Chair: 'La lucidité est la blessure la plus rapprochée du soleil', *Coto vedado*, 8th edn (Barcelona: Seix Barral, 1985), p. 5.

possibility of the natural self upon which traditional autobiography is predicated,[15] the fact remains that dissidence itself – conceived of in the abstract
but realized through the arrogation of other voices and fragmented
subjectivities – gives a core meaning to Goytisolo's life and deeds. To this
point we shall return after considering, first, the self-conscious elements of
Goytisolo's autobiographies, and, second, the homosexual identity that they
seek to establish.

Constructivism versus Essentialism (1): The Form of Goytisolo's Autobiographies

The structure of *Coto vedado* visually demonstrates the desire to retell the
past within a self-reflexive discourse in a flamboyant effort to avoid the
inscription of an essentialist identity. In reality, however, it creates a productive tension that plays off a constructivist, or performative, notion of identity,
against an essentialist one. The volume contrasts sections of text in Roman
type, which seem to narrate Goytisolo's childhood and adolescence in the
traditional manner, with passages in italic type that reflect on the act of
writing an autobiography.[16] Attention in these latter sections is drawn to questions of the inaccuracy of memory, of the author's motivation for writing, of
his possible readership, and of the difficulties and moral advantages to be
attained by writing about a painful past.[17] Indeed, the tone of the italicized
sections is one of discursive instability, an eye constantly attending to the
theoretical problems of seeking an 'authentic' self. In this division, Goytisolo
marks textually what has been termed the 'enunciatory abyss' of autobiographical writing, namely the split in the 'subject' between the 'I' of the
present who shapes the autobiography and the 'I' of the past whose life is
(re-)created. Traditional autobiography has, according to Paul Smith, dealt

---

[15] Jo Labanyi, 'The Construction/Destruction of the Self in the Autobiographies of
Pablo Neruda and Juan Goytisolo', *Forum for Modern Language Studies*, 26 (1990),
212–21 (215).

[16] Adopting Annie Perrin's approach to the analysis of Goytisolo's discourse, Robert
Richmond Ellis suggests that the Roman script represents a 'heterotextual' form of writing
(linear discourse, which aims to reproduce reality) and the italic script is a 'homotextual'
discourse (a writing of deviance founded on the notion of a self-generating, subversive
text). See Ellis, *The Hispanic Homograph: Gay Self-Representation in Contemporary
Spanish Autobiography* (Urbana: University of Illinois Press, 1997), p. 43; Perrin, 'El
laberinto homotextual', in Manuel Ruiz Lagos (ed.), *Escritos sobre Juan Goytisolo:
coloquio en torno a la obra de Juan Goytisolo, Almería, 1987* (Almería: Instituto de
Estudios Almerienses, 1988), pp. 73–81. This view seems to presuppose that homosexuality is, and must always be, *essentially* subversive.

[17] For example, 'los meandros de la memoria', or 'hallar en la resistencia interior a
desnudarlo el canon moral de tu escritura' (*Coto vedado*, pp. 29 and 41 respectively).
Other such examples are easily found throughout the volume.

with this split by establishing as moral guarantor a third, synthesizing 'I' to preserve the wholeness of the autobiographical 'subject'.[18] Against this conventional move, Goytisolo appears to stress the fluidity of identity through the *textual* non-identity of the 'I' writing and the 'I' written about, apparently refusing to construct a coherent third 'I'. However, as we shall see, this textual division is not absolute, for it conceals a hidden synthesizing imperative, which offers a coherence to the autobiographical project in the form of the establishment of a space of dissidence from which to speak. And this gesture should not be hastily condemned as an essentializing one, for it serves a particular political purpose that underpins Goytisolo's entire *obra*.[19]

Goytisolo begins his autobiography by mocking the idea of a search for family origins, which would ultimately lead, he wryly notes, to Adam and Eve, yet he continues in a traditional vein with a narrative of the immediate 'troncos materno y paterno' (p. 9) of his family tree. The opening section of *Coto vedado*, though not beginning with Goytisolo's birth, does set his background within a particular 'family myth', that of bourgeois origins based on the fortune that his great-grandfather amassed as owner of a Cuban sugar plantation. Against this myth, Goytisolo – who would later discover Marxism and ally it with a residual sense of guilt instilled by his Catholic upbringing – can only rebel:

> El proceso revolucionario cubano, iniciado unos años más tarde, sería vivido así, íntimamente, como una estricta sanción histórica a los pasados crímenes de mi linaje, una experiencia libertadora que me ayudaría a desprenderme, con la entusiasta inserción en él, del pesado fardo que llevaba encima.   (p. 11)

---

18 Paul Smith, *Discerning the Subject* (Minneapolis: University of Minnesota Press, 1988), p. 105.

19 Following Diana Fuss in *Essentially Speaking: Feminism, Nature and Difference* (New York: Routledge, 1989), Paul Julian Smith argues, in *Laws of Desire: Questions of Homosexuality in Spanish Writing and Film* (Oxford: Clarendon Press, 1992), pp. 14–20, that the 'risk of essentialism' may be worth taking in literature and art, and that readers should not conduct a witch-hunt of texts that fall into essentialism, but ask what strategic gain may be had from its deployment. In 'Estados de deseo', Epps takes an opposing view, suggesting that there are inherent problems in Goytisolo's association of homosexuality with a 'nation' of outsiders. The result, he argues, is akin to the reification and essentialization of both homosexuality and nationalism, which paradoxically results from the work of Michel Foucault, in the *History of Sexuality*, and Benedict Anderson, in *Imagined Communities: Reflections on the Origin and Spread of Nationalism* (London: Verso, 1983). Of Foucault's work Epps notes (pp. 804–5): 'ha recalcado la condición moderna de la "homosexualidad" (y de la "heterosexualidad") de forma tan persuasiva que muchos se han visto obligados a acreditar o a descreditar no sólo en la validez del término, sino también la realidad de una existencia "homosexual" a través de los siglos.' I can only agree, but this does not invalidate the argument that essentialism is put to strategic use in Goytisolo's work.

As if to counter this subjective view of historical forces, Goytisolo marshals documentary evidence in the form of letters detailing his grandfather's exploitation of black plantation workers in order to justify his abhorrence of his family's past 'crimes'.[20] However, Goytisolo's presentation of his Cuban connections raises the inevitable problem of the 'enunciatory abyss' within his text, for, in noting down the socio-political values that will inform his rebellion early in the autobiography, long before the young Goytisolo could have been conscious of them, the author points to the presence of a shaping consciousness reflecting on its past. Of the letters and their support for his later Marxist political stance he notes, 'estoy anticipando una lectura realizada muchos años más tarde' (p. 13). Self-consciousness, then, is not limited to italicized sections, but will discreetly infiltrate the traditional narrative pieces as well.

This tension between the exploration of the process of writing and a more traditional, confessional narrative is also manifest in the italicized sections of *Coto vedado*. Goytisolo notes that his autobiography is, in the traditional manner, a '*reconocimiento, cura, desinfección con mercromina y algodón*' (p. 28), which will lead to the acceptance of a dissident, gay position, yet he had earlier nodded to a structuralist view of language as a system of signs with the comment, '*imperceptiblemente, los signos se acumulan*' (p. 25). This is intended, it would seem, to unite formal self-reflexivity and the notion of the self as a mere construct of language, but the thought is undone only a moment later when Goytisolo treats these signs not as impeding the writing process but as rendering difficult the *reading* process – the words create '*espacios adrede para dificultar su lectura*' (p. 25). Suddenly, the formal subversion is reversed as it becomes the mere task of the reader to decipher what Goytisolo intends by his text. At the end of this same section, the autobiographer notes that his text may '*corregir, completar la realidad elaborada en sus sucesivas ficciones, este único libro, el Libro que desde hace veinte años no has cesado de crear y recrear*' (p. 29), adding a further level of confusion for, instead of autobiography becoming fiction, fiction – Goytisolo's own *obra*, viewed as a single, quasi-sacred Text – now becomes autobiographical.

Autobiography's 'enunciatory abyss' is thus signalled in *Coto vedado* by more than just the physical appearance of the text and its division into two

---

[20] Ellis notes this in *The Hispanic Homograph*, p. 42. James Fernández, in 'La novela familiar del autobiógrafo: Juan Goytisolo', *Anthropos*, 125 (1991), 54–60, argues that the opening sections of *Coto vedado*, dealing with Goytisolo's family, ridicule the notion of origins through 'desacralización de la paternidad'. He does not note, however, that this superficial ridicule conceals the beginning of an oppositional politics that relies upon a particular perspective of the Goytisolo family and thus requires an inscription of origins. Navajas, on the other hand, suggests, in 'Confession and Ethics' (p. 265), that Goytioslo's unmitigated contempt for his family demonstrates a lack of real understanding for others and shows his own inability to assess his origins dispassionately.

blocks of type-face. Crossings between the supposedly clearly defined roles of Roman and italicized sections seek to undermine the initial binary structure, and this is reinforced in the division of the self into different speaking voices, marked by, and then subverted by, particular pronominal usages. If *En los reinos de Taifa* joins up with *Don Julián* in its concluding reference to the mythical traitor,[21] *Coto vedado* already adopts a key strategy from that novel in establishing a dialogue of first- and second-person pronouns. The identity of the 'I' is, of course, the crux of the autobiographical enterprise, and the desire to both pin it down and, simultaneously, indicate the impossibility of doing so has preoccupied writers of the ilk of Gertrude Stein, Nathalie Sarraute, and, more in fiction than in autobiography proper, Samuel Beckett.[22] Rimbaud's famous declaration, 'JE est un autre', often taken to encapsulate the characteristic alienation of modern man, is strikingly appropriate to express the dilemma of the autobiographer. For Goytisolo, as for Sarraute in *Enfance*, the 'I' that is another generates a 'you' that affirms its otherness at the same time as it engages it in dialogue.[23] So, the first-person pronouns of the Roman-type sections in *Coto vedado* compete with a second-person voice in the italicized interludes. If the opening lines of the autobiography – in traditional type – seem initially to avoid any personal identification through generalizing comments, it is not long before 'mi caso', 'mis antecesores' and 'mi infancia' become the subject of interest. The second section – italicized – then inscribes 'tú' as the dominant subject, but implies in this very gesture a corresponding analytical 'I' who speaks about this 'you'.

Nevertheless, more interesting than the contrast and dialogue between the 'yo' and the 'tú' is the insistent appearance of definite articles and impersonal verb forms where more personal grammatical markers might be expected. There is a tendency, for example, for the definite article to replace personal pronouns in 'el abuelo Ricardo' or 'la bisabuela' (p. 30), or, perhaps more strikingly, in the comment, 'pese al trasiego y agitación reinantes, *los* recuerdos, confusos hasta entonces, parecen decantar*se*' (p. 50, my italics). Whilst the use of the impersonal might be dismissed as no more than a

---

[21] It also points towards *Las virtudes del pájaro solitario*, the novel that Goytisolo would write immediately after the autobiographies. See, for instance, the references to San Juan de la Cruz and the mystical imagery of the phrase, 'dolor y gozo, crudeza, llama, consumación' (*En los reinos de Taifa*, p. 306).

[22] James Olney offers a detailed reading of Beckett in this respect in *Memory and Narrative: The Weave of Life-Writing* (Chicago: University of Chicago Press, 1998), chapter 3.

[23] Emer O'Beirne argues that although *Enfance* privileges the role of dialogue in the construction of selfhood, the text of Sarraute's autobiography ultimately reaffirms narrative authority through monologism, since the first-person voice comes to dominate over the second-person, which is supposedly a challenge to it. See *Reading Nathalie Sarraute: Dialogue and Distance* (Oxford: Clarendon Press, 1999), chapter 2.

stylistic desire to avoid repetition of 'mi' in contexts where ambiguity is not an issue, the consistent use of impersonal verb forms in the italicized sections seems to point, more significantly, to a desire to create a clear division between voices that correspond to 'I' and 'non-I', or other.

Taking as his basis – rather appropriately, given Goytisolo's preference for Islamic culture – Arab grammarians, the French linguist Émile Beneveniste has argued that pronouns are empty shifters whose identity is filled by context. The first person is 'the one who speaks', the second person 'the one who is addressed', and the third person is 'the one who is absent'.[24] If 'I' and 'you' imply the presence of the speaker to the listener, whose relationship is reciprocal and reversible, then 'he' and 'she' denote the disembodied, empty space of the other. This would seem to be even more the case with the impersonal voice, which uses third-person verb forms.[25] Yet, Beneveniste's work complicates this picture by revealing a concealed slippage between the second and third persons, which reveals the 'I'/'non-I' division (p. 201):

> The second person [Beneveniste notes] can be made to enter into a variety of the 'impersonal'. For instance, *vous* in French functions as an anaphoric of *on* [. . .]. In many languages, 'you' can serve, as it does in English, to denote an indefinite agent. [. . .] It is necessary and sufficient that one envisage a *person* other than 'I' for the sign 'you' to be assigned to that person. Thus every *person* that one imagines is of the 'you' form, especially, but not necessarily, the person being addressed 'you' can thus be defined as 'the non-*I*-person'.

The pronominal shifting of the italicized sections of *Coto vedado* suggests a desire to conflate not 'yo' and 'tú', the reciprocal voices of the dialogue, but 'tú' and the impersonal 'se'. If the 'yo' is associated with the traditional sections, representing an identity and a past to be set down, fixed in time through writing, and thus tamed, then the 'tú' and the impersonal both belong to the italicized sections and represent an aspirational identity that has yet to be realized.[26] The emptiness of the 'tú' is thus emphasized by this conflation with the impersonal voice. For instance, Goytisolo ponders his motives for writing:

---

[24] Émile Beneveniste, *Problems in General Linguistics* (Coral Gables, Florida: University of Miami Press, 1971), p. 197.

[25] Beneveniste writes (p. 199): 'The third person, by virtue of its very structure, is the non-personal form of verbal inflection. Indeed, it is always used when the person is not designated and especially in the expression called impersonal.'

[26] Interestingly, the fact that Goytisolo echoes Flaubert in French – 'Don Julián *c'est moi*' – allows him to retain the impersonal 'ce', whereas, in Spanish, a first-person pronoun, 'soy yo', would have appeared. For an extended discussion of Beneveniste's ideas as applied to *Don Julián*, see José Manuel Martín Morán, *Semiótica de una traición recuperada: génesis poética de 'Reivindicación del Conde don Julián'* (Barcelona: Anthropos, 1992).

sustituto laico del sacramento de la confesión? : necesidad inconsciente de autojustificarse? de dar un testimonio que nadie te solicita? : testimonio de quién, para quién? : para ti, los demás, tus amigos, los enemigos? : deseos de hacerse comprender mejor? (p. 40, my underlining)

In the final pages of *Reinos*, when Goytisolo embraces the mythical rebel Don Julián as himself, and thus realizes this aspirational identity, he uses the *second* person voice to refer to Julián – the desired rebel identity – and reifies the past self of the first person by casting it as a *definite* third person – 'el expatriado'.[27] Hence, although, in *Coto vedado* and *En los reinos de Taifa*, Goytisolo does not construst the natural self of traditional autobiography, as Labanyi correctly notes, he does offer a view of identity that suggests that lurking behind the fragmentation and flux of different pronominal usages is an essential core of stability and consistency deriving from the basic contrast of self and other – or, in existentialist terms, of an inauthentic self to be rejected and an authentic one to be embraced.

Constructivism versus Essentialism (2): Metaphorical Shaping of the Forbidden Territory

The tension in Goytisolo's autobiographies between self-reflexiveness and confession, and between constructivism and essentialism, may be seen as an attempt to inscribe at the centre of the autobiographical text the inherent difficulties of the enterprise. In this view, the text, by constantly contradicting itself, would in fact undermine itself – both as 'true' and 'fictional' life narrative. Nevertheless, certain discursive structures, or shaping metaphors, point towards a confessional, truth-seeking imperative as being Goytisolo's dominant aim, and this emerges more forcefully as the autobiography progresses. The first of these shaping metaphors is the appeal to near-death experiences as a motive for writing, the second is a Freudian idiom that pervades the text,

---

27 Ellis contends (*The Hispanic Homograph*, p. 56) that, in qualifying his identification with Julián with the words, 'el expatriado de quien ahora te despides es *otro*', Goytisolo recognizes that this identity is problematic, since it is an aggressively oppositional identity, which casts the other as enemy and envisages no possibility of a reciprocal relationship. This seems implausible. In 'De *Don Julián* a *Makbara*: una posible lectura orientalista' (*Crónicas sarracinas* [Barcelona: Seix Barral, 1989], pp. 27–46), an essay first published in 1982, Goytisolo indeed recognized that in *Don Julián* he used violence to counter violence and thus reinforced the duality of subjecting and subjected selves upon which authority is founded. Nevertheless, in his autobiographies, published in 1985 and 1986, he *still* insists on accepting the Julianesque identity as his own. As if to confirm this further, the conclusion of *Reinos* stylistically and thematically joins up with *Don Julián* rather than breaking with it. This demonstrates that an existentialist sense of conflict is fundamental to Goytisolo's sense of identity even in his autobiographies.

and the third is the role of a visit to Cuba in Goytisolo's depiction of his growing awareness of political and sexual dissidence.

In the first italicized section, Goytisolo narrates, without explanation for his motive, two crises that seem to have had a consciousness-raising effect upon him. The first is a car crash, and the second a dangerous encounter with a bull during the 'encierros' in Elche, from which his friends extricate him. These events are slipped into the text as if by chance – '*conducir, por ejemplo, a la amanecida* [. . .]' introduces the first; '*O, quince meses más tarde, en el curso de un viaje sentimental al espacio de tu propia escritura* [. . .]' presents the second (pp. 25–6, my underlining). Nevertheless, both turn out to have been crucial experiences, which stimulated the writing of the autobiography in the first place: '*No permitir que cuanto amas, tu pasado, experiencia, emociones, lo que eres y has sido deaparezcan contigo, resolución de luchar con uñas y dientes contra el olvido,*' declares Goytisolo (p. 29).[28] There is in this an existentialist sense of *angst* in the face of death driving a need to understand the self and to construct the tale of a life so that it may live on after the body's mortal demise. And the existentialist sense of a self constructed in the face of death will be reinforced, later, in Goytisolo's descriptions of homosexual liaisons, which are combative and presented as a negative reading of the Sartrean gaze as it seeks to objectify the lover (the other) in order to realize the self.[29]

The use of a Freudian idiom in *Coto vedado* serves two functions. First, it displaces the motivation for writing from the conscious to the unconscious self. This may be intended as a means to disguise the deliberate project of establishing a dissident identity, but it brings as a consequence the presentation of selfhood in an essentialist perspective. Second, the Oedipus complex is used to structure relations between Goytisolo, his father, and, ultimately, Franco's Spain. Most important of all, however, is the fact that this use of a Freudian perspective demonstrates again the ambiguous nature of Goytisolo's approach to his autobiography. He is driven, he says, like a frustrated mother who has just suffered a miscarriage and wishes to become pregnant again. He thus feels '*la violenta pulsión de la escritura tras largos meses de esterilidad sosegada, urgencia y necesidad de escribir*' (p. 29). Early childhood is depicted as '*opacidad del limbo infantil : negrura de túnel momentáneamente interrumpida por claros, horados, imágenes fugaces*' (p. 45), and his emerging homosexuality will be '*lava seminal [. . .] ardiente pulsión abrigada en la sima*' (p. 230). Implicit in the image of the dark tunnel is a Freudian uterine reference, the notion of childhood learning being repre-

---

[28] Paul Julian Smith considers these episodes and comes to the conclusion that they point to the author's need to impose order on the contingency of existence (*Laws of Desire*, p. 32).

[29] Jean-Paul Sartre, *Being and Nothingness*, trans. Hazel E. Barnes (London: Routledge, 1989), p. 364.

sented here by biological birth. Furthermore, 'pulsión' is an odd word in Spanish, used by Goytisolo perhaps in evocation of 'pulsion', the standard French translation for the Freudian 'drive'.[30]

Later, however, Goytisolo queries his use of the Freudian idiom, pondering whether the influence of the unconscious through involuntary memory might not actually impede his autobiographical task: '¿es función de la memoria involuntaria conservar las impresiones soterradas que el mecanismo del recuerdo destruye? ¿[la hipótesis freudiana] no condena acaso tu ingenuo proyecto de recobro en razón de sus posibles resultados opuestos al fin persrguido?' (p. 152) Despite yet another indication of the autobiographical 'enunciatory abyss' in this confession of his metaphorical shaping of the past in a section where such remarks might not be expected, Goytisolo will go on to establish the Oedipus complex as a metaphor that determines his relations to his family.

These are divided into two camps that loosely symbolize a masculine and a feminine principle. The paternal line – the masculine principle – represents the bourgeois myth of family origins, which is rejected as repressive, unimaginative, authoritarian, and ultimately linked to the political figure of Franco, whose politics Goytisolo's father supports. The maternal line – the feminine principle – contains the seeds of the future 'true' Goytisolo, though one which must be realized through writing, thus uniting a notion of identity as essence with one of performance. There is a great-great-grandmother who wrote a lost novel in the style of Walter Scott; a bohemian uncle who is a nonconformist, a Catalan nationalist, and has an Irish lover; and an open-minded, cultured mother whose library of French twentieth-century classics (including works by Gide, though not specifically his autobiography), will form Goytisolo's literary apprenticeship.[31]

---

[30] A more normal Spanish translation for 'drives' is 'instintos'.

[31] Goytisolo, however, does make reference to Gide's autobiography, *Si le grain ne meurt* (Paris: Gallimard, 1955), a key homosexual work, in his 'Presentación crítica de José María Blanco White', in *Obra inglesa de José María Blanco White*, 3rd edn (Barcelona: Seix Barral, 1982), p. 13. Like Goytisolo's autobiography, Gide's text reveals a preoccupation with veracity. Gide does, for example, question the fidelity of his memories, use others' narratives to bolster them, and even contradict himself; at other times, he creates the illusion of precision in his evocation of the past and takes a firm hold of the narrative in asserting his authorial right to deform chronology. In *En los reinos de Taifa*, Goytisolo remarks, 'No sigo una cronología estricta de los hechos sino el desorden coherente de la memoria' (p. 138). In the description of childhood sexuality, in particular, Gide's reference to 'mauvaises habitudes' (p. 65) is echoed in Goytisolo's account of his early sexual activity and his mother's gentle objections, contrasting with his father's anger at his cross-dressing on one occasion (*Coto vedado*, p. 47). And like Gide, Goytisolo frames events in such a way that they represent precocious glimpses of a 'true' sexual identity, which has been 'buried' – comparable to a Freudian unconscious – and will emerge in time. In this regard, both writers shape their autobiographies as revelation or enlightenment – specifically, the revelation of their sexuality. Gide writes (pp. 63–4): 'Autour de moi, en moi, rien que ténèbres. [. . .] Je le répète: je dormais encore; j'étais

The most significant figure from the maternal line, though, is grandfather Ricardo, guilty of molesting Goytisolo as a child but treated with considerable sympathy – not because Goytisolo condones his actions but because he pities his situation, forced to conceal his true nature and live a lie. Ricardo's lack of honesty and passive acceptance of the shame society heaps upon him will be the impetus for Goytisolo's 'coming out' in *Coto vedado*.[32] In this regard, the opposing blocs of family members serve as a metaphor for Goytisolo's rebellion against authority and his establishment of a dissident position. The autobiography will enact the assassination of the father figure and his values in what Ellis terms 'an extended gesture of parricide', in order to bring about the triumph of the feminine principle, linking writing, homosexuality, and marginality.[33] This structure, however, replicates the structures of repression within Goytisolo's own family and shows the autobiographer to be enslaved to those very mechanisms he wishes to subvert. At the end of *Coto vedado* Goytisolo notes, with no trace of irony, that his father died in ignorance of his homosexuality and was spared 'el desarrollo y florecimiento en uno de sus hijos de esa monstruosa semilla de desorden, aberración y desvío de la rama maternal que fuera la obsesión de su vida' (p. 246). This, along with Goytisolo's Oedipal structuring of his family relations, perhaps illustrates Foucault's suggestion that the discourses of psychoanalysis, rather

pareil à ce qui n'est pas né.' See note 14 above for an example of Goytisolo's use of the enlightenment metaphor.

[32] Goytisolo writes of his grandfather (p. 105): 'Esta conformidad suya al juicio ajeno, aceptación sumisa de su condición natural de paria, incapacidad de reaccionar a los ataques que continuamente sufría provocarían mucho más tarde en mí una inmensa piedad por él. [. . .] Careciendo del temple moral necesario para asumirla, no tenía más recurso que ofrendar la cabeza al hacha del verdugo cada vez que, por su mala fortuna, cedía a ella y era expuesto después a la picota pública. El recuerdo de este automenosprecio consecutivo al desdén de los demás, de este oprobio asumido y transmutado en culpabilidad interna pesó muy fuerte en la decision de afirmar mi destino contra viento y marea, de poner las cosas en claro frente al prójimo y a mí mismo.' Despite Goytisolo's sympathy for his grandfather, however, the fact remains that he was guilty of child abuse, as Ellis points out (*The Hispanic Homograph*, p. 47).

[33] Ellis, *The Hispanic Homograph*, p. 43. He goes on to note that in his valuation of the mother's world, Goytisolo departs from a tradition of male life-writers who take as their point of departure an ideal or missing father. The negative view of the father figure in Goytisolo is also developed by Cristina Moreiras-Menor in 'Juan Goytisolo, F.F.B. y la fundación fantasmal del proyecto autobiográfico contemporáneo español', *Modern Language Notes*, 111 (1996), 327–45 (332). Jo Labanyi argues that Goytisolo's aim in his autobiography is not to give a voice to homosexual men, but to the various women in his life who have been silenced by patriarchy. It is certainly true that Goytisolo treats both his mother and Monique, his eventual wife, with considerable tenderness, but Monique, an author herself and the centre of a literary gathering, is hardly a figure silenced by patriarchy. Furthermore, although Goytisolo attributes writing to his mother's family line, elsewhere he has characterized it as an exclusively male act: the phallic pen, the virgin page, and the seminal ink. See, for example, section VI of *Juan sin Tierra* where this is the dominant metaphor for writing.

than revealing the nature of the family, have led man to impose a particular format upon it.[34]

In a self-reflexive text that appeals to Freudian precedents and establishes a dialogue of pronominal voices, one might have expected an exploration of the cathartic role of narrative in psychoanalytical cure, yet there is no evidence that Goytisolo seeks seriously to deconstruct the metaphorical structures that underpin his autobiography. Instead, he presents the emergence of his homosexuality as the inevitable result of an inherent instinct, which he had, at the instigation of society, been repressing as a '*yo-otro*' (p. 40). This repression, and the autobiographer's passive adoption of homosexuality because it 'chooses' him, and not he it, is associated both with politics and with culture. Just as Goytisolo writes in Castilian, not Catalan, because the former language chose him, so 'la oscilación entre dos culturas e idiomas se asemeja bastante a la indecisión afectiva y sensual del niño o adolescente: unas fuerzas oscuras, subyacentes, encauzarán un día, sin su consentimiento, su futura orientación erótica' (pp. 38–9). This link between language, politics, and sexuality is curious and offers a contradictory view of selfhood. Goytisolo seems to suggest an essentialist conception of the self determined by an inherent homosexuality; but he also implies that this homosexuality is an *oppression* which, unlike the cultural and linguistic oppression of the Franco regime, he will *choose* to accept in order to live authentically. Goytisolo's homosexuality is an inherent part of his nature, it drives him, and, paradoxically, it represses him. These are hardly the sentiments of gay liberation, but it is liberatory for Goytisolo who feels the '*imperativo de dar cuenta, a los demás y a ti mismo, de lo que fuiste y no eres*' (p. 29).

The realization of this authentic self forms the basis of the second half of *Coto vedado* and is continued into *En los reinos de Taifa*. A visit to Cuba in 1963 becomes the epiphanic moment when Goytisolo discovers his divided self, the authentic core of his being concealed by an inauthentic mask. The realization works on two levels, the sexual and the political. Having heard of the ostracization of two Cuban lesbians because of their sexuality, Goytisolo feels vaguely uneasy with his approving companions, a sentiment reinforced when he is presented at a political meeting as a young revolutionary intellectual from Spain. He feels that this is far from being his true identity, first, because of his family background,[35] and, second, because of his sexuality, which sets him apart from his 'brothers' in revolution. Although Goytisolo,

---

[34] Foucault, *History of Sexuality: The Will to Knowledge*, p. 113. In noting the controlling power of the (religious) confession, Foucault suggests that it was a source of repression in relation to sexuality. From this perspective, Goytisolo's autobiography would remain within the repressive paradigm whose binary parameters it simply reverses.

[35] In *En los reinos de Taifa* Goytioslo notes his pleasure at the Castro Revolution as both hope for social revolution in general and, more personally, as an 'ajuste de cuentas con el pasado execrable de tu propio linaje' (pp. 61–2).

aware of the double autobiographical subject, undermines almost immediately the sense of anagnorisis that shaped the initial presentation of the Cuban episode[36] – 'las cosas no ocurrieron al ritmo acelerado en que las cuentas sino con suavidad' (p. 139) – the structure of a divided self, with an authentic '*yo genuino*' (p. 139) as its core, remains. The concealed self must be allowed, in echo of the imagery of the novel, *Makbara*, perhaps, to '*abandonar las catacumbas, emerger, respirar, escupir a la cara del otro, del doble, el fantasma, enemigo alevoso de tu intimidad, [. . .] afrontar el destino de las acusadas*' (p. 139). As a result, the autobiographer feels a '*brusco e imperioso afán de autenticidad*' (p. 140).[37]

A Divided and Embattled Self

One consequence of Goytisolo's conflicting sense of self – provisional, yet with a stable core – is the establishment of a series of oppositions through which he articulates his identity: either authentic or inauthentic, homosexual

36 '*Fulgurante anagnórisis*', '*deslumbramiento epifánico*', and '*segunda, desmorada nacimiento*' will also be terms used by Goytisolo at the close of *Coto vedado*, though with respect to the author's developing socio-political conscience during a visit to Murcia and Almería (p. 275). Randolph D. Pope argues, in 'Theory and Contemporary Autobiographical Writing: The Case of Juan Goytisolo', *Siglo XX/20th Century*, 8 (1990–1), 87–101, that Goytisolo does, in fact, manage to destabilize the self through 'discontinuous histories' that 'are not forced into shape, hammered into a harmonious vase of despair' (p. 96). In the autobiography, he concludes (p. 100), 'there is no one sense, not one big conversion that explains all, not one single attainment'. Pope develops this postmodern view of Goytisolo's autobiographies in 'El autorretrato postmoderno de Juan Goytisolo', *L'Autoportrait en Espagne: Littérature & Peinture* (Aix-en-Provence: L'Université de Provence, 1992), pp. 319–30. However, as demonstrated above, careful reading of the metaphors and formal structuring that Goytisolo employs, as well as the concentration of interest on a moment of revelation associated with Cuba, suggests that the autobiographies do indeed offer a 'big conversion' and a 'single attainment' of dissidence. The fact that *En los reinos de Taifa* leaves off where the novel, *Don Julián*, begins further suggests that the autobiography relates the evolution of a dissident writing voice that reaches maturity in that novel. Ryan Prout, echoing my own view, argues that Goytisolo makes 'outsiderdom' his essence from childhood and then turns this into a principle for his fiction. See *Fear and Gendering: Pedophobia, Effeminophobia, and Hypermasculine Desire in the Work of Juan Goytisolo* (New York: Lang, 2001), p. 13.

37 The Cuban experience is anticipated in Goytisolo's university years when, having formed the literary *Tertulia del Turia* with some friends and under the guidance of a well-known theatre director, the latter made homosexual advances to one of group. 'Aunque por estas fechas,' Goytisolo recounts in *Coto vedado* (p. 169), 'mi inclinación sexual no estaba en modo alguno resuelta, las medidas profilácticas de mis amigos me disgustaron.' Immediately following this episode in the autobiography is more evidence of an underlying essentialism in Goytisolo's view of the self. He writes (p. 170): 'A los veinte años cumplidos, mi identidad no sólo en lo que tocaba a mi carácter y criterios morales sino también a los godeos y fantasmas que luego marcarían mi vida, permanecían envuelta en una bruma que no alcanzaba a disipar.'

or heterosexual, Jekyll or Hyde, victim or hangman, the voice of marginality or that of authority. Although the autobiography seeks to break down binarism through certain formal strategies discussed above, it in fact narrates the process that leads to the overthrow of the second set of terms by the first. Goytisolo does not fragment his identity in an erratic or arbitrary manner; he structures it as a violent battle between two options in which only one can triumph. This is reflected both in the fiction that he will compose from the mid-1960s on, and in a more discreet form in the homosexual relationships depicted in the autobiographies. They are predicated upon a relationship not of reciprocity but, as both Ellis and Smith argue, of violence.[38] Ultimately, it is a relationship of subjecting and subjected sexual partners that problematically parallels the evolution of a dissident literary perspective: 'mi pasión por [la literatura], vivida como un verdadero salto al vacío, me arrojaría un día al goce *zahorí* del castellano en virtud de la misma lógica misteriosa por la que hallaría en el sexo la afirmación agresiva de mi identidad' (p. 198). While Goytisolo, speaking of the political affiliations of his contemporaries, may propose that an oppositional politics is the unavoidable consequence of a repressive background, since it leads to the exchange of one kind of oppression for another (Francoist intolerance is replaced by communist dogma in the thinking of his generation), he does omit to mention that in *Crónicas sarracinas* he has already recognized the limitations of his own oppositional aesthetic. Towards the end of *Coto vedado*, with a certain satisfaction at his decision not to join the Communist Party, Goytisolo writes of his contemporaries:

> Amamantado desde la niñez en la creencia de una clave explicativa del mundo única y totalizadora, de un conjunto de referencias autosuficiente y cerrado, de una verdad infalible, dogmática, desertará de las filas de la doctrina inculcada para abrazar con el mismo fervor y ausencia de espíritu crítico la del adversario irreductible pero simétrico de su primitivo credo official.   (p. 246)

Yet, these words could be used against the author himself, for it is not until the publication of *Las virtudes del pájaro solitario* in 1988 that Goytioslo, through the use of a mystical idiom, fully breaks free of oppositional thinking and establishes a reciprocal vision of human relations.

In *Coto vedado* and *En los reinos de Taifa* it is the inauthentic Sartrean relationship of self against other that predominates; so, while Goytisolo may move towards an authentic sense of reciprocity by the end of the 1980s, he

---

[38] Ellis, in *The Hispanic Homograph*, p. 47, notes particularly the connection between sexuality and violence in Goytisolo's account of his childhood fascination, during the early years of the Civil War, with his father's bodyguard, Jaume. Smith objects to Goytisolo's depiction of homosexual love as inherently violent in *Laws of Desire*, p. 35.

does not depict this in his autobiography. In recounting his emerging homo-sexuality in *Coto vedado*, in the episode with Lucho, Goytisolo employs the Jekyll-and-Hyde metaphor to explain his 'strange' behaviour when he drunk-enly embraces his friend under the watchful eye of a café waiter. The person-ality that manifests itself in this gesture is, to Goytisolo, an 'intruso burlón y malévolo' (p. 187) who must be repressed. Drawing explicit attention to a conflictual relationship based on *le regard*, Lucho's incriminating gaze – 'ojos negros, metálicos, insondables y duros como la mica' (p. 189) – forces our author to censor his actions, but, having visited a brothel, and proved his 'normality' to Lucho, he can once again look him straight in the eye. While Goytisolo is at pains, in this episode, to stress that he does not wish to 'atribuir a lo acaecido un sentido premonitorio y establacer a partir de ella una impeccable cadena de causas y efectos [. . .] sino exponer los hechos tal y como los percibía en el momento' (p. 188), thus suggesting an evolving and provisional identity, his repeated use of the conflictive self–other opposition in sexual relationships suggests that he does harbour hidden motives and a concealed essentialism.

The element of violence and exoticism in what Goytisolo, echoing Richard Burton, terms the 'zona sotádica' is reinforced in the description of Raimundo, another figure to whom Goytisolo is attracted, as 'la absoluta marginalidad' (p. 223). A frustrated liaison, since Raimundo remains appar-ently unaware and certainly unreceptive to Goytisolo's erotic interest in him, the latter, nevertheless, lives a Wildean 'pasión imposible y sin nombre' (p. 226), which demonstrates to him the inappropriateness of his bourgeois origins. These homosexual encounters now acquire a literary status in the writing of the autobiography as Goytisolo moves towards the adoption of the rebellious Don Julián stance (pp. 227–8):

> Del mismo modo imperceptible que Lucho, tu amigo [Raimundo] se ha ido convirtiendo poco a poco en un personaje literario con el que contiendes a diario en la página en blanco independientemente del modelo real. Este cambio de *status* implica un distancimiento tácito del segundo, el cese de tu anterior subordinación a su apremiante, avasalladora personalidad.

It would seem that the 'true' self is to be realized in fiction, not life, through the figure of the arch-dissident Don Julián (note the use here of the second person, associated with an 'authentic', rebel stance); yet, this is achieved through the verbal repression of Raimundo's dominant personality. The same sense of conflict and verbal, or literary, opposition also emerges in *En los reinos de Taifa* where, as Ellis argues (p. 52), Goytisolo submits to the power of the other in sexual intercourse but dominates them through language (p. 228): 'poseídos de ellos y su placer áspero, buscaba instintivamente la manera de contrapesar mi sumisión física con una dominación intelectual capaz de establecer el equilibrio entre los platillos de la balanza'. Although

Goytisolo goes on to write that 'el acto de escribir y asumir la voz con la misma plenitud con que unas horas o unos minutos antes habían dispuesto de mi cuerpo mezclaría a menudo la benevolencia aparente de la escritura con el regodeo secreto de la erección', it is clear that the power of the voice both supersedes and combats his earlier sexual submissiveness. Writing, unlike its original formulation at the beginning of *Coto vedado*, where it was associated with Goytisolo's lost mother, is not, in fact, a feminine principle, but an aggressively gay, masculine one. The fact that the only truly reciprocal sexual relationship that Goytisolo recounts in his autobiography, that with Monique, is a heterosexual one, reinforces through exception the image of writing as self-centred and exclusively phallic. Thus, Goytisolo concludes with a joyous celebration of 'deviant' sexuality as 'la vandálica, jubilosa apropiación de la grafía árabe' (p. 228).

Looking in the mirror towards the end of *En los reinos de Taifa*, Goytisolo's old self becomes 'un rostro que no es el tuyo' (p. 303), and his new one, '*irremediablemente homosexual*' (p. 240), finds 'la brusca y violenta jubilación, el nítido ramalazo destructor presentidos desde la infancia [en la] fuerza ligada a tu vivencia peculiar del sexo' (p. 304). It would seem that Goytisolo's self is irremediably divided and destined to rebel through the emergence of a homosexuality that is predicated upon violence and oppression. In joining up with the text of *Don Julián*, quite literally, through a Gongorine language that 'dispensa sus señas en medio del caos' (p. 306),[39] Goytisolo's autobiography does not move beyond the problems of his fiction. Nor does it ultimately offer a provisional sense of identity. Instead, autobiography acts as testimony to Goytisolo's development of a dissident voice that unites sexuality, politics, and writing in a discourse of violence. Ironically, having uncovered – ultimately not fabricated, but revealed – a core essence, or identity, for himself in his homosexuality, Goytisolo seeks to present this through direct statements and textual devices that emphasize the element of choice: an existentialist performance of identity. Thus we see a clear tension between constructivism and essentialism. However, the choice that Goytisolo makes – to adopt a position of dissidence – inevitably inscribes his homosexuality as 'outside the fold'. This may be unavoidable, for Goytisolo's dilemma is perhaps that of any writer concerned with identity politics in the post-structuralist era. Having queried the grand narratives of Enlightenment thought, post-structuralism offers a critique of the social and

---

[39] This echoes the following lines from the novel, themselves an reference to the Golden Age poet Luis de Góngora: 'enredados aún en tu memoria, tal implicantes vides, los versos de quien, en habitadas soledades, con sombrío, impenitente ardor creara densa belleza ingrávida : indemne realidad que fúlgidamente perdura y, a través de los siglos, te dispensa sus señas redentoras en medio del caos : rescátandote del engañoso laberinto' (*Reivindicación del Conde don Julián*, ed. Linda Gould Levine [Madrid: Cátedra, 1985], pp. 114–15).

political structures that have been a source of oppression for marginalized groups. Yet, in going as far as to challenge notions of coherent identity and the existence of a unitary self, it also impedes the articulation of marginal group identity and political activism. In this regard, Goytisolo's autobiography is exemplary of a 1980s dilemma, namely the attempt to walk an impossible line in giving expression to an dissident identity while fielding a defence against the accusation of having fallen into the trap of a naïve Enlightenment humanism. Goytisolo, in short, embraces the responsibility for speaking and acting ethically that Paul Smith accuses post-structuralism of having abrogated.[40] He runs the 'risk of essentialism', and indeed falls foul of it, as Epps has eloquently demonstrated, but he does so for the purpose of carving out a particular dissident position from which to speak. An evaluation of the effectivenes of this strategy will depend upon an analysis not just of the autobiographies but of Goytioslo's work as a whole, whether in fiction or critical essays. It is to the latter that we shall turn first.

[40] Smith, *Discerning the Subject*, chapter 3.

2

CANONIZING DISSIDENCE:
FOUR DECADES OF ESSAY-WRITING

*To become good literary historians, we must
remember that what we usually call literary history
has little or nothing to do with literature and that
what we call literary interpretation – provided only
it is good interpretation – is in fact literary history.*
Paul de Man[1]

The Essay Genre

Essay-writing is a flexible and subjective art. It ranges from reasoned
intellectual argument to the travel essay, specializing, as Philip Lopate puts it,
in misadventure, to the personal essay, which constitutes, in Samuel Johnson's felicitous phrase, 'a loose sally of the mind'.[2] To essay is to test out a
position, and the essayist, according to Theodor Adorno, writes in full
consciousness of the fragmentary nature of his art, seeking a utopian illumi-
nation through its practice yet acutely aware that his gesture can only ever be
provisional and incomplete.[3] For Adorno, the essay's incompleteness is a
mark of subversive thought, a challenge to culture's claims to naturalness and
a rejection of what he calls the 'royal road to origins' (p. 11). Instead, the
essayist always speculates on pre-existing material, and he or she is a 'child-
like person who has no qualms about taking his inspiration from what others
have done before him' (p. 4).[4] The essayist thus envisaged is a reader, or even

---

1   Paul de Man, 'Literary History and Literary Modernity', in *Blindness and Insight:
Essays in the Rhetoric of Contemporary Criticism*, 2nd edn (London: Routledge, 1989),
pp. 142–65 (p. 165).
2   Philip Lopate, introduction to *The Art of the Personal Essay: An Anthology from the
Classical Era to the Present* (New York: Random House, 1995), p. l; Johnson, quoted in
Lopate, p. xxxvii.
3   In 'The Essay as Form', *Notes to Literature*, 2 vols, trans. S. Weber Nicholsen (New
York: Columbia University Press, 1991), I, 3–23 (16–17), Adorno writes: 'The word
Versuch, attempt or essay, in which thought's utopian vision of hitting the bullseye is
united with the consciousness of its own fallibility and provisional character, indicates, as
do most historically surviving terminologies, something about the form, something to be
taken all the more seriously in that it takes place not systematically but rather as a characteristic of an intention groping its way.'
4   Georg Lukács also notes this aspect of essay-writing in 'On the Nature and Form of

a re-reader, in a rebellious and intertextual mode – an image which, as we shall see, anticipates Goytisolo's own view of the role of the intellectual as subversive re-reader of the literary canon.

In his study of essay-writing in twentieth-century Spain, Thomas Mermall argues that the essayist seeks to dramatize ideas in a form of writing that is synthetic, urgent, and economical. Agreeing with Adorno that the essay is prey to chance and idiosyncrasy, Mermall suggests that it manifests a tension between subjective and objective modes of discourse. The writer offers both observed facts and personal intuition in support of his argument, which is characterized by the 'interdependence of observation and introspection, intuition and logic'. The 'genuine' essay, Mermall states, 'conveys an aesthetic emotion [. . .], a certain tone, style, or personal manner'. The essay is also instructive as a cultural artefact, reflecting a consciousness 'bent on a re-evaluation or subversion of values through a critique of ideology'.[5] The personal aspect of criticism in general leads the structuralist Paul de Man to view it – and by implication the essay genre in which criticism is usually presented – as a form of autobiographical writing in which the essayist approaches his own self through the study of others. If this argument is pushed to its ultimate conclusion, literary criticism becomes a form of self-knowledge or, as de Man puts it in his essay, 'Criticism and Crisis', an 'alternating process of mutual interpretation' in which 'the observing subject is no more constant than the observed'.[6] But the issue then arises, of course, of where the resulting dizzying *vertige*, what de Man terms the 'endless oscillation of an intersubjective demystification', ends, or can, at least provisionally, be brought to a halt. 'In literature,' de Man goes on (p. 11), 'everything hinges on the existential status of the focal point; and the problem is more complex when it involves the disappearance of the self as a constitutive subject.'

In this chapter I wish to suggest that although Goytisolo's literary essays exemplify the conflict between personal intuition and objective thought that many have found inherent to the genre, there is ultimately a focal point, or centre, which is organized around an autobiographical imperative – the retention of a constitutive subject – and expressed through the subversive intertextuality that Adorno highlights as fundamental to the essay itself. Goytisolo's essays reflect a cultivation of marginality and dissidence that finds expression in the adoption of a series of literary doubles and in a discur-

the Essay', in *Soul and Form*, trans. Anna Bostock (London: Merlin Press, 1974), pp. 1–18.

   5   Thomas Mermall, *The Rhetoric of Humanism: Spanish Culture After Ortega y Gasset* (New York: Bilingual Press, 1976), pp. 3–4. Mermall confirms these views in 'Culture and the Essay in Modern Spain', in David T. Gies (ed.), *The Cambridge Companion to Modern Spanish Culture* (Cambridge: Cambridge University Press, 1999), pp. 163–72.

   6   'Criticism and Crisis', in *Blindness and Insight*, pp. 3–19 (pp. 9–10).

sive act of ventriloquism. That is to say, there exists a series of projected
voices that Goytisolo speaks both for and through – for them, in that he
rescues them from either oblivion or orthodox interpretations and, in turn,
reads them in the light of his dissident canon; through them, in that he
conceals himself behind them and appropriates their words in the process. In
this sense, it is a mystifying process which, in Epps' words, 'takes one thing
for another, one's words for another's.'[7] Nevertheless, this is neither a
silencing of the original voice, nor of literary origins, but rather a ventriloquism where the sources are evident and the dummy, as it were, can speak
back. In this sense, Goytisolo's approach is akin to a Bakhtinian notion of
heteroglossia in which the occupation of the voice of the other is a form of
self-creation – in short, an autobiographical act – but one that does not, in the
process, silence or destroy the other. As Bakhtin remarks:

> The word in language is half someone else's. It becomes 'one's own' only
> when the speaker populates it with his own intention, his own accent, when
> he appropriates the word, adapting it to his own semantic and expressive
> intention. Prior to this moment of appropriation the word does not exist in a
> neutral and impersonal language [. . .] but rather it exists in other people's
> mouths, in other people's contexts, serving other people's intentions: it is
> from there that one must take the word, and make it one's own.[8]

The Intellectual as Iconoclast

Throughout his writing career Juan Goytisolo has consistently sought to
carve out a position for himself as a literary and political iconoclast, establishing a series of literary precursors who seem to support his own concerns
and preoccupations. He defines thus in *Cogitus interruptus* the corrective
activity of a writer 'sin mandato',[9] who, despite a subversive approach,
remains ever loyal to the literary canon of his time:

7 Of *Reivindicación del Conde don Julián* Brad Epps writes in *Significant Violence*
(pp. 55–6): 'Goytisolo's text, despite its self-professed intertextuality, underestimates the
obliquity of discourse, its capacity to conceal its sources by creating the illusion that it
emanates from others. Ventriloquism is a curiously complex speech act. It refers, that is, to
the slipperiness of reference, to the mystifying ability to take one thing for another, one's
words for another's. [. . .] It is, hence, an act of speech that entails a violent silence, or
silencing. If I were Harold Bloom, I would say that it is an act of strength, a sign of value,
a thing of greatness. If I were Bakhtin, I would say (much more convincingly, I might add)
that it is a form of heteroglossia, one of a "multiplicity of social voices" that by virtue of
its complexity tends to obscure specifics of gender, class, and race.' However, Epps is
unclear on just how Bakhtinian heteroglossia is a *silencing* of voices, since it relies
precisely upon their multiple and heterogeneous articulation.
8 Mikhail Bakhtin, 'Discourse and the Novel', in *The Dialogic Imagination: Four
Essays*, trans. C. Emerson and M. Holquist (Austin: University of Texas Press, 1981), pp.
259–422 (pp. 293–4).
9 Goytisolo admits to borrowing the phrase from Günter Grass in 'Memoria, olvido,

> Dicha lealtad a la lengua y al *corpus* literario [. . .] implica el estudio de sus conotaciones y cambios, la reapropiación de los términos expulsados por medidas coercitivas, la combinación de la sincronía con la diacronía, el descubrimiento de la modernidad atemporal oculta en textos multi-centenarios, la forja de un árbol literario alimentado con raíces diversas en contraposición al árbol de cartón de piedra de una tradición apergaminada y huera.   (p. 56)

This is an excellent summary of Goytisolo's literary activity, in both essays and fiction, from the 1960s to the present day, and it is based on three premises: first, that 'loyalty' is not slavish acceptance of orthodox interpretations, but involves an awareness of literary continuity and change; second, that there should be a collapsing of temporal categories; and third, that one should nurture a heterodox literary tree to oppose the prevailing orthodox one.

It might seem surprising that a writer constantly at odds with 'official' culture might value loyalty to the canon, but this is only one of several paradoxes of Goytisolo's literary essays, which reveal an unexpectedly traditional and essentialist thrust. In comparing the literary tradition to a tree, Goytisolo conforms to the traditional, nineteenth-century organicist approach to literature and culture. The metaphor of the tree of literature implies a progressive notion of development over time. Given the author's preoccupation with, as he puts it, 'la combinación de la sincronía con la diacronía', this seems contradictory to say the least, and indicates an underlying teleological movement in his own reading of the canon.[10] The 'tree' of official culture is thus to be replaced with a dissident literary tree, which grows through time but simultaneously draws intertextually on the cultural past as it evolves radically new forms of expression. Although Goytisolo accepts that a variety of interpretations should co-exist, he still gives priority to the idea of marginality, so that the forging of an anti-canon of dissidents in fact canonizes heterodoxy, mirroring the paradigm of orthodoxy without subverting it.[11] And for a writer

amnesia, recuerdo y memoricidio', in *Cogitus interruptus* (Barcelona: Seix Barral, 1999), pp. 41–57 (p. 53).

[10] This is all the more evident if Goytisolo's metaphor is compared to Gilles Deleuze and Félix Guattari's discussion of organicist metaphors of literary development in *A Thousand Plateaus* (trans. and foreword Brian Massumi [London: Athlone, 1988]). They contrast the classical 'root-book' with the 'radical-system' (p. 5). In the former, the tree or root image 'endlessly develops the law of the One that becomes two, then of the two that becomes four . . . Binary logic is the spiritual reality of the root-tree' (p. 5), which thus follows a teleological progression. The radical system, or rhizome, on the other hand, allows for 'an immediate, indefinite multiplicity of secondary roots', which grafts onto it in a 'radical-chaosmos' rather than a 'root-cosmos' (pp. 5–6). See pp. 97–8 for a further discussion of rhizomic textual structure.

[11] Indeed, he literally canonizes his preferred mystical and religious dissidents in chapter 11 of *La cuarentena* (Barcelona: Mondadori, 1991), when he imagines visiting a wax museum where they are represented.

conventionally taken to fall within the postmodernist mode, Goytisolo lays surprising emphasis on ethics, embodied in his conception of loyalty as a questioning of established norms. Indeed, on this question of ethics, Goytisolo laments in *Cogitus interruptus* our current world's lack of real moral values.[12] In this regard, his essays – particularly, but not exclusively, the literary ones – offer a consistently ethical position in that they seek to uncover and articulate dissidence both within and without canonical culture. Furthermore, the essays frequently take an autobiographical turn which illustrates the difficulties of walking the line between personal intuition and objective analysis.

In his mature fiction, and most notably in *Don Julián*, Goytisolo creates a canon of dissident literary and historical heroes. Thus, the traitor Julián, supposedly responsible for the Moorish invasion of the peninsula, becomes Goytisolo's alter ego, and Cervantes, Góngora, Quevedo, and Luis de León are all turned into literary rebels. None of this is concealed. Indeed, it is flaunted as a form of intertextuality that is quite the opposite of Bloom's Freudian 'anxiety of influence'.[13] Goytisolo's adoption of a series of literary disguises has long been accepted and discussed with regard to his fiction, but critics often ignore the fact that it also occurs in his essays, which are simply marshalled in explanatory support of the intertextual practice of the novels. Recalling Paul de Man, that 'the observation and interpretation of others is always also a means of leading to the observation of self' ('Criticism', p. 9), we may note that there is an autobiographical impulse operating at the heart of Goytisolo's literary criticism that reinforces the subversive intent of his writing as a whole. If, in some essays, Goytisolo does attempt an objective analysis or adopts a particular position on intellectual and cultural history,[14]

12 Goytisolo's anticipated reply to those who might criticize this humanist view comes in the conclusion of 'Memoria, olvido' (p. 57): 'La voluntad iconoclasta y el respeto a la verdad *siempre relativa* asequible al nivel de nuestros conocimientos son la mayor arma contra la amnesia interesada de los poderes e instituiciones públicas y el blanqueo a cañonazo limpio de los artilleros memoricidas.'

13 Harold Bloom, *The Anxiety of Influence: A Theory of Poetry*, 2nd edn (New York: Oxford University Press, 1997).

14 Even in his more historically oriented essays, especially those on the theme of 'Spain as problem', Goytisolo's arguments are refracted through the ideas of Américo Castro, who is also highly influential in many of the literary essays dealing with potential overlaps between Spain's Latin, Christian heritage and her Arabic, Muslim past. The more properly historical essays are to be found in *Crónicas sarracinas*; the literary ones, for example, on the *Libro de buen amor* and San Juan de la Cruz's 'Cántico espiritual', in *Contracorrientes* and *El bosque de las letras*. For critical discussion of Goytisolo's interpretation of Spanish history, particularly in relation to Moorish Spain and the Castro hypothesis on *convivencia*, see Claudia Schaefer-Rodríguez, *Juan Goytisolo: del 'realismo crítico' a la utopía* (Madrid: Porrúa Turranzas, 1984); Jo Labanyi, *Myth and History in the Contemporary Spanish Novel* (Cambridge: Cambridge University Press, 1989); Michael Ugarte, 'Juan Goytisolo: Unruly Disciple of Américo Castro', *Journal of Spanish Studies: Twentieth Century*, 7 (1979), 353–64. Also of relevance is the Castro–Goytisolo corres-

in others he offers a blatantly personal and subjective perspective that betrays his subversive aesthetic as an autobiographical gesture. His essays on Larra, Blanco White, and Cernuda, all from the 1960s and 1970s, are examples of ventriloquism, where the essay-writer adopts the voice of his admired forefather; his later readings of Cervantes, Góngora, and Juan Ruiz, in both essays and fiction, follow the Renaissance practice of *imitatio* in order to offer important interpretations fundamental to Goytisolo's construction of a personal dissident canon.

The Heroic Satirist: Mariano José de Larra

The traditional *exordium* accompanying a collection of essays is, as Mermall notes in *The Rhetoric of Humanism* (p. 104), a highly personal form of argumentation, since it attempts to justify the speaker's motives in choosing and ordering his material. Goytisolo's preliminary remarks in his first serious collection of essays, *El furgón de cola*, where he discusses Larra and Cernuda, two of his most revered dissident literary heroes, are most revealing in this regard. Deliberately setting himself within the context of the liberal, pessimistic tradition of writing on the subject of 'Spain as problem' – the title of the collection is from a comment by Antonio Machado on the deplorable state of Spanish culture[15] – Goytisolo qualifies himself to speak on the state of the nation by establishing himself as one of a generation of writers for whom 'no pasan días'.[16] Despite the fact that, economically and socially, Spain had begun to change with the technocrat revolution of the 1960s, politics did not keep pace, and intellectuals found themselves facing the choice between either impotent and self-indulgent alienation from the people or a complete identification with the masses, which would bring with it a total loss of freedom. With the advent of capitalism, says Goytisolo, 'la esfera de acción del intelectual disminuye, el tecnicismo reemplaza al compromiso sentimental y desinteresado, la tentativa romántica apunta en el horizonte'.[17] Thinking, characteristically, in terms of literary predecessors,

pondence in the Boston Archive, *El epistolario: cartas de Américo Castro a Juan Goytisolo (1968–1972)*, ed. Javier Escudero Rodríguez, prologue Juan Goytisolo (Valencia: Pre-Textos, 1997).

[15] Antonio Machado refers to Spain's position as 'furgón de cola' in Europe in 'La reacción', in Manuel and Antonio Machado, *Obras completas*, ed. Heliodoro Carpintero (Madrid: Plenitud, 1967), p. 1247.

[16] The phrase is, of course, Larra's. In his essay in *The Cambridge Companion to Modern Spanish Culture*, Mermall traces the tradition of discussing the woes of the nation back to Feijóo. Dolores Franco usefully anthologizes commentaries on the question of 'Spain as problem' in *España como problema* (Madrid: Alianza, 1988).

[17] Untitled introduction, *El furgón de cola*, 2nd edn (Barcelona: Seix Barral, 1982), pp. 11–17 (pp. 14–15).

Goytisolo presents the choice as one between Larra and Cernuda, between an anguished commitment to Spain and the trauma of exile, yet he acknowledges that present historical circumstances make the choice an invidious one, for the response of each writer seems equally valid. In *El furgón de cola* both will figure as alter egos of Goytisolo's own political dilemma in a book with a twofold aim: to contribute to the 'saneamiento de nuestra atmósfera cultural', and to assuage the author's own 'romanticismo incurable' (p. 17) with regard to his mother country.

The opening essay of *El furgón de cola*, 'La actualidad de Larra', although at times imprecise and wandering, is an indirect statement of Goytisolo's view of the role of the intellectual in society. Larra represents, for Goytisolo, the intellectual as outsider and as demythificator. Instead of adopting the disinterested perspective of the humanist commentator, Larra anguishes over the state of his country and grounds his view of literary morality in the writer's debt to society. In this sense, he offers a concrete, historically based view of life that is distant from the metaphysical speculations of the Generation of 1898, who, Goytisolo contends, failed to understand their nineteenth-century hero. Facing the problem of censorship, Larra adopted the weapon of irony, which enabled him to 'restituir su verdadero valor a los nombres como a los hechos o las palabras'.[18] This form of ironic linguistic subversion is unfortunately not developed to any significant extent by Goytisolo, who generally opts for the voice of the satirist in a more open and, ultimately, less effective form of subversion.[19] Nevertheless, concealed in a footnote to the comment on Larra's language, Goytisolo gives us one of his most important statements concerning his generation's need to question the idiom and myths of the Franco regime:

> El lenguaje creado y utilizado por el Régimen durante sus venticinco años de gobierno no ha sido objeto, hasta ahora, de ningún análisis serio por parte de la izquierda española. La crítica y denuncia del edificio semántico en que se apoya llevaría, no obstante, consigo, la crítica y denuncia de los fundamentos mismos de su existencia. Esta verdad, descubierta por Larra hace más de un siglo, sigue siendo letra muerta para nosotros. En lugar de iniciar la crítica de los valores a partir de las palabras caemos en una retórica fácil – simétrica y complementaria de la que denunciamos.

18 'La actualidad de Larra', in *El furgón de cola*, pp. 19–38 (p. 32).
19 Andrew Ginger, in *Political Revolution and Literary Experiment in the Spanish Romantic Period* (Lewiston: Mellen, 1999), suggests that Larra's most valuable legacy was not his political agenda but the literary dimension of his writing, 'the shifting ironies, the building of narrative structure around divergence not convergence' (p. 112). This is not developed in any real sense by Goytisolo, who, Ginger notes, was wrong, in 'La actualidad de Larra', to assume that Larra's pessimism about the prospects for a favourable liberal political climate was warranted, and his suicide a tragic consequence of the desperate state of the nation. As Ginger points out, Larra was a depressive who died just before a new, more liberal constitution was drawn up in Spain.

> Esfuerzo inútil: tarde o temprano la experiencia nos obligará a reconocer que la negación de un sistema intelectualmente opresor comienza necesariamente con la negación de su estructura semántica.   (p. 32, n. 2)

That such a clear statement of the future direction of Goytisolo's own demythificatory intentions should be hidden in a footnote is evidence of the place that *El furgón de cola* holds as a formative series of essays, working towards the more confident arguments of *Disidencias*. Goytisolo does, however, follow the opening essay in praise of Larra in *El furgón de cola* with what is surely his only imitation of Larra's ironic model of subversion, 'Escribir en España', thus appropriating the voice of his hero for the space of a few pages. This powerful essay, an indictment of the Franco regime's policy of censorship and cultural control, opens on a personal note with the recollection of some comments by a French friend on the helpfulness of the censor to the intellectual scene of a country. What at first seems an outrageous suggestion comes to seem to Goytisolo, after mature reflection, to represent a profound truth and one which, furthermore, was voiced by Larra.[20] The essay thus begins with a highly subjective viewpoint, a remembered comment that is initially ridiculed; it then moves, via the appeal to a previous authority on the question – Goytisolo's hero himself – to an ironic analysis of the state of writing in contemporary Spain. Taking literally the metaphor of illness, so often applied in the past to Spain's political state, Goytisolo depicts a nation of ill and healthy writers, who may be instantly cured or fall sick according to the whims of officialdom. Various remedies are available to heal the infirm, including that of silence and electric-shock treatment. The healthy are kept fit through excessive praise, and death is the ultimate leveller, allowing both the infirm and able-bodied in life to be added to the canon. It is death, then, that offers the only hope of future acknowledgement for those officially rejected.

In this essay one can see the tension between subjectivity and objectivity to which Mermall alludes, although in Goytisolo's satirical vision the suggestions for social improvements that lie scattered in Larra's work are absent. Unlike his hero's progressive agenda, Goytisolo ultimately espouses a Nietzschean view of history that does not propose a gradual evolution

---

[20] The idea may not be as far-fetched as Goytisolo here pretends. In his autobiography he notes wryly that authoritarian regimes are the only ones to take literarture seriously, and that duping the censor can provide a subversive sense of pleasure (*Coto vedado*, p. 155). Goytisolo himself made a conscious decision mid-career not to submit to the Spanish censor as he had internalized the censoring process, leading to a certain literary dishonesty by which he felt compelled to write in a manner so as not to be banned (*En los reinos de Taifa*, pp. 24–5). George Steiner argues throughout *Language and Silence: Essays 1958–1966* (London: Faber & Faber, 1985) that political censorship does not necessarily have a simple silencing effect on writers, and that there may be more subtle forms of censorship and intellectual orthodoxy in so-called 'free' societies. See particularly his essay, 'Night Words' (pp. 89–99).

towards a brighter future. Instead, he uses Larra as a form of shorthand for the despairing intellectual who remains loyal to his nation despite its – in his view – congenital illness. And his imitation of Larra's ironic approach is little more than a straightforward homage to the nineteenth-century thinker. This is intertextuality of the most obvious kind, the subversive impact of the essay arising not out its textual operations but from the satirical position adopted on censorship.

Ventriloquism and Double-Voiced Discourse: José María Blanco White

Leaving, for a moment, *El furgón de cola*, let us turn to a contemporary of Larra's, José María Blanco White, of whom Goytisolo offers an extended and ostentatious autobiographical reading that reveals the complexities of his ventriloquist method of canonizing dissidence in Spanish literary history. In a recent essay, 'Blanco White y la desmemoria española', Goytisolo refers to the varying fortunes of artists and writers throughout history, and notes that Blanco, like Goya at a particular stage in the historiography of Spanish painting, was largely a forgotten figure – except, that is, for readers of the work of Menéndez Pelayo, for whom Blanco was the ultimate cultural renegade. Nevertheless, Pelayo's bilious attack on Blanco fails to hide, Goytisolo suggests, a 'soterrada admiración' for the ninteenth-century intellectual.[21] It also reveals Blanco's importance within the anti-establishment tradition that Goytisolo has sought to rehabilitate. Indeed, Goytisolo's essay stresses the contemporary relevance of Blanco, 'un escritor marginado',[22] and especially of his ethical stance at a time when, in our author's eyes, Spain is approaching again a National–Catholic ethos and an associated cultural poverty.[23] 'En una España que económicamente va a más y culturalmente a menos,' he notes, 'una voz clara e independiente como la de Blanco resulta más necesaria que nunca.' Furthermore – and Goytisolo's words themselves reveal the passion

21 'Blanco White y la desmemoria española', *El País*, 5 June 2001. Goytisolo quotes Pelayo as having called Blanco a 'renegado de todas las sectas, leproso de todos los partidos'. It transpires in Goytisolo's introduction to *Obra inglesa de José María Blanco White* (p. 3) that it was Pelayo who first alerted Goytisolo to Blanco's writing, a point elaborated by Randolph D. Pope in 'Juan Goytisolo y la tradición autobiográfica española', *Revista Chilena de Literatura*, 41 (1992), 25–32. Carmen Martín Gaite also notes the paradoxically positive influence of Pelayo's *Historia de los heterodoxos españoles* in kindling her interest in eighteenth-century Spain, in 'El miedo a lo gris', *Agua pasada* (Barcelona: Anagrama, 1993), pp. 78–87.

22 Thus declares the header to the article. In reply to Goytisolo, José Luis Abellán objected, in the letters column of *El País*, 27 June 2001, that by that time Blanco was far from being a marginal figure in the Spanish canon, and was in fact the object of study of several academics, himself included.

23 The essay was, of course, written before the 2004 electoral defeat of Aznar's Partido Popular, leading to a change of government.

with which he shares Blanco's ethical position – 'la valía excepcional de su obra la convierte no sólo en un punto de referencia indispensable para los defensores del concepto de ciudadanía en el marco de una España abierta y plural, sino también en una serie de dominios y disciplinas que conciernen a nuestra visión crítica de la cultura, la religión y la sociedad.'[24]

It was in 1972, and in Buenos Aires, as a result of censorship in Spain, that Goytisolo published *Obra inglesa de José María Blanco White*, his Spanish translation of selected works by Blanco, a liberal thinker who had spent much of his life in England. Concluding his lengthy critical introduction to the volume, Goytisolo wrote:

> Acabo ya y sólo ahora advierto que al hablar de Blanco White no he cesado de hablar de mí mismo. Si algún lector me lo echa en cara y me acusa de haber arrimado el ascua a mi sardina, no tendré más remedio que admitir que la he asado por completo. Pero añadiré en mi descargo que resulta difícil, a quien tan poco identificado se siente con los valores oficiales y patrios, calar en una obra virulenta e insólita como la que a continuación exponemos sin caer en la tentación de compenetrarse con ella y asumirla, por decirlo así, como resultado de su propia experiencia.   (p. 98)

In the second volume of his autobiography, Goytisolo would go as far as to call Blanco 'una remota encarnación de ti mismo' (*Reinos*, p. 81). Martin Murphy, Blanco White's biographer, has called this a 'brilliant case of icono-clastic special pleading', and it might appear as such when contrasted with the Blanco anthologized by Vicente Llorens in 1971.[25] Llorens, like Goytisolo, was working in exile and undoubtedly felt Blanco was a kindred spirit, yet he arguably achieves a more balanced view of the man who

---

[24] Goytisolo goes on to stress that Blanco's abhorrence of Catholic dogmatism can be applied to the Taliban in Afghanistan, to the Serb Orthodox Church and its support for Serbian ethno-nationalism, and to Zionist fundamentalists in Palestine. Closer to home, however, Blanco's views on the Cortes de Cádiz are enlightening if read with Basque nationalism in mind. And Goytisolo concludes his essay with the following observation on Blanco's importance for the republican and constitutional heritage in Spanish political life: 'La línea del pensamiento constitucionista y republicano de Pí y Margall, la Institución Libre de Enseñanza y Manuel Azaña –soporte indispensable de cualquier proyecto educativo y cívico, opuesto a la ignorancia protectiva y heredado apoltronamiento de los mandarins y burócratas culturales–, no puede permitirse el error de prescindir de un intelectual del fuste excepcional del autor de las bellísimas *Cartas de España*.'

[25] Martin Murphy, *Blanco White: Self-Banished Spaniard* (New Haven: Yale University Press, 1989), p. 204; José María Blanco White, *Antología de obras en español*, ed. and prologue Vicente Llorens (Barcelona: Labor, 1971). In personal correspondence, Llorens compliments Goytisolo on his reading of Blanco (Goytisolo Collection, Boston University, box 13, file 2). For a discussion of the major differences between Blanco and Goytisolo, see Ángel G. Loureiro, 'Intertextual Lives: Blanco White and Juan Goytisolo', in *Intertextual Pursuits: Literary Mediations in Modern Spanish Narrative*, ed. Jeanne P. Brownlow and John W. Kronik (Lewisburg: Bucknell University Press, 1998), pp. 42–56.

Goytisolo dramatically labels, in his novel, *Las virtudes del pájaro solitario*, a 'tránsfuga de diversas Iglesias'.[26] Nevertheless, Llorens and Goytisolo write for different reasons, and Goytisolo reveals a more than noteworthy engagement with the passion and urgency of Blanco's work. Fiction and commentary will also combine, as we shall see, in the introductory essay to the *Obra inglesa de José María Blanco White*, suggesting that it is, in echo of Adorno, intertextual in mode and subversive in its means of proceeding.

If Blanco is an archetypal cultural renegade, then this is also the position to which Goytisolo aspires, whether it be in the Spain of the last years of Franco or that of Aznar. Hence, in his presentation essay, Goytisolo highlights his own mental process of becoming Blanco, assuming his voice in an aggressively unapologetic manner and at the end of his essay. This changes the light with which we go on to read Blanco, so that, in presenting selections from his works, Goytisolo seems in fact to be presenting his own position, for editing is not, of course, a neutral form of interpretation. Goytisolo's 'editing' here could, in fact, be regarded as a form of ventriloquism, and the extracts from Blanco's works become 'purloined letters' – quite literally, indeed, since four of the selected passages are from Blanco's *Letters from Spain*.

If we take, for example, the extract that Goytisolo translates from Blanco's *Observations on Heresy and Orthodoxy*, we find remarks applicable to Goytisolo's case. When Blanco notes of heresy, 'desde que es el vínculo que une bajo su guía vastas corporaciones humanas, y la heterodoxia o herejía suscita agrupaciones contrapuestas bajo gobernantes que se convierten así en rivales peligrosos de los ortodoxos, dichos principios de unión y oposición actúan necesariamente como patriotismos rivales y opuestos' (*Obra inglesa*, p. 267), we could be forgiven for taking this as a commentary on the manner in which Goytisolo has sought to construct an alternative to the orthodox literary canon. When Blanco objects to those who base their notion of 'Christian truth' on biblical texts without recognizing the extent to which these are open to interpretation, he seems to anticipate Goytisolo's own interrogation of authoritative texts. And, in his comments on language and religious symbolism, Blanco reveals himself to be strikingly contemporary – one might even go so far as to suggest that he anticipates Saussurian linguistics and its development into structuralist analysis. Language, for Blanco, is 'un conjunto de signos arbitrarios' that have no meaning beyond 'la que les

---

26 *Las virtudes del pájaro solitario*, 3rd edn (Barcelona: Seix Barral, 1990), p. 116. In the *Pájaro solitario* Blanco is represented by the figure of the Archimandarita. One can see in this a Cervantine mixing of criticism and fiction which, as will become clear shortly, Goytisolo has consistently praised as generically subversive in its self-questioning, and hence democratic and ethically aware. On Blanco White's role in the *Pájaro solitario*, see Manuel Ruiz Lagos, 'Pájaros en vuelo a Simorgh: Transferencias y metamorfosis textual en un relato de Juan Goytisolo, *Las virtudes del pájaro solitario*', in *Escritos sobre Juan Goytisolo*, pp. 171–228.

confiere el hábito mental de quienes las usan' (*Obra inglesa*, p. 265). Hence, orthodox religion, by which Blanco means Roman Catholicism, must come to understand that words such as 'body' and 'blood' are purely arbitrary and may be used in a figurative sense, only acquiring their (Catholic) literalness after familiar usage.[27] Although Blanco might not go so far as a deconstructionist position, the implications of the notion, expressed by him here, are explored in a novel such as *Juan sin Tierra*.

In reading Blanco, then, we seem to learn a considerable amount about Goytisolo, and this identification with a predecessor would seem to exemplify de Man's argument that criticism is a form of self-definition, since 'both parties tend to fuse into a single subject as the original distance between them disappears'. The result, according to de Man, is a '*vertige*, a dizziness of the mind caught in an infinite regression' ('Criticism', p. 10). One can certainly appreciate something of this sense of *vertige* in Goytisolo's edition of Blanco's works. It must be remembered that we are dealing with extracts from Blanco, not complete texts, and that the selection is therefore interesting in itself. The inclusion of a passage on heresy and orthodoxy is perhaps only to be expected, as are the passages in the opening chapter of Blanco's autobiography that detail his youthful dissatisfaction with the spiritual exercises demanded by Catholicism. The tone and subject matter, which is reminiscent of Joyce's famous depiction of his religious education in *Portrait of the Artist as a Young Man*, echoes Goytisolo's own difficult relationship to religion described in his autobiography.[28]

However, the complexity of the relationship between Blanco and Goytisolo emerges if we consider the extracts Goytisolo includes from Blanco's *Letters from Spain*, originally published in English. In translating Blanco, Goytisolo gives him a voice in Spanish, acting as the ventriloquist who projects Blanco's voice into a different language. But the nature of those letters casts this act of translation as a double, or quasi-Barthesian second-level, ventriloquism, for the *Letters from Spain* were, of course, written under an assumed identity – thus they started life themselves as an act of ventriloquism. Signed 'Leucadio Doblado', Blanco explains that Leucadio derives from the Greek meaning 'white', and Doblado indicates the repetitive Blanco White of his surname. But Blanco is more of a trickster than that, for, in a

---

[27] Blanco writes of rival interpretations of biblical texts (*Obra inglesa*, p. 266): 'Los contendientes miran con auténtica sorpresa lo que juzgan desatino y perversidad notorios de su adversario. Las llamas mal apagadas de un celo igualmente genuino les hacen hervir la sangre de las venas cuando observan que palabras tan simples como "cuerpo" y "sangre", por ejemplo, no se toman en su sentido obvio–olvidando que, por tratarse de signos arbitrarios, especialmente cuando pueden ser usados de modo figurativo, dicho sentido solo puede ser obvio si el uso lo ha vuelto familiar.'

[28] See, for instance, *Coto vedado*, p. 122. Goytisolo makes the Blanco White–Joyce link clear in chapter 21 of *La cuarentena*, and in *Telón de boca* (Barcelona: El Aleph, 2003), p. 46.

preface worthy of Cervantes in the games it plays with the reader, he admits that the letters supposedly written from Spain were in fact composed in England. In his presentation essay Goytisolo thus identifies with, or rather, camouflages himself behind, someone who is already an impostor and a ventriloquist. Nevertheless, Blanco, like Goytisolo, it should be noted, is driven by an ethical imperative. He conceals his identity not merely for the sake of textual jocularity, but because his social protest requires such a protective disguise.[29]

Unfortunately, Goytisolo does not include Blanco's preface in his anthology, but he does include passages from the *Letters from Spain* in which Blanco satirizes Spain – passages which, in fact, sit easily beside Goytisolo's own satire of the Spain of his time in, for example, *Juan sin Tierra*. Mocking the notion of *limpieza de sangre*, Blanco writes: 'I verily believe, that were St. Peter a Spaniard, he would either deny admittance into heaven to people of tainted blood, or send them to a retired corner, where they might not offend the eyes of the *old Christians*.'[30] There is also Blanco's cynical description of the execution of a nobleman and his so-called friends who paid for the conduct of the execution, assuring themselves that afterwards his certificate of *noblesse* would reflect well on them.[31] Lastly – but interestingly *not* anthologized by Goytisolo – are Blanco's comments on the bullfight, which can only be enjoyed with 'feelings [. . .] greatly perverted'.[32] Such preoccupations with purity of blood, the honour code, and national spectacles will form the three main elements of the satirical '*auto da fé* as tourist attraction' in part IV of *Juan sin Tierra*, a spectacle which – in the topsy-turvy world of that novel – apparently suffers under a lack of suitably 'qualified' victims since the censorship of the Regime has improved dramatically the moral health of Spain. With these connections in mind, one should stress that *Juan sin Tierra* was the novel Goytisolo published immediately after his Blanco White anthology.

Aspects of Blanco's work that are not anthologized may be as important as those selected, for they call attention to the process of editing as a form of interpretation. One significant omission points to a major difference between Blanco and Goytisolo, namely their religious beliefs. Blanco was a firm believer in God, despite professing the faith of different churches and denominations during his life; Goytisolo professes no religious faith, Christian or

---

[29] Murphy (p. 116) notes that Blanco is keen to hide his identity particularly when discussing the Catholic education of a young Spanish gentleman – based on himself – in the third letter of the collection. Goytisolo, of course, chose to avoid censorship by living and publishing outside Spain from the 1950s on.

[30] Leucadio Doblado, *Letters from Spain* (London: Colburn, 1822), pp. 30–1. Goytisolo includes this passage in his anthology, *Obra inglesa de José María Blanco White*, p. 184.

[31] *Letters from Spain*, pp. 41–3; in Goytisolo's anthology, pp. 190–1.

[32] *Letters from Spain*, p. 158.

otherwise. In the extract that Goytisolo offers from the first chapter of Blanco's autobiography, we find that a comment indicating the cleric's Christian faith has been omitted. One can only speculate that this may be because this aspect of the writer is of less interest to Goytisolo. In the Spanish translation, we read of Blanco's childhood hatred of spiritual exercises (*Obra inglesa*, p. 118): 'Indignarme, al cabo de tantos años, sería absurdo; pero puedo contenerme difícilmente cuando recuerdo lo que he sufrido en nombre de la religión.' These are sentiments with which Goytisolo clearly sympathizes. Blanco's original text, however, continues: 'Alas! My sufferings from that source [i.e. religion] are still more bitter in my old age. No wonder that I utterly dislike that vague name, and prefer to use that of *true Christianity*. RELIGION may mean every mischievous absurdity which still degrades and afflicts mankind: *true Christianity* alone is its antidote.'[33]

Arguably, Blanco is silenced here by the translator; yet there also are occasions when Blanco's voice is not silenced and differences between him and Goytisolo are allowed to emerge. If Blanco's statement of Christian belief is omitted in the passage referred to above, then his Protestant sympathies are represented elsewhere – for instance, in the extract from *Second Travels of an Irish Gentleman in Search of a Religion*. One might also cite the short piece on Cervantes and Dickens at the close of Goytisolo's anthology, which offers a Romantic reading of the *Quixote* that views the mad knight as a symbol of heroic idealism in an unjust world. Such a view is greatly at odds with Goytisolo's own emphasis on the formal aspect of Spanish literature's most famous book.[34] In a third example of double-voiced discourse in the anthology, Blanco's anti-nationalist sentiments, which echo Goytisolo's own oft-stated abhorrence of ethno-nationalism, are articulated in a short passage quoted from his autobiography. But these comments are then juxtaposed with a passage, originally from much later in the autobiography, which reveals Blanco's sense of patriotism: 'Me temo muchísimo por la infeliz España,' Blanco writes.[35] Unless one regards extreme satire as an expression of love, it is hard to imagine the author of *Juan sin Tierra* sharing such tender sentiments towards his mother country.

In this act of literary ventriloquism, the dummy can – and does, on occasion – speak back. Blanco finds room to speak in the intersticies between his original texts, Goytisolo's translation and editing of them, and the presenta-

---

[33] Joseph Blanco White, *The Life of the Rev. Joseph Blanco White, written by himself, with portions of his correspondence*, ed. John Hamilton Thom, 3 vols (London: Chapman, 1845), I, 29.

[34] See *Obra inglesa de José María Blanco White*, pp. 326–7; Anthony Close, *The Romantic Approach to 'Don Quijote': A Critical History of the Romantic Tradition in 'Quijote' Criticism* (Cambridge: Cambridge University Press, 1977), p. 244.

[35] The two passages in question are close together in Goytisolo's edition, despite being a hundred pages apart in the original. See *Obra inglesa de José María Blanco White*, pp. 302 and 304.

tion essay. This creates a Bakhtinian heteroglossia in which Blanco is not silenced; rather he at times speaks for Goytisolo, and at others speaks for himself. That we are able to distinguish such moments is most instructive. It is, of course, Blanco's ethical position, constantly questioning accepted norms of any kind, that attracts Goytisolo. He therefore seeks to establish a formal connection between himself and his nineteenth-century forefather, adopting the position of one who is already a game-playing impostor in the construction of his marginal identity, and so turning such literary machinations into ethical gestures. Yet, one must wonder if this really is a question, following de Man, of the 'disappearance of the self as constitutive subject' ('Criticism', p. 12). Arguably, the marginal self that Goytisolo refracts through the mirror of earlier writers such as Blanco is not fragmented to the point of vertigo, but rather represents a self-conscious attempt by him to balance the dilemma of an ethical project carried out in a philosophical climate unsympathetic to the utterances of a unified, self-constituting marginal subject. Instead of offering a single speaking voice, Goytisolo creates heteroglossic texts in which the marginal subject is fragmented into a plethora of marginal subjectivities. Yet, underlying these disparate voices is still a unified ethical position, and arguably a generic 'marginal subject'.

Towards the end of Goytisolo's essay on Blanco we find a passage that would later surface in the novel, *Juan sin Tierra*, indicating not just the generic overlap that characterizes Goytisolo's work, but also the unifying motif of dissidence that gives much of it an underlying coherence. Interestingly, in the passage, stress is placed on the figure of the author, or scribe, tracing out his dissident canon:

> En el silencio denso, la mariposa nocturna ronda en torno a la lámpara: gira, planea, describe círculos obsesivos, se aleja si la espantamos, pero vuelve en seguida, una vez y otra y otra, hacia el fulgor que la fascina y atrae, absorta en su alucinada tarea, hasta obligarnos a ceder por cansancio – así, desde el instante en que empuñamos la pluma, la idea fantasmal, reiterada, surge y nos acomete, se desvanece cuando la rechazamos, regresa tenaz y muda, con la certeza de su victoria paciente, sabedora de nuestro cansancio. Nos resignamos, pues: la acogemos. El paralelo entre los dos escritores se impone: ¿por qué nos resistiríamos a trazarlo?
>
> (*Obra inglesa*, p. 79)[36]

Taken out of context, there is a certain ambiguity in the identity of the two writers referred to. Initially, it seems that the parallel is between Blanco and Goytisolo, although, in fact, the connection is between Blanco and Cernuda,

---

36 The connection between Blanco and Goytisolo's novel is reinforced in the title of the latter, which apes *Cartas de Juan Sintierra*, an edition of Blanco's letters criticizing the Cortes of Cádiz and the war with France, and written under pseudonym to the editor of *El Español*, the journal that Blanco himself edited.

who were both Sevillians as well as exiles and literary rebels, as Goytioslo goes on to note. Blanco, Goytisolo concludes (*Obra inglesa*, p. 82), 'sujeto a una íntima e irreductible dualidad que puede compendiarse en el apellido repetido con que firma y el recíproco, angustiado examen de White por Blanco y Blanco por White', anticipates Cernuda's doubling of his poetic self in his late poetry, to which we shall shortly turn.

In this passage a second kind of double-voiced discourse is at work: not that of one writer who assumes the voice of another, but that of a writer who doubles his supposedly unitary self in order to interrogate and better understand not his self, but selves. The marginal subject becomes at least two marginal subjectivites for Blanco and Cernuda. Goytisolo, likewise, will employ a form of doubling – labelled *desdoblamiento* in *Don Julián* – as part of his interrogation of identity.[37] Merging Blanco and Cernuda as archetypal *déracinés*, Goytisolo thus seeks to merge himself with both in order to create a generic figure of dissidence encompassing multiple subjectivities. In this regard, the most intriguing aspect of the reappearance of the passage from the Blanco essay in *Juan sin Tierra* is the transformation it undergoes.[38] First, the reference to Blanco and Cernuda is omitted. As if to assume the double-voiced qualities of their discourse for himself, Goytisolo ends the passage, 'te resignas, pues, y la acoges : la soledad propicia su vuelo y el paralelo, a todas luces, se impone : por qué te resistirás aún a trazarlo?' Second, the pronouns shift from the first-person plural ('¿por qué nos resistiríamos a trazarlo?') to the second-person singular ('por qué te resistirás aún a trazarlo?'). Third, Goytisolo adds the image of a writer sitting 'en el silencio del escritorio-cocina', presumably the author figure, or 'writing consciousness', of the novel that gives it a centre.[39] This is the most significant change, for the image of the moth circling the light is offered in *Juan sin Tierra* both as a motif for fragmented voices that cohere around a central core of dissidence, and as a metaphor for the structure of that novel and an image of the writing process that it explores. Far from suggesting a Barthesian 'death of the author', the text of *Juan sin Tierra*, as we shall see, thus places

[37] The relevant passage from the novel is: 'desdoblándote al fin por seguirte mejor, como si fueras otro' (p. 126).

[38] Repunctuated in accordance with Goytisolo's fictional style, the passage in *Juan sin Tierra* (Barcelona: Mondadori, 1994), p. 203, reads: 'en el silencio del escritorio-cocina la mariposa nocturna ronda en turno a la lámpara : gira, planea, describe círculos obsesivos, se aleja cuando la espantas pero vuelve en seguida, una vez y otra vez y otra, hacia el fulgor que la fascina y atrae, absorta en su alucinada tarea, desdeñosa de tus manotadas : así, desde el instante en que regresas del baño, la idea fantasmal, reiterada surge y te acomete, se desvanece cuando la rechazas, porfía, tenaz y muda, con la certeza de su victoria paciente, sabedora de su inmediato cansancio : te resignas, pues, y la acoges : la soledad propicia su vuelo y el paralelo, a todas luces, se impone : por qué te resistirás aún a trazarlo?'

[39] In *En los reinos de Taifa* (p. 229) Goytisolo uses this term to refer to the room in which he worked in his home in Paris.

on a pinnacle, or offers as a point of origin, the figure of the scribe in his 'escritorio-cocina'.

The repetition of this passage in essay and novel clearly brings about an intertextual questioning of generic division. More than this, however, it also fragments, in a centrifugal movement, the speaking voices in Goytisolo's discourse while, at the same time, underpinning centripetally their unity around a focal point of dissidence. Finally, it queries the classic humanist notion of a unified subject and yet also defies the postmodernist dispersion of the subject into contingent voices through its images of multiple and *convergent* subjectivities and of a central writing consciousness. It would seem that de Man's abolition of the constitutive subject in a dizzying intersubjectivity finds a limit, at least in Goytisolo's work, because the author's ethical imperative – the search for a dissident position from which to speak – demands an end to the *vertige*. It ultimately necessitates a point at which the observing subject can, in fact, be recuperated from the observed.

The Self as Other: Luis Cernuda

In *El furgón de cola* Luis Cernuda is presented as a poet and literary critic whose open-mindedness contrasts with the various mutually exclusive theoretical schools competing for Goytisolo's intellectual attention in 1960s Paris. If existentialism, Marxism, psychoanalysis, formalism, and structualism all ran the risk of blinkered thinking, Cernuda, possibly influenced by his exposure to the English tradition of Arnold, Eliot, and Wilson, had read literary works with a delicate sensitivity that employs a variety of interpretative approaches (although this admiration for eclecticism will later be modified by Goytisolo in favour of the suggestion that different approaches to literature be seen as complementary but never synthesized into a blunted attempt at coherence).[40] Cernuda, according to Goytisolo, had also avoided the quagmire of Spanish literary criticism, which laboured under a self-serving myth of national greatness that was in reality long dead. He achieved this by jettisoning polemical intentions and reading with independence and an honourable sense of nonconformity – something that Goytisolo himself has constantly strived for, even if he has not always achieved it.

Cernuda is not, however, merely to be admired as a literary critic. He was, first and foremost, a poet whose exile, irreverent attitude to the native land that shunned him, and dialectical vision of life – encapsulated in the title of his collected poems, *La realidad y el deseo* – is imitated by Goytisolo in his

---

40 See 'Cernuda y la crítica literaria española', in *El furgón de cola*, pp. 133–50 (p. 140, n.); for Goytisolo's revised view of the use of theoretical models, see 'Escritores, críticos y fiscales', in *Libertad, libertad, libertad* (Barcelona: Anagrama, 1978), pp. 80–94.

own work. Taking up Cernuda's cause becomes, for Goytisolo, a deliberate gesture of defiance against the prevailing norms of so-called social realist writing in the 1950s.[41] In the second of two essays on the poet in *El furgón de cola*, 'Homenaje a Luis Cernuda', Goytisolo comments that Cernuda's poetry offers a way out of the log jam affecting Spanish letters: 'por espacio de quince años los poetas [and novelists, one could add] han cantado la revolución sin que la revolución se produzca.'[42] Cernuda will provide Goytisolo with a means of rejecting documentary-style writing in *Señas de identidad* and *Reivindicación del Conde don Julián*, both through an irreverent and vituperative attitude towards Spain – *Sansueña* is their shared term for her – and through the double vision of life expressed in a dialogue between a first-person 'yo' and a second-person 'tú'.[43]

Cernuda's difficult relationship with his mother country is placed by Goytisolo in a context wider than that of pure politics. A supporter of the Republic, the poet was bound to find Francoist Spain inhospitable, but his increasing discomfort with Spanish society emerges before the war, in the poems of *Los placeres prohibidos* (1931), the title of which is a loosely disguised reference to Cernuda's homosexuality. 'El desacuerdo del instinto amoroso del poeta con las convenciones sociales y morales de su país y de su tiempo,' observes Goytisolo ('Homenaje', p. 158), 'acentúa todavía su acritud respecto a las instituciones que simbolizan a sus ojos la negación de su libertad: matrimonio, familia, religión, leyes.' One cannot help but imagine Goytisolo in the 1960s identifying his own concealed homosexuality, not made public until much later, with that of the poet. Like the younger novelist, Cernuda offers a rebellion that is political, religious, and aesthetic. So, we read in Goytisolo's essay that 'la rebeldía de Cernuda se manifiesta asimismo en el terreno religioso en forma de una apología de los placeres terrenos radicalmente opuesta al puritanismo cerril del medio español en que vive' (p. 160). Feeling himself torn between reality and desire, elaborating two points of view not only different, but in fact opposed, Cernuda nevertheless forges

---

[41] Critics now question whether social realism existed in the simplistic, documentary guise by which it has often been defined. Jeremy Squires reads Rafael Sánchez Ferlosio's *El Jarama*, generally acclaimed as the best of Spanish social realism, as a much more complex text in *Experience and Objectivity in the Writings of Rafael Sánchez Ferlosio* (Lewiston: Mellen, 1998). Jo Labanyi highlights the mythical elements of one of Goytisolo's own supposedly social realist novels, *Duelo en El Paraíso*, in 'The Ambiguous Implications of the Mythical References in Juan Goytisolo's *Duelo en El Paraíso*', *Modern Language Review*, 80 (1985), 845–57.

[42] 'Homenaje a Luis Cernuda', *El furgón de cola*, pp. 151–74 (p. 172).

[43] The name *Sansueña* is apparently of French origin, denoting Saxony. It was, according to Menéndez Pidal, imported into Spanish through ballads whose source was the Carolingian epic, and came to be the name used to indicate a Moorish city or region in the peninsula, frequently Zaragoza. This is how Cervantes uses it in the *Quijote* (II, 26). See Pidal's *Romancero hispánico (hispano-portugués, americano y sefardí)*, 2 vols (Madrid: Espasa-Calpe, 1953), I, 256.

out of this paradox a clear vision of his *madrastra* and of the need to awaken the Spanish people from the dream world in which they live, a theme that also pervades the essays of *El furgón de cola*.[44]

In the poem 'Ser de Sansueña', Cernuda elaborates his notion of Spain as a vicious step-mother, a view repeated by Goytisolo in *Don Julián*, where he refers to Spain as his 'madrastra inmunda' (p. 88). Indeed, the opening of Goytisolo's novel, in which the protagonist, ensconced in Tangier, imagines Spain – 'tierra ingrata entre todas espuria y mezquina' – lying threateningly across the Straits of Gibraltar, echoes the initial lines of 'Ser de Sansueña':

> Acaso allí estará, cuatro costados
> Bañados en los mares, al centro la meseta
> Ardiente y andrajosa. Es ella, la madrastra
> Original de tantos, como tú, dolidos
> De ella y por ella dolientes.[45]

The rejected son who, despite his suffering, feels tied to the nation he abhors and which abhors him is the theme of much of Goytisolo's mature fiction, and Cernuda's poetry clearly strikes a chord. And just as Cernuda will use agricultural and climatological references in 'Ser de Sansueña' to suggest the wild extremes of Spain's politics – 'Árida tierra, cielo fértil [. . .] Allí todo es extremo' (p. 269) – Goytisolo will make a similar comparison in *Don Julián*, where Spain's weather is subject to 'influencias mudables, opuestas : a la dictadura versátil de los caprichos imponderables' (p. 83).

It is, however, Cernuda's creation of a dialogue between first- and second-person voices that provides the most intriguing textual link with Goytisolo, for he creates a similar *desdoblamiento* in *Señas de identidad* and *Don Julián*. In the poem, 'La familia', from *Como quien espera el alba*, for example, Cernuda uses the device to express many of the sentiments concerning a rigid social order, with no tolerance for difference from the norm, which Goytisolo would later echo in his autobiography. The poet interrogates himself as to the nature of his childhood and relationship with his parents:

---

44 Cernuda also lauds Larra as a forefather who had wrestled with the problems of living in an inhospitable country. In 'A Larra con unas violetas', which commemorates the centenary of Larra's suicide, Cernuda writes: 'La tierra ha sido medida por los hombres,/ Con sus casas estrechas y matrimonios sórdidos,/ Su venenosa opinión pública y sus revoluciones/ Más crueles e injustas que las leyes,/ Como inmenso bostezo demoníaco;/ No hay sitio en ella para el hombre solo,/ Hijo desnudo y deslumbrante del divino pensamiento.' He goes on to refer to Spain as a *madrastra* and laments: 'Escribir en España no es llorar, es morir/ Porque muere la inspiración envuelta en humo.' The poem is from the volume *Las nubes*, collected in *La realidad y el deseo*, 4th edn (Mexico City: Fundo de Cultura Ecónomica, 1964), pp. 145–6.

45 'Ser de Sansueña', from *Vivir sin estar viviendo*, in *La realidad y el deseo*, pp. 268–70 (p. 268); *Don Julián*, p. 83.

> ¿Recuerdas tú, recuerdas aún la escena
> A que día tras día asististe paciente
> En la niñez, remota como sueño al alba?[46]

The oppressive atmosphere of family life, and the rigidly hierarchical structure of relations between father, mother, and offspring, is encapsulated in the
image of the home as made of glass (p. 203): 'tal vidrio/Que todos quiebran,
pero nadie dobla.' For the young Cernuda, the choice is either to accept or
rebel, with no possibility of change – 'doblar' here seems to indicate a desire
to question and turn around the prevailing norm in order to create a new
balance of family relations. Like Goytisolo, Cernuda feels a fundamental lack
of understanding between himself and his taciturn father, and he is compelled
to mask his true self and sexuality behind the ill-fitting garments of others'
values:

> Aquel amor de ellos te apresaba
> Como prenda medida para otros, [. . .]
> A odiar entonces aprendiste el amor que no sabe
> Arder anónimo sin recompensa alguna.   (p. 203)

The division of the poet's self in the dialogue of first- and second-person
voices thus reflects the double life he initially leads – 'Pero algo más había,
agazapado/Dentro de ti, como alimaña en cueva oscura,/Que no te dieron
ellos, y eso eres' (p. 203) – and, on a more profound level, brings about its
end through a form of self-analysis that uncovers an authentic identity under-
neath the surface mask. Total isolation, and in Cernuda's case exile itself, is
the price the poet pays:

> Y libre al fin quedaste, a solas con tu vida,
> Entre tantos de aquellos que, sin hogar ni gente,
> Dueños en vida son del ancho olvido.   (p. 203)

However, there is a key difference between Cernuda's use of doubling and
that of Goytisolo. While, in both cases, the technique facilitates the interrogation of personal identity through an analysis of the past and of prescribed
social roles, for Cernuda, the creation of another poetic voice is, in the words
of Alexander Coleman, 'a perspective upon the self which can impassively
observe it' and thus avoid 'sentimental communicaiton'.[47] There is none of
the aggressiveness of Goytisolo's self-analysis, where the interplay between
the self and other, as we have seen in *Coto vedado* and *En los reinos de Taifa*,

---

[46] 'La familia', from *Como quien espera el alba*, in *La realidad y el deseo*, pp. 201–4
(p. 201).

[47] Alexander Coleman, *Other Voices: A Study of the Poetry of Luis Cernuda* (Chapel
Hill: University of North Carolina Press, 1969), p. 84.

and shall see in the next chapter in relation to *Señas de identidad* and *Don Julián*, is intended to bring about the destruction of an abhorrent past identity and articulate the emergence of a new, more authentic self. The imagined other with whom Cernuda conducts a dialogue varies, taking the form of a desired lover, an imagined self, or a personal demon. Only the last of these corresponds to Goytisolo's case, and the divergence between the two writers is all the more evident in the series of poems in which Cernuda creates a series of masks or *personae*, such as Lazarus, the *Reyes Magos*, or Philip II, as alter egos.[48] For Coleman, these figures serve as a 'focal point which, like a magnet, attracts the poet's mind away from a concentration on his own image' (p. 84), an approach largely at odds with the impassioned self-analysis of Goytisolo's writing. Cernuda's *personae* do not necessarily express aspects of the poet's self, but represent an abandonment of self through the liberation of speaking as an imaginative character. This is in opposition to Goytisolo's readings of Larra, Blanco White, and Cernuda himself, where literary forefathers fulfil the role of authenticators of the novelist's personal dilemmas and quest to canonize literary dissidence.

Imitatio *as Cultural Re-reading: Cervantes, Góngora, Juan Ruiz*

If Goytisolo's readings of Larra, Blanco White, and Cernuda reveal a progressive desire not just to value the work of previous masters, but to draw upon it and imitate it, then this is carried much further in relation to an array of literary predecessors whose writing has particularly engaged Goytisolo: first Cervantes, Góngora, and Quevedo; then Fernando de Rojas and Francicso Delicado; later San Juan de la Cruz and Miguel de Molinos; most recently the author of the 'Carajicomedia de Fray Bugeo'. Each of these can be identified, in Goytisolo's eyes, with 'Juan Sin Tierra', the legendary figure of exile who marks a symbolic point of convergence for Goytisolo's canon of dissidents.[49] While space precludes a lengthy discussion of each of these

---

48 See 'Lázaro' and 'La adoración de los magos', from *Las nubes*, and 'Silla del Rey', from *Vivir sin estar viviendo*, in *La realidad y el deseo*, pp. 164–8, 171–80, and 270–3 respectively.

49 Juan Sin Tierra is a Spanish version of the legendary wanderer who also appears in English as John Lackland and French as Jean Sans Terre. Michael Ugarte, in *Trilogy of Treason: An Intertextual Study of Juan Goytisolo* (Columbia: University of Missouri Press, 1982), p. 120, relates the title of the novel, *Juan sin Tierra*, to a volume of poetry, *Jean sans terre*, by the Alsatian poet, Ivan Goll (ed. Francis B. Carmody [Berkeley: University of California Press, 1962]). Elsewhere, Genaro J. Pérez ('Form in Juan Goytisolo's *Juan sin Tierra*', *Journal of Spanish Studies: Twentieth Century*, 5 [1977], 137–59) and Brad Epps (*Significant Violence*, pp. 129–30) relate the title to John Lackland of England (1167–1216), who was forced to accept the Magna Carta. While these are certainly suggestive connections, Blanco's use of the title seems, as already noted, a more convincing, Spanish source for Goytisolo.

cases of intertextuality, a brief consideration of three of the most significant forefathers whom Goytisolo imitates will serve to demonstrate the personal and intuitive nature of his readings in Spanish literature. What is most notable is that from the 1970s on, that is to say after *El furgón de cola*, many of the writers whose work Goytisolo explores are central to the Spanish canon and not, like Blanco or Cernuda, exiled and arguably much more marginal. Such is the case with Cervantes, Góngora, and Juan Ruiz, who are discussed in turn below.

Disidencias, a series of essays published as a single volume in 1977, represents the first full flowering of Goytisolo's mature essayistic style. The book deals with the theme of literary dissidence and its ethical implications, offering three perspectives on the question: formal experimentation, originating in Cervantes and found in the modern Latin American novelists, Carlos Fuentes and Guillermo Cabrera Infante; linguistic innovation, to be found in Góngora and the contemporary Hispanic writers, Joaquín Belda and José Lezama Lima; and thematic rebellion, found in Quevedo's sexual and scatological vocabulary and revisited by Octavio Paz. In later essays in *Contracorrientes* and *El árbol de la literatura* Goytisolo would add a formal-thematic type of dissidence located in the overlap between Muslim and peninsular literature to be found in the works of Juan Ruiz and San Juan de la Cruz. The main thrust of his reading of the canonical writers whose work and reputations he tackles is to combine a formalist perspective with the project of political subversion inherited from his earliest works.

Cervantes, it is frequently suggested, is the father of both the modern novel and of self-conscious textuality. *Don Quixote* lends itself to a structuralist, and even a post-structuralist, reading because of the plethora of narrators, editors, and translators who traverse the work, undermining any pretence to objective narration. At first glance, Goytisolo seems to follow this perspectivist approach, termed by E. C. Riley a 'game with mirrors'.[50] In fact, however, he elaborates an ethical stance that is quite at odds with classic (post-)structuralist thought and which offers a moral basis for the intertextual method of writing that has dominated Goytisolo's fiction since *Don Julián*. In the *Quijote*, Goytisolo argues, 'la lectura única tradicional cede el paso a una disyuntiva o variedad de interpretaciones que preserva nuestra libertad de elección y juicio, confiriendo así a una empresa aparentemente estética una profunda justificación moral.'[51] This open, 'democratic' approach to writing, a template for a moral textual rebellion, is achieved through the practice of Renaissance *imitatio* from which the parody of chivalric romance in the *Quixote* derives. And *imitatio*, remodelled as

---

[50] *Cervantes's Theory of the Novel* (Oxford: Clarendon Press, 1962), p. 39. The self-conscious tradition in Spanish literature is much older than Cervantes, of course. One need look no further than Goytisolo's own writings on medieval literature to note this.

[51] 'Terra Nostra', in *Disidencias* (Madrid: Taurus, 1992), pp. 269–312 (p. 305).

Bakhtinian intertextuality, is the practice that Goytisolo will employ in relation to both Cervantes and Góngora, thus applying to them an important aspect of their own poetics.[52]

In the *Quijote*, Cervantes catalogues the faults of chivalric romance and yet displays a certain affection for it, and this ambivalence also characterizes modern intertextuality, which implies both homage to the text parodied and irreverence through its adaptation in the new piece of writing.[53] Both are dialogic processes involving the re-reading and re-writing of earlier texts, which must necessarily be recognized by the reader and which are transformed by being placed in a new context.[54] Arthur Terry explains Renaissance imitation in terms of rupture and continuity, seeing it as a means by which writers can attempt to bridge a perceived cultural gap between their own modern age and that of the classics. 'Allusion is the central procedure of most Renaissance writing,' Terry suggests. 'The writer in this context is always a re-writer, concerned with the dismemberment and reconstruction of what has already been written. This is a very different matter from conventional notions of "sources" and "influences" – terms which can scarcely suggest the strenuousness which such re-writing can involve.'[55]

This sense of the consumption and transformation of previous texts in a new context, rather than mere allusion to them, describes accurately Goytisolo's approach to creative writing, and it is a technique he learned from Cervantes. Although the refrain 'el país de cuyo nombre no quiero acordarme' haunts *Don Julián*, and the Cardenio episode from the *Quixote* is parodied in the sixth section of *Juan sin Tierra*, Cervantes is more important as a *model* of the dialogic method of writing than as an immediate source to pillage. Nevertheless, Goytisolo, as is the case with many of the writers that interest him, is content to ignore aspects of Cervantes' works that do not accord with his own intentions. So, Cervantes' Christianity, more clearly expressed in such stories as 'La Gitanilla' or 'La fuerza de la sangre', from the *Novelas ejemplares*, and in the late romance, *Los trabajos de Persiles y Segismunda*, are set aside in favour of a Bakhtinian-based formalist reading.[56]

---

52 Paul Julian Smith explores this point rather literally in his notion of '(be)hindsight' as homosexual literary homage in 'Cervantes, Goytisolo and the Sodomitical Scene', in Edwin Williamson (ed.), *Cervantes and the Modernists: The Question of Influence* (London: Tamesis, 1994), pp. 43–54.

53 By intertextuality I understand the Bakhtinian notion of a dialogue of texts that brings about literary renewal through 'defamiliarisation', or the placing of old ideas in new contexts.

54 See Linda Hutcheon, *A Theory of Parody* (New York: Methuen, 1985), p. 6, and *Intertextuality: Theories and Practices*, ed. Michael Whorton and Judith Still (Manchester: Manchester University Press, 1990), for the connection between intertextuality and imitation.

55 Arthur Terry, *Seventeenth-Century Spanish Poetry: The Power of Artifice* (Cambridge: Cambridge University Press, 1993), p. 40.

56 For a discussion of Goytisolo's use of Cervantes in his fiction, and of his tendency

And previous Spanish interpretations of Cervantes are rejected, notably the Generation of 1898's romantic view, or the prevailing mid-century approach, which was largely intuitive and thematic and tended to glorify the *Quijote* as an expression of the Spanish character.[57]

Another canonical writer with whom Goytisolo engages in a literary dialogue is the Baroque poet, Luis de Góngora. Like Cervantes, Góngora was a practitioner of *imitatio* whose work now seems strikingly modern – indeed, it has been interpreted as a post-structuralist play of signifiers.[58] Unlike Cervantes, however, Góngora suffered from a negative image during the early years of the Franco regime, his highly ornate, baroque poetry being read unfavourably when compared to Garcilaso's pared-down classicism. The Falangist Luis Rosales pitted Góngora against Garcilaso in his 1936 essay, 'La figuración y la voluntad de morir en la poesía española', arguing that, while in the latter's work there was an ephiphanic moment of revelation 'anterior a la aparición de la palabra en el proceso de la creación', the former had turned his attention to the word itself and lost the mystery that lay behind it.[59] Thence, argued Rosales, had stemmed the decadence of Spanish poetry from the seventeenth to the nineteenth centuries, for Romanticism was deemed guilty of the same formal introversion as Góngora. Concerned more with the weight of the literary tradition that preceded him, Góngora is unfaithful to the true nature of the Spanish poetic spirit and as such must be

to misread certain aspects, see Pina Rosa Piras, 'El cervantismo de Juan Goytisolo', in *Cervantes*, 19 (1999), 167–79, and my ' "En el principio de la literatura está el mito": Reading Cervantes through Juan Goytisolo's *Reivindicación del Conde don Julián* and *Juan sin Tierra*', *Bulletin of Hispanic Studies* (Liverpool), 77 (2000), 587–603.

[57] For a comparison of the treatment of the *Quijote* by Goytisolo and Unamuno, see my 'Juan Goytisolo, Miguel de Unamuno and Spanish Literary Criticism', in *A Lifetime's Reading: Essays for Patrick Gallagher*, ed. Don W. Cruickshank (Dublin: University College Dublin Press, 1999), pp. 135–52 (published as Alison Kennedy). Examples of mid-century Cervantine criticism within Spain can be found in the centenary publication, *Actas de la Asamblea Cervantina de la Lengua Española* (Madrid: Revista de Filología Española, 1948), in which Oscar Miró Quesada, for example, patriotically writes ('Dualidad en Cervantes y en el *Quijote*', pp. 407–14): 'Cervantes es una voz que todos los hombres han escuchado y un noble espíritu que todos han comprendido, ya leyéndole en el idioma hispano, para veintidós naciones materno; ya a través de versiones innúmeras en la mayor parte de las lenguas conocidas.' For him, Cervantes' genius lies in his ability to harmonize 'la belleza y la profundidad; el estilo y la idea; la importancia de lo dicho y la elevada manera de decirlo'.

[58] See, for example, Paul Julian Smith, 'Góngora and Barthes', in *The Body Hispanic: Gender and Sexuality in Spanish and Spanish American Literature* (Oxford: Clarendon Press, 1989), pp. 44–68; Lorna Close, 'The play of difference: a reading of Góngora's *Soledades*', in Peter W. Evans (ed.), *Conflicts of Discourse: Spanish Literature in the Golden Age* (Manchester: Manchester University Press, 1990), pp. 184–98; and Crystal Chemris, 'Self-Reference in Góngora's *Soledades*', *Hispanic Journal*, 12 (1991), 7–15.

[59] Luis Rosales, 'La figuración y la voluntad de morir en la poesía española', *Cruz y Raya*, 33 (1936), 65–101 (80).

condemned (Rosales seems immune to Garcilaso's Petrarchan sources). Whether his glorification by the Generation of 1927, by then well out of favour with Nationalist cultural politics, has any bearing on Rosales' judgement is unclear, but a later, similarly negative assessment of the Baroque poet does make reference to this 'disconformista' group as valuing Góngora purely out of a desire for another modern '-ism'. Speaking twenty-five years after Rosales' article, on the occasion of the quatercentenary of Góngora's birth, the art historian José Camón Aznar argued that the Cordoban had come to the attention of modern literary sensibility thanks to his more *irritating* works. In his 'versos de laboratorio', Góngora employed words in an arbitrary fashion, separating them from their referent and producing poetry which, he claims, is 'la más alejada del gusto de hoy, tan apetente de humanismo y de temas directos'.[60] 'No hay en toda la historia del pensamiento', Camón Aznar observes (p. 12), 'una tal confianza en la virtualidad de la pura creación poética. Ni una tan desdeñosa versión de la naturaleza.'[61] Góngora had, of course, in the meantime been the subject of a favourable, largely formalist interpretation by Dámaso Álonso, a minor member of the Generation of 1927, but Goytisolo's reading of the poet is, rather strikingly, the opposite of that of Rosales and Camón Aznar, and leads one to wonder if more than just a feeling for the modernity of Góngora's poetry lies behind his view.[62]

Goytisolo's interpretation of Góngora begins with a focus upon language as, in Saussurian terms, a system of relationally defined signifiers that stand arbitrarily for the objects they signify. Góngora's heavily metaphorical and metonymic style thus celebrates, Goytisolo argues, the gap between signifier

[60] José Camón Aznar, *Góngora en la teoría de los estilos* (Madrid: Dirección General de Archivos y Bibliotecas, 1962), p. 9. Another critic to object to the Generation of 1927's glorification of Góngora was José Luis Varela, in 'Con la soledad y en las *Soledades* de Góngora', *Cuadernos de Literatura*, 1 (1947), 41–53. Although Varela offers a neutral reading of Góngora as the culmination of a literary tradition, he slams his twentieth-century poetic followers for producing a minority art which, in its formalism, has lost touch with humanity.

[61] Possibly feeling the need to conclude his lecture on a positive note, given the occasion, the author begrugingly remarks that Góngora's genius was his stylistic independence, despite his disinterest in the cultural and human justification of the themes he treated. A further example of the continuation, in diluted form, of criticism of Góngora's metaphoric style is to be found with Alberto Sánchez in *La obra de Góngora* (Madrid: n.pub., 1960), a lecture course for pre-university students. There Sánchez argued that, in contrast to the poems of San Juan de la Cruz, the *Soledades* contained no mystery, no luminosity, but were organized according to mathematical clarity and precision. Rosales, in 'La figuración y la voluntad de morir', had earlier also praised the sense of mystery in San Juan's poetry.

[62] It is not the intention here to suggest that Goytioslo is writing *directly* in opposition to Rosales and Camón Aznar – there is no proof that he ever read them – but, rather, that they represent a form of intuitive literary criticism, negative to Góngora, which contrasts strikingly with Goytisolo's more rigorous, formalist reading.

and signified, revealing the opacity and even sensuality of the medium with which the writer works. However, despite the apparently structuralist view of language that underpins this interpretation, Goytisolo continues in a manner that is decidedly un-structuralist and, in fact, somewhat essentialist. Hinting that Góngora's sensual use of language may be Arabic in origin, and reversing the negative evaluation that Rosales and Camón Aznar offer of his obscurantist use of metaphor, Goytisolo attributes to Gongorine language an ethical value akin to that located in Cervantine narrative games. 'La boscosa frondosidad del lenguaje de Góngora', he writes in 'La metáfora erótica' (p. 330), 'su verso escurridizo, serpentino, permiten al novelista del siglo XX adueñarse del mundo complejo en que vive mediante la creación de un cuerpo verbal vivo y, por consiguiente, sensual.' Rather than seeing Góngora as an example of structualist and post-structuralist communicative melt-down, Goytisolo sees his poetry as erotic. It represents a means to awaken the reader's intellect, to encourage him to question accepted dogma through an interrogation of multiple meanings,[63] and to instill an appreciation of the malleability, physicality, and not just sensuality, but even sexuality, of words. Góngora's poetry is indeed like this, but, crucially, it achieves its aim without losing touch with reality. Layers of metaphors impose themselves, certainly. Yet, Góngora will use them to *master* reality – hence, *adueñarse* is the verb Goytisolo uses to describe this mimetic process.[64]

The hint, here in relation to Góngora, that Spanish literature retains Arabic influences is developed much more forcefully by Goytisolo in interpretations of other canonical writers, including Cervantes, San Juan de la Cruz, and Juan Ruiz.[65] The latter case perhaps illustrates best what is really a larger argument concerning the intersection of Christian, Jewish, and Muslim societies in Spanish cultural and intellectual history. The thesis derives from the controversial work of Américo Castro, who postulated, in *La realidad histórica de España*, that Ruiz's poem was evidence of a rich cultural osmosis in the peninsula. In its combination of eroticism and religiousness, Castro saw the *Libro de buen amor* as reminiscent of *The Dove's Neck-Ring*, a work by the eleventh-century Islamic author, Ibn Hazm, and he described the

---

[63] Goytisolo cites as an example Góngora's legacy to writers such as Luis Martín-Santos, for whom a baroque syntax was a means to fool the censor and encourage readers to probe beneath surface meanings.

[64] For a fuller discussion of the complex relationship between language and reality in Góngora's poetry and Goytisolo's fiction, see my 'Language, Meaning, and Rebellion in Goytisolo's *Don Julián*: The Gongorine Intertexts', *Bulletin of Spanish Studies*, 80 (2003), 47–68.

[65] For Goytisolo on Cervantes' Moorish connections, see 'Vicisitudes del mudejarismo: Juan Ruiz, Cervantes, Galdós', in *Crónicas sarracinas* (Barcelona: Seix Barral, 1989), pp. 47–71, and 'Cervantes, España y el Islam', in *Contracorrientes* (Barcelona: Montesinos, 1985), pp. 25–9. For Goytisolo's interpretation of San Juan de la Cruz, see pp. 143–58.

poem as 'fruto ambiguo de la alegoría vital y de los frenos moralizantes'.[66] In other words, it represented a combination of sensuality and aestheticism that he regarded as characteristic of Oriental thought. Castro's controversial hypothesis has been refuted by a number of scholars, notably Claudio Sánchez Albornoz, who counters Castro's Moorish reading of the *Libro* by linking it to both the Goliardic tradition and to Ovid, whose *Pamphilus* is referred to in the poem.[67]

Although the existence of Christian, Jewish, and Muslim communities in the peninsula in Ruiz's time is undisputed, the amount of cross-community activity and, more importantly, cultural understanding that existed is difficult to gauge. The *Libro* has many sources in Western, Latin-based culture, and it is impossible to assess the extent of Ruiz's personal knowledge and appreciation of Arabic language and thought. Nevertheless, for Goytisolo, the *Libro* is evidence of the *possibility* of an intercultural osmosis that is highly suggestive. In a key essay, 'Vicisitudes del mudejarismo: Juan Ruiz, Cervantes, Galdós', he suggests that Ruiz is stimulated by an active engagement with cultural difference and diversity. 'El gran escritor crea,' he remarks (pp. 47–8), 'a partir de todo: su voracidad insaciable le impulsa al pillaje desenfrenado de librerías, museos, culturas; a penetrar en ellos como en terreno conquistado; a apropiarse sin remordimiento de lo que le interesa y conviene; a fundar en el trasvase, permeabilidad, ósmosis, su única e irreductible especifidad.'[68] This cultural pillaging recalls the active engagement of *imitatio* with other texts, giving Goytisolo a literary rationale for his highly personal reworking of the *Libro de buen amor* in *Makbara*. There he imagines it being read aloud by one of the oral storytellers in Marrakesh's Xemaá-el-Fná, thus reciting, and even re-siting, it in an Arab context.[69]

---

[66] Américo Castro, *La realidad histórica de España*, rev. edn (Madrid: Porrúa Turanzas, 1962), p. 382.

[67] See Claudio Sánchez Albornoz, *España: un enigma histórico*, 2 vols (Buenos Aires: Sudamericana, 1956), I, chapter 8.

[68] The apparently post-structuralist, promiscuous, orientation that this quotation seems to suggest is, however, off-set by the more traditional view that Goytisolo offers in the same essay of the process of reading. In search of something akin to Hans Robert Jauss's 'horizon of expectations' in relation to the author whose work he approaches, Goytisolo remarks (p. 52): 'Cuando me enfrento a una novela y/o relato de un escritor alejado de mí en el tiempo y/o espacio, la falta de un contexto común a ambos me obliga a reconstruirlo si aspiro a los beneficios de una lectura óptima, totalizadora, global. Sólo el coetáneo y paisano del autor puede captar el maremágnum de conotaciones, propósitos y referencias integrados en sus libros, sin necesidad de recurrir a una minuciosa, y siempre aleatoria, reconstrucción. Recrear la atmósfera cultural y social en que se produjo el texto, situar a éste dentro de aquélla, revivir los sentimientos de inmediatez, familiaridad y simpatía del público originariamente destinatario serán así empeño obligado del crítico resuelto a penetrar en sus zonas de sombra y dilucidar sus presuntos secretos.'

[69] For an analysis of Goytisolo's intertextual reading of Juan Ruiz in *Makbara*, see my 'Reciting/Re-siting the *Libro de buen amor* in the *zoco*: Irony, Orality and the Islamic in Juan Goytisolo's *Makbara*', *Modern Language Notes*, 117 (2002), 406–31.

Goytisolo regards Juan Ruiz as an experimental writer who, through his stylistic innovation, straddles the divide between Moorish and Christian Spain, creating 'un lenguaje desinhibido y suelto, promiscuo, malicioso, insolente, jocundo' ('Vicisitudes', p. 55).[70] The intriguing combination of sexual frankness and religious reference in a poem apparently composed by a cleric is perhaps the *Libro*'s most obvious attraction for Goytisolo, although he has indicated other, more formal, aspects that interest him. The poem's 'estructura atípica e informe, lúbrido de generos distintos y opuestos' and 'carácter espúreo, mestizo, abigarrado' (p. 53) particularly attract the contemporary novelist and suggest to him the persuasiveness of Bakhtin's theory of the medieval carnival as a space of rupture and rebellion. The *Libro*'s textual 'quiebras, desniveles, rupturas, tensiones centrífugas, transmutaciones de voces', or, in a word, 'polifonía', is strikingly modern (p. 54).[71] And the fusion of vulgar and learned vocabulary, the language of the street and the language of religious devotion, breaks literary codes of decorum in a gesture of subversion.

Goytisolo is, of course, quite wrong to imply that Ruiz is special in this regard, and the number of medieval antecedents he has uncovered over the years for his own sacriligeous, polyphonic method of writing – the *Celestina*, the *Lozana andaluza*, the 'Carajicomedia de Fray Bugeo Montesinos', to name but a few – is proof enough of the existence of a long tradition of burlesque writing in Spain. Furthermore, the main point of Bakhtin's argument concerning the medieval carnival, elaborated in *Rabelais and His World*, is that rebellion is inscribed within, and thus controlled or contained by, the orthodox social order.[72] Nevertheless, Goytisolo's reading of Ruiz is marked by an ethical impulse, that of unseating orthodox literary interpretations and thus subverting the canon. His rebellion is both universal – in that it taps into a more general questioning of canonicity by feminism, post-colonialism, subaltern studies, lesbian and queer theory, among other postmodern discourses – and personal – in that it creates a literary lineage for the novelist himself.

---

[70] The notion of linguistic and literary promiscuity is fundamental to Goytisolo's own aesthetic. In 'El lenguaje del cuerpo (sobre Octavio Paz y Severo Sarduy)', in *Disidencias*, pp. 205–31, he includes Ruiz among his canon of dissident writers since he represents 'el único momento de nuestra historia en el que el binomismo "cuerpo" / "no cuerpo" mantiene un equilibrio armonioso' (p. 215).

[71] Goytisolo develops his discussion of modernity as an attitude of scepticism and rebellion with regard to literary rules and, therefore, as fundamentally achronic, in 'Medievalismo y modernidad: el Archipreste de Hita y nosotros', in *Contracorrientes*, pp. 15–24.

[72] Mikhail Bakhtin, *Rabelais and His World*, trans. Hélène Iswolsky (Bloomington: Indiana University Press, 1984).

A Dissident Canon and a Personal Literary Identity

The project of creating a series of literary voices through which the novelist can articulate his own concerns, and whom he can use to legitimate his own poetics of the novel, is paradoxical. It brings about the establishment of a personal dissident canon upon which the writer can draw. As a rejection of orthodoxy, however, it fails, for it simply leads to the creation of an alternative literary tradition without exploding the concept of the canon itself. Nevertheless, Goytisolo's readings in Spanish literature are most valuable as an expression of his own concerns, and, following de Man, this may well be the case with all criticism. A such, they stand as a defiant gesture of self-creation.

Goytisolo has noted in *El furgón de cola* that the Civil War and its Nationalist aftermath left his a 'fatherless' generation, in a literary sense.[73] The most prominent writers of the first third of the twentieth century either did not survive the war, were executed, or went into exile, leaving a dearth of artistic talent and no role-models for the *Generación de medio siglo*, as Goytisolo and his contemporaries are sometimes known. The intellectual climate of the 1940s and 1950s, the formative years for this generation, was dominated by Nationalist ideology, leaving writers either to conform or seek to forge a personal literary identity outside its restricted parameters. Feeling exiled at home, as it were, and ultimately choosing exile from the late 1950s on, Goytisolo's endeavours to re-read the Spanish canon can be seen as a search for roots that is typical of migrant communities generally.

Moving, first, from simple identification with a writer like Larra, through a complex reading of Blanco, to the imitative praxis of his mature writing, Goytisolo forges a voice that is intertextual in the Bakhtinian sense: it both offers soundings in the Spanish tradition – orthodox and heterodox – and creates a heteroglossic discourse in which the old and the new (no longer divided along the lines of the traditional and the innovative that modernism established so firmly) co-exist, interact, and mutually enlighten one another. Ironically, in returning to the past, Goytisolo reveals himself to be as quintessentially contemporary as the old texts he reads. His work travels through the ages, but preserves at its centre an ethical concern with dissidence and marginality that is as much at home in discussions of Cervantes as it is in those of poverty in Almería or political persecution in Algeria and Bosnia.[74] And in appropriating the voices of others, as Bakhtin argued, Goytisolo makes them his own. The paradox inherent in this – that purloined letters can become an expression of individual identity – is one noted

---

[73] 'La herencia del 98 o la literatura considerada como una promoción social', in *El furgón de cola*, pp. 121–31.

[74] Space precludes an extended discussion of Goytisolo's more overtly political works. Some of them will, however, be touched upon in succeeding chapters.

recently, in a very different context from that of Hispanic fiction. Ann
Tremkin recently remarked thus of Barnett Newman, the American Abstract
Expressionist painter who came from an immigrant background: 'short of
declaring oneself entirely fatherless, making one's own choice of a parent
facilitates the modern artist's necessary task of self-invention. The more
unlikely the subject of this inverse adoption, the better the argument for one's
autonomy.'[75] Newman became interested in primitive American art in his
search for roots. Goytisolo, on the other hand, turned first to obvious predecessors – to the disenchanted Larra, and the exiles Blanco White and Cernuda
– and later to figures who were central to the established canon – Cervantes,
Góngora, and Juan Ruiz, among many others. In seeking to interpret their
work as marginal, he subverts the canon from within. This approach is open
to criticism, since it fails to undo the master-narrative of orthodoxy and
heterodoxy, but what it does articulate – if one shifts the focus from the
general to the particular – is an individual response to a personal experience
of inner exile and moral intellectual alienation.

---

[75] 'Barnett Newman on Exhibition', in *Barnett Newman*, catalogue accompanying the
exhibition of the same name, Philadelphia Museum of Art, 24 March–7 July 2002, and
Tate Modern, London, 19 September 2002–5 January 2003 (Philadelphia: Philadelphia
Museum of Art, 2002), pp. 18–75 (p. 28).

PART II

IDENTITY AND ALTERITY

3

MEMORY, HISTORY, AND IDENTITY:
SEÑAS DE IDENTIDAD AND
REIVINDICACIÓN DEL CONDE DON JULIÁN

> *Everywhere there are meanings, dimensions, and forms in excess*
> *of what each 'consciousness' could have produced; and yet*
> *it is men who speak and think and see. We are in the field of*
> *history as we are in the field of language or existence.*
>
> Maurice Merleau-Ponty[1]

Memory, History, and Identity

With the publication of *Señas de identitdad* in 1966 and *Reivindicación del Conde don Julián* in 1970, Goytisolo gave centre stage to the closely connected themes of memory, history, and identity. Identity, Goytisolo suggests, is intimately linked to one's individual recall of the past set against the backdrop of the shared history of a community. Memory is the key to unlock this sense of identity by offering access to the past, from the perspective of the present, with a view to the future direction that the individual's or community's life may take. This is a phenomenological and non-teleological view, akin to the autobiographical approach to the past discussed in chapter 1 above. The recuperation of the past, rather than a mere act of remembering, is thus seen as an active negotiation with the present and future, out of which a provisional and constantly shifting sense of identity may emerge.[2] Of course,

---

1 Maurice Merleau-Ponty, *Signs*, trans. and intro. Richard C. McCleary (Evanston: Northwestern University Press, 1964), p. 20.

2 It is not my intention to argue that Goytisolo is, in the strict philosophical sense of the term, a phenomenologist. However, certain aspects of his fiction in the 1960s can be productively related to existentialist phenomenology as developed by Maurice Merleau-Ponty. His work offers insights into the exploration and expression of a dissident identity in its depiction of the body-subject as an intentional agent inextricably bound to the life-world in which it finds itself. As Merleau-Ponty argues in *Phenomenology of Perception* (trans. Colin Smith [London: Routledge, 1962], pp. 330–3): 'Through my perceptual field with its temporal horizons I am present to my present, to all the preceding past and to a future. And, at the same time, this ubiquity is not strictly real, but is clearly only intentional. [. . .] Things and instants can link up with each other to form a world only through the medium of that ambiguous being known as subjectivity, and can become present to each other only from a certain point of view and in intention. Objective time

the task is a difficult and problematic one. Memory is notoriously subjective and unreliable, and shared interpretations of the past – what has become known as cultural memory[3] – are frequently the site of contested claims motivated by ideological concerns. Both *Señas de identitdad* and *Don Julián* explore these issues through an examination of the creation of a dissident identity.

Each novel dramatizes the attempted destruction by its protagonist of an abhorrent past and creation of a hopeful, even utopian, future. The focus, though, shifts considerably from the first work to the second. *Señas* concentrates on personal memory, depicting the anguish of its chief character, Álvaro Mendiola, as he recalls his childhood in a Nationalist family during and after the Civil War, and comes to realize his own incompatibility with the values of his upbringing and social class. *Don Julián* retains this protagonist and broadly existentialist approach – although unnamed, its protagonist-narrator recalls Álvaro in his family and social affiliations – but focuses on Spain's collective past in an examination of the mythical foundations of her national identity.[4] Despite these varying emphases, however, each novel reveals the impossibility of achieving a complete rupture with the past. The intersubjective nature of memory entails a retention of the very past that one seeks to escape. Many have argued that Goytisolo's confrontational approach only serves to reinforce this, since the longed-for future identity is projected in his novels as the opposite of the rejected past, establishing a violent

which flows and exists part by part would not even be suspected, were it not enveloped in a historical time which is projected from the living present towards a past and towards a future.' We are, then, agents always acting within the field of history, outside which there is no transcendental view, since, according to Merleau-Ponty, the phenomenological reduction's most important lesson is the impossibility of a complete reduction.

[3] Cultural memory is distinguished from collective memory by Jan Assmann, the German Egyptologist, in that the latter has a limited life-span of three or four generations, and is informal and frequently oral. The former is more enduring, having a fixed point or horizon that does not change with the passage of time. It is, argues Assmann in 'Collective Memory and Cultural Identity', *New German Critique*, 65 (1995), 125–33, made up of 'fateful events [. . .] whose memory is maintained through cultural formation (texts, rites, monuments) and institutional communication (recitation, practice, observance)', which then become 'islands of time' (129).

[4] *Señas de identitdad*, *Don Julián*, and *Juan sin Tierra*, the latter published in 1975, are conventionally termed the 'Mendiola Trilogy' because their protagonist retains the same fundamental 'marks of identity'. However, the grouping of the three works as a trilogy seems increasingly unsatisfactory and unnecessary. While there are undoubted thematic connections between them, which have been comprehensively studied by Abigail Lee Six in *Juan Goytisolo: The Case for Chaos* (New Haven: Yale University Press, 1990), these also extend beyond the 'trilogy' to much of Goytisolo's work in the 1960s and 1970s. In formal terms, the novels diverge greatly, and I have, therefore, chosen to discuss them in two separate chapters in order to highlight not similarities, but the shifting treatment of themes, particularly of authorship and authority, in Goytisolo's writing during these decades.

dialectic between self and other. However, certain features of the novels do militate against this. Had they been developed less in terms of a Sartrean reading of the Hegelian master–slave dialectic, and more along the lines of a Merleau-Pontian view of reciprocal collaboration in a willingly shared interworld, it is possible that memory and history in Goytisolo's fiction might have appeared not as a bind or dead weight but as a liberating horizon of possibility.

Both *Señas* and *Don Julián* present their examination of the past through the eyes a protagonist who, far from being a disembodied consciousness, as a structuralist view might suggest, is an individual located in a particular socio-political context. In each work Goytisolo frames his protagonist's interrogation of memory as an existentialist search for identity, and, by formally stressing the quest rather than its end result, he strives to draw the reader into an active engagement with the texts. In *Don Julián* particularly, this emphasis on the process of interpretation serves to create a parallel between the protagonist and the reader, thus underlining the importance of a critical attitude towards both personal and cultural memory.

Mental Exile and Being-Towards-Death in Señas de identidad

Señas de identidad narrates the anguish of an emigrant – a voluntary exile from Francoist Spain – as he reflects on his family upbringing and memories of his nation's recent past. Álvaro Mendiola, the novel's protagonist, is reminiscent of Goytisolo himself. He lives in Paris, is in contact with the Spanish exile community there, and has revisited the country to document the poor living conditions in southern Spain in the late 1950s.[5] This potential identification between author and protagonist is deliberately used by Goytisolo to raise the question of the generic status of his novel and signal its experimental nature.[6] Conceived in the margins between fact and fiction, autobiography and novel, *Señas* formally and thematically exploits such liminality to reveal

---

5 In *Señas* Álvaro makes a film documentary of life in Andalusia, whereas Goytisolo chose the genre of travel writing in *Campos de Níjar* (1960) and *La Chanca* (1962). However, another of Goytisolo's works from this period, *La resaca* (1958), coincided with the release of a documentary on the poverty of southern Spain, *Notes sur l'émigraion*, which was shown at the Teatro del Corso in Milan. On the screening, its sabotage, and later erroneous association with Goytisolo, see María Silvina Persina, *Hacia una poética de la mirada: Mario Vargas Llosa, Juan Marsé, Elena Garro, Juan Goytisolo* (Buenos Aires: Corregidor, 1999), pp. 151–2.

6 In conversation with Emir Rodríguez Monegal (*El arte de narrar: diálogos* [Caracas: Monte Avila, 1968], pp. 165–98) Goytisolo commented that works such as *Campos de Níjar* and *Señas de identidad* were experimental, intended to help him rethink his attitude to the novel and to provide a springboard towards a new aesthetic. *Señas* is written, he says, as an 'examen de conciencia', so that he and Álvaro are inevitably alike in some ways and different in others.

certain ambiguities inherent in the projection of a dissident self. In this sense, it is an important step on the road which, from a chronological point of view, led Goytisolo from fiction to autobiography between the 1960s and 1980s.

For Michael Ugarte, an exile lives in a liminal space, seeking a new life yet constantly defining himself by comparison with the country, language, values, and society he or she has left behind.[7] Developing a latent sense of the Spanish word, *destierro*, as an unmooring from the homeland, Ugarte sees the exile as condemned to live a kind of existential death. Life can only have meaning for him through a separation that negates his former identity, yet leaves him paralysed by dependence on the very past that threatens his hopes of a better future. In Rafael Alberti's words, 'pasado muerto, porvenir helado'; or in the lines from Quevedo that Goytisolo borrows as an epigraph to *Señas*: 'Ayer se fue; Mañana no ha llegado.'[8] While neither Goytisolo, nor his protagonist Álvaro, were actually forced into exile, they each feel so alienated from Francoist Spain that they cannot continue to live there. In this sense, they are mental exiles, and *Señas* uses this anguished lack of belonging to justify Álvaro's interrogation of his 'señas de identidad'. Yet, there is a certain optimism in Goytisolo's use of the theme of exile, possibly because his is a voluntary exclusion that affirms his active opposition to the Franco regime. Our author certainly believes in the possibility of a future renewal, but to achieve it he must disentangle himself from the reins that bind him to Spain, his family, and his past literary works. This threefold effort constitutes the novel *Señas de identidad*, as Goytisolo explained to Julio Ortega:

> *Señas de identidad* es, entre otras cosas, la expresión literaria del proceso de extrañamiento de un intelectual de hoy con respecto a su propio país: la exposición de la herida moral de un hombre de mi generación –al que le ha tocado vivir uno de los períodos de paz sepulcral más largos de la historia de España.[9]

Playing upon the paradoxial situation of exile as both separation from and dependence upon a lost country and sense of identity, Goytisolo depicts Álvaro as engaged in a creative process of re-viewing his past in order to invent anew the future. And this parallels Goytisolo's own desire to forge a new literary voice for himself that will be an effective weapon of subversion in his attempt to undermine the cultural foundations of the Franco regime.

In *Señas*, Goytisolo presents Álvaro as acutely aware of life as an existen-tialist being-towards-death. The novel's protagonist lives an 'existencia a

---

[7]   Michael Ugarte, *Literatura española en el exilio: un estudio comparativo* (Madrid: Siglo XXI, 1999), p. 9.

[8]   Alberti, quoted by Ugarte, *Literatura española en el exilio*, p. 27; Quevedo, quoted in *Señas de identidad*, 6th edn (Barcelona: Seix Barral, 1987), p. 7.

[9]   Interview with Ortega, *Disidencias*, pp. 353–96 (pp. 354–5).

plazo' (p. 3), marked by his 'doble experiencia de español y de emigrado' (p. 107). Not only this, but he is also recovering from a recent heart attack and, overcome by a sense of the futility of life, toys with the possibility of suicide as a means of escape. Death thus acts as a limiting frontier, which allows Álvaro literally to halt the relentless march of time. This is presented as a kind of phenomenological bracketing of the world that will facilitate a greater understanding of the self and personal identity through reflection. Hence, Álvaro characterizes the garden where he sits recuperating and meditating on his family's past as 'aquel analgésico y tierno remanso de paz' (p. 13) – a pain-free space in which he can lose himself 'hasta el vértigo en la difícil geometría de las constelaciones' and 'desenterrar uno a uno de la polvorienta memoria los singulares y heteróclitos elementos que componían el decorado mítico de tu niñez' (pp. 12–13). The idea of phenomenological bracketing – which is not the same as an escape to an undefined, conceptual present, but is a 'standing-back' within a contextualized present – is underlined here in the fusion of a moment of supposedly pure analytic consciousness – the mental process of remembering – with closer proximity to the physical world – the fact that the memories are dusty and burried. On other occasions, Goytisolo describes Álvaro as physically entering the past through memory and of being taken over by it: 'Bastaba [. . .] incorporarse del sofá, [. . .] *recorrer* el oblicuo pasillo en el que moraran los duendes de su universo infantil para *desembocar* en el adusto comedor indiano [. . .]' (p. 40, my italics); or 'el pasado había irrumpido en ti' (p. 18).[10] Furthermore, Álvaro is not a disembodied consciousness. He is both a being-*in*-the-world and a being-*of*-the-world; that is to say, the examination of his past is conducted in a particular political and ideological context, which, in turn, partly determines his sense of self.[11]

Memory is not an abstract notion for Goytisolo. Rather, it relies on both physical objects (photographs, old school reports, books) and imagination to bring about a recuperation of the past. It is also intimately connected not just to the past, but also to the present and the future. Confronting documents

[10] Richard Kearney, in *Modern Movements in Philosophy: Phenomenology, Critical Theory, Structuralism*, 2nd edn (Manchester: Manchester University Press, 1994), notes how phenomenology regards imagination as an intending of something absent as if it were present (p. 25): 'Every time we remember the past or anticipate the future we are already engaged in making experience imaginatively present in its absence (the past as *no longer present* and the future as *not yet present* in the full perceptual sense).'

[11] This recalls Merleau-Ponty's view of the embodied self in *Phenomenology of Perception* (p. 453): 'To be born is both to be born of the world and to be born into the world. The world is already constituted, but also never completely constituted; in the first place we are acted upon, in the second we are open to an infinite number of possibilities. But this analysis is still abstract, for we exist in both ways *at once*. There is, therefore, never determinism and never absolute choice, I am never a thing and never a bare consciousness.'

from a past that seems alien to him – 'pruebas documentales, fehacientes, del niño pintoresco y falaz que habías sido y en el que no se reconocía el adulto de hoy' – Álvaro finds himself 'suspendido en un presente incierto, extento de pasado como de provenir' (p. 14). The implication is that Álvaro's lack of certainty in the present derives from his inability to identify with his own past and, hence, his failure to imagine a future for himself. The faculty of memory – *memoria* – thus envisaged acts as a point of negotiation between the lived past and the aspired for future, permitting, as a result, that the self forge an identity in the present. And it contrasts with memories – mere *recuerdos* – that are jumbled and in need of organization into a coherent perspective.

This is initially demonstrated in *Señas* in Álvaro's recollection of his childhood visit to his senile maternal grandmother in a nursing home. The visit reveals the grandmother's mental degradation and brings home to the young Álvaro the precariousness of human existence, 'expuesto a un azar, todo aleatorio, irremediablemente prometido a la muerte' (p. 44). The grand-mother's loss of memory drives a wedge between her and Álvaro, for, he says, they no longer share a common past and are estranged from each other. This lack of memory contrasts with the young Álvaro's confused recall of the past. Of the Civil War years, spent at various resorts on the French Riviera, Álvaro has only a vague recollection in the 'recuerdo embrionario de su memoria confusa' (p. 42). That Goytisolo should draw attention to the difference between disorganized memories and the organizing faculty of memory itself is surely important. It is as if the grandmother, having lost her memory, has lost her sense of self – at least in the young Álvaro's eyes, for he refers to her as a sleep-walker.[12] On the other hand, the child Álvaro, having only inco-herent memories of his past, has yet to forge an identity. A similar distinction between memories and the faculty of remembering is drawn later when Álvaro, recalling the surveillance he was placed under by the Spanish police, notes that these are 'asociaciones de ideas y recuerdos no filtrados aún por el severo tamiz de la memoria' (p. 128). If memory is a selective process of filtering and sieving, then this is presented positively in *Señas de identidad* as a necessary part of the individual's development of a sense of self.

The manner in which Álvaro seeks to order his memories into a coherent vision of the past is twofold. First, he decides, after attending the funeral in Barcelona of his former teacher, Ayuso, that he must engineer a radical break with his past. Anything less than a total rejection of his present identity is insufficient, as the example of Ayuso's futile lifetime of opposition to the

---

[12] The connection between memory, temporal and spatial location, and self is explored in similar terms by Ciarán Benson in *The Cultural Psychology of Self: Place, Morality and Art in Human Worlds* (London: Routledge, 2001). Comparing stroke and other brain-damage sufferers who are aware of their condition with those who are not, he notes that 'without a sense of one's past, present and future all personal events are adrift and self is dislocated' (p. 39).

regime and its values demonstrates: '[él] ha vivido con dignidad años difíciles, destierro, cárcel, persecuciones [. . .], sin claudicar jamás en el combate todo para acabar así, cubierto de tierra, cemento y ladrillo bajo la custodia de ellos' (p. 85). Second, he opts for a combative approach to this task by reifing the old self and pitting it against a new aspirational, dissident one. The dialogue between these two voices is conducted through a complex use of pronouns in *Señas*, inscribing the struggle at the level of the text itself.

Rupture with the Past

The solitary battle that Álvaro enjoins 'con los fantasmas del pasado' (p. 186) involves, primarily, his own family, but also, secondarily, the values of the Franco regime with which his paternal line is associated. Anticipating the analysis of his own family in *Coto vedado*, Goytisolo characterizes Álvaro's as a binary of good and bad. His maternal ancestors are judged by his father to be an 'árbol condenado y enfermo' (p. 40), a condemnation that Goytisolo and Álvaro both reverse in celebrating this heritage as the source of literary creativity and imagination. *Señas* also hints obliquely at the rebellion that both *Don Julián* and *Coto vedado* will later enact. 'Un miembro anónimo de tu linaje' (p. 45), we are told, experiences the same 'anomaly' as Álvaro but suppresses it as if it were a cancer threatening the destruction of the household. While the specific deviation from family morality is not named, the terms in which it is presented evoke Goytisolo's discussion of his grandfather Ricardo's paedophilia in *Coto vedado*. Álvaro is the heir to this marginal family line, and will attempt to break the ties of conformity just as another ancestor, uncle Néstor, did. Goytisolo would seem to be weaving here an origin for his protagonist's rebellious identity, yet the ambiguity that pervades the text reinforces this sense of identity as provisional and uncertain – in contrast to the ultimately more confident, yet less ambiguous, assertions of the autobiographies. The 'anomaly' from which Álvaro suffers is deliberately left vague, dispersing the idea of a core (unspecified, but possibly homosexual) identity into a more suggestive opposition to social norms.

The emphasis that *Señas* places on Álvaro's social and political context is, indeed, crucial, for it ensures that his rebellion, and the identity that he seeks to forge as a result, is contextualized. Not only is Álvaro existentially 'in-the-world', he is also 'of-the-world' in the sense that Spain's collective past influences his current sense of self and the identity to which he aspires. This relationship between self and circumstance is evident in chapter 3 of the novel, in which Álvaro explores the death of his father at Yeste in 1936. The Civil War is the most significant event of recent Spanish history, and as such it marks Álvaro's life. The violence that resulted from the military coup in July 1936 has quite literally left its stain upon the land, as the spilt blood of Álvaro's father and his companions mingles with the soil to become part of

the 'estructura geológica del paisaje', leaving the dead 'fundidos definitiva-
mente a la tierra e integrados a ella' (p. 88). Though time may have removed
the visual evidence of the war's brutality, it remains in the collective memory
and literally *imposes* itself upon Álvaro's mind – 'el escenario del fusila-
miento se había impuesto de modo paulatino a tu memoria' (p. 88) – as he
sits now recalling his visit to the area in 1964 and perusing old newspaper
cuttings and photographs relating to his father's shooting. Not only are the
events of the past presented as geological strata, but so are Álvaro's memories and the coordinates of the 'extraviada identidad' (p. 89) that he is trying
to redefine.[13]

Searching through evidence from the past involves both reconstruction and
imagination, however, for memory is not simply the objective recall of
previous events. Aware of the capriciousness of memory – 'tu caprichosa
memoria' (p. 168) – and of the fallibility of conjecture – the 'arenas movedizas
de la conjetura' (p. 103) – Álvaro finds himself engaged in the elusive task of
sorting out fact from fiction with regard to a past in which he is himself implicated. This is a key point, first, because it indicates the extent to which
Álvaro's attempt to forge a new identity is determined by his relationship to
both a personal and a collective past, and, second, because it testifies to the
doubling of his identity, which will be one of the key means by which he
attempts to redefine himself. Referring to the attempt to uncover the full
circumstances of his father's death, Álvaro remarks:

> Pese a tus esfuerzos de síntesis los diversos elementos de la historia se
> descomponían como los colores de un rayo luminoso refractado en un
> prisma y, en virtud de un extraño desdoblamiento, asistías a su desfile
> ocioso simultáneamente como actor y como testigo, espectador, cómplice y
> protagonista a la vez del remoto y obsesionante drama.   (p. 89)

---

[13] The depiction of the Civil War in *Señas* is much more subtle than in *Don Julián*,
where oppositions between good and bad, friend and foe, are presented as absolutes. In
Señas, the warring factions are seen as victims *and* perpetrators of violence, as if fulfilling
a national destiny. The confusing events in Yeste, which resulted in shootings by
firing-squad on both sides at different points in the war, are set against the backdrop of
bull-running. Goytisolo is careful to fuse the war and fiesta scenes not just cinematically,
by cutting dramatically between them, but also linguistically, so that references to a
'bandera roja' (flag, but also bullfighter's cape?) and 'detonaciones' (explosions or fire-
works?) (p. 115) straddle both and join them through the depiction of violence as inherent
to the Spanish nation. Thus, 'las imágenes brutales se cruzan' (p. 118) in Álvaro's mind.
The national destiny is presented as long centuries of violence in which 'todos (los de los
vencidos, como los de los vencedores, los excusados como los injustificables) obedecían a
las leyes de un mismo ciclo cínico en el que, al frenesí y desatino de las crisis, suceden
largos períodos de calma, embrutecimiento y modorra. . .' (p. 124). Contrary to the
Nationalist view of the nation's destiny as the forging and preservation of conservative,
Catholic, Castilian values, Goytisolo establishes an alternative vision of hatred and
brutality, and, in the references to the bullfight as a national festival, recalls Martín-
Santos' *Tiempo de silencio*.

The reference to a doubling of the self here reaffirms the manner in which Goytisolo utilizes different pronouns in *Señas* to represent the battle between Álvaro's old and new identities, a point to which I shall return presently.

If Álvaro's identity is in part defined by the past that he shares with the Spanish nation, then is it also influenced by the present circumstances of that country, and it is worth noting the numerous allusions that *Señas* makes to the political and economic situation of the 1950s and early 1960s. Several passages, articulated in the anonymous voice of officialdom and placed in quotation marks, make reference to the celebrations marking 25 years of peace and thus reflect what Paloma Aguilar has termed the appeal to a 'performance-based' political legitimacy.[14] Indeed, the 1964 festivities confirmed the Regime's stability and hold on power and demonstrated the futility of the efforts of the like of Profesor Ayuso's generation to bring about political change, hence justifing Álvaro's decision to adopt a more radical form of rebellion. This, he is confident, will 'iluminar no sólo tu biografía sino también facetas oscuras y reveladoras de la vida en España' (p. 127). Álvaro's self-analysis is, then, also a sounding of the national psyche, and his use of memory is far from unmotivated. That this could be problematic is an issue not directly raised, though Goytisolo does present Álvaro's efforts as a genuine ethical commitment to greater self-understanding. Further, the play of perspectives in the novel between official and non-official discourse – for example in the images cast of Álvaro by the Regime set against his own documentary evidence and view of himself – does point to the existence of varying interpretations of the past. The dangers inherent in the manipulation of memory and history are, however, the central focus of *Don Julián*, and in *Señas* interest is confined to the optimistic possibility of a positive outcome for Álvaro's attempts at self-redefinition.

Dialogue with – and within – the Self

The protagonist of *Señas* seeks to redefine himself through the creation of a series of oppositional structures. Evoking uncle Néstor as an anti-hero in whose steps he wishes to follow, Álvaro sketches out the combative and rebellious identity that will later be painted more boldly in *Don Julián*. This dual vision of an old self to be rejected and a new one to be embraced is sketched using structuralist techniques,[15] yet, recalling the episodes of the car

---

14 Paloma Aguilar, *Memory and Amnesia: The Role of the Spanish Civil War in the Transition to Democracy*, trans. Mark Oakley (New York: Berghahn Books, 2002), p. 35.

15 By structuralist narrative techniques, I mean those that turn inwards to focus on the word as linguistic sign and seek to expose the deep structures within a text that form part of its system of signification. They concentrate on narrative form, questioning such notions as a clear identification between word and world, the homogeneity and causal

accident and *encierros* narrated in *Coto vedado*, this is set in the existentialist context of death as a stimulus to anguished self-analysis. As we have seen, *Señas* presents Álvaro's identity, like Goytisolo's in his autobiography, as partly determined by family origin, through the rejection of conformity and the association with figures such as grandfather Ricardo and uncle Néstor. But it is also affected by the image of him created by others, specifically the voice of authority of the Franco regime. The interaction between family and society thus serves to reinforce Álvaro's new identity as dissident, but, crucially, this dissidence is inscribed in a faltering manner through pronominal shifts, which suggest a fluid, rather than a fixed, identity for Álvaro.

The novel opens not with the voice of Álvaro, but with that of the regime's propaganda machine promoting the image of Álvaro as a dissident. Goytisolo contrasts the voice of 'ellos', an aggressive discourse of authority that attempts to fix an identity for Álvaro – 'tales son las características del individuo en cuestión' (p. 9) – with the analytical discourse of a meditative Álvaro considering his own image as divulged by the official press, an image that he has never accepted – 'así hablaban de ti [. . .] confiando, como tantos otros, en un cambio regenerador y catártico que, por misteriosos imponderables, no se había producido y, al cabo de largos años de destierro, estabas de nuevo allí, en el doliente y entrañable paisaje de tu juventud' (p. 11). The sources of the opening passage, taken from actual newspaper reports on Goytisolo himself by the Francoist press, have been well documented. The voice of officialdom echoes a piece in *Arriba* from 1961 describing Goytisolo 'con más años de residencia en Francia que en España, con más costumbres francesas que españolas, incluso en el amancebamiento con una mujer muchos años mayor'.[16] The ambiguity we noted earlier in relation to

---

structuring of discourse, the existence of a unified subject, and the possibility of coherent narrative meaning. However, the use of such formal techniques does not necessarily imply strict adherence to structuralist doctrine. Structuralism was unapologetically synchronic in its approach, seeking to elucidate structures or systems under ahistorical conditions and rejecting a humanist perspective that might take account of intentional human agency. While Stanley Black identifies a comprehensive use of structuralist techniques in Goytisolo's work in his study, *Juan Goytisolo: The Poetics of Contagion* (Liverpool: Liverpool University Press, 2001), ultimately Goytisolo's use of language in context and his interest in an existentialist embodied subject set him apart from a structuralist philosophical outlook. The work of the philosopher Paul Ricoeur demonstrates that a textual focus, particularly in relation to pronouns and the issue of identity, does not necessarily imply a structuralist or post-structuralist outlook. See, for instance, his *Oneself as Another*, trans. Kathleen Blamey (Chicago: University of Chicago Press, 1992).

   [16] *Arriba*, 15 March (1961), copy included in the Goytisolo Archive, Diputación Provincial de Almería, cata. no. 1195. *Señas* opens as follows (p. 9): ' "Instalado en París cómodamente instalado en París con más años de permanencia en Francia que en España con más costumbres francesas que españolas incluso en el ya clásico amancebamiento con la hija de una notoria personalidad del exilio residente habitual en la Ville Lumière [. . .]." ' The press clippings and published sources of *Señas* are identified and discussed at length

the autobiographical aspects of the novel is thus reinforced by the opening itself, but, by placing this Francoist discourse in quotation marks, Goytisolo calls into question the veracity of its image of his protagonist. Álvaro is 'prisionero de un personaje que no eras tú, confundido con él y por él suplantado' (p. 12) – 'confused' or united with an imposed self, yet at the same time replaced by him. His identity, as presented in this novel, is not fixed as either conformist or rebel but as a dialogue between both.

From the beginning, then, Señas inscribes Álvaro's identity as textual and undermines the certainty of a fixed self by placing this constantly under erasure. In this respect, it certainly employs structuralist devices. However, it uses them for existentialist ends, thus fusing the approach of two literary and philosophical schools often seen as mutually exclusive.[17] As Álvaro reflects upon former instances of his self – identities such as those projected by old school reports and family photographs that confirm his origins as 'eslabón de una ininterrumpida cadena de mediocridad y conformismo' (p. 14) – he attempts to throw off this conformist self, rather as Goytisolo attempts to do in his autobiographies, by fixing it firmly within the past as a Sartrean inauthentic identity imposed from without. Only when this is achieved can Álvaro move on from his current obsession with death and destruction to establish a new identity in the future. This existentialist project is enacted through the creation of a dialogue of three pairs of voices – between Álvaro and 'ellos', between a 'tú' and an 'él' within Álvaro's own self, and between this 'tú' and the 'yo' that it necessarily implies.

The protagonist of Señas is generally careful to develop in his meditations a division between his inauthentic past self, signalled by a third person 'él' or by the distancing effect of his own name – 'Álvaro examinó de nuevo los tres hombres de la tarima [. . .]' (p. 212) – and the potential seeds of a future authentic self, referred to as 'tú'. The Cernuda-esque alternation between these two voices dramatizes Álvaro's battle with his past. While the old self is

---

by Linda Gould Levine in the first chapter of *Juan Goytisolo: la destrucción creadora* (Mexico City: Mortiz, 1976), and Ugarte in *Trilogy of Treason*, pp. 67–70. It is also to be noted that in *Señas* Néstor is described as 'amancebado con una tumultuosa poetisa irlandesa' (p. 45), thus creating a linguistic link between the rebellious uncle, his nephew, and the real-life Goytisolo.

17 Luc Ferry and Alain Renault argue, in *French Philosophy of the Sixties: An Essay on Antihumanism*, trans. Mary Schnachenberg Cattani (Amherst: University of Massachusetts Press, 1990), that structuralism owes more to phenomenology than it is willing to admit, not least because it defined itself in opposition to its particular interpretation of existentialist and phenomenological humanism. 'If the truth must be shattered,' they conclude (p. 228), 'if there are no facts but only interpretations, if all references to universal norms are inevitably catastrophic, then is not the essential thing to "participate" as they say? And, from this point of view, do not deconstructions of modernity accompany democracy, in the Tocquevillean sense of the word, to its farthest point, making authenticity the supreme value, *whatever its content may be*?'

one of conformity, wishing, for example, to live out the lives of the child saints his nursemaid Lourdes reads to him,[18] the new self is associated with 'deviant' activities such as a youthful attraction to Jerónimo and visits to brothels with his friend Sergio. This can be said to intimate, without the heavy-handedness of *Coto vedado*, an authentic self located within sexual dissidence, for, as Paul Julian Smith illustrates, the early episode with Jerónimo both anticipates and is deliberately recalled during Álvaro's first homosexual experience.[19]

Nevertheless, a certain ambiguity is maintained, since the division within Álvaro's self is less than categorical. While Álvaro most frequently attempts to fix his past through the use of the third person, there are occasions on which an overlap occurs between the apparently separate voices. In recalling his early passion for Jerónimo, Álvaro switches voices through subtle pronominal changes: 'Recostado en el jardín en el que el inconsciente niño que fuiste *tú* vegetó y languideció con los suyos hasta la revelación súbita de *su* pasión por Jerónimo [. . .]' (p. 269, my italics). Earlier in the novel he had addressed himself directly as 'tú, Álvaro Mendiola, residente habitual en el extranjero [. . .]' (p. 110), and later we read 'Álvaro, dijiste para tu sayo [. . .]' (p. 298). In chapter 4, which contains interpolations from the authorities' 'diario de vigilancia' detailing Álvaro's supposedly subversive activities, the juxtaposition of voices creates the impression that it is also Álvaro who must be vigilant in his 'esfuerzos de reconstitución y síntesis' (p. 127), since 'cuántas veces tú, el propio Álvaro, no habías pactado con el conformismo ambiente, censurándote en público y en privado' (p. 181). The battle has been enjoined, but has yet to be won.

Implied by the use of 'tú', yet left unspoken until the final pages of *Señas*, is the voice of the 'yo', the integrating consciousness that Álvaro seeks. The appearance of a first-person pronoun at the end of the novel is interpreted by Reed Anderson to mean the achievement of the status of marginality that Álvaro desires.[20] Nevertheless, this final move to the first-person remains aspirational and takes the form of a parody of the *Anima Christi* earlier recited in Spanish by the child Álvaro. The appearance of a first-person pronoun at this point is therefore somewhat formulaic: 'cuerpo de Changó sálvame' (p. 332).[21] More significant, in fact, is the widespread absence of an

[18] *Señas*, pp. 17–20, which draws material from G. Gross, *Niños Santos* (Madrid: La Hormiga de Oro, n.d.), included in the Goytisolo Collection, Boston University.

[19] For the passage on Jerónimo, possibly an echo of Goytisolo's early infatuation for Jaume recounted in *Coto vedado*, see *Señas*, pp. 35–40; on the trips to brothels with Sergio, which are reminiscent of Goytisolo's visits to prostitutes with Lucho, also in *Coto vedado*, see *Señas*, pp. 60–4. See also Paul Julian Smith, *Laws of Desire*, p. 67.

[20] '*Señas de identidad*: Chronicle of Rebellion', *Journal of Spanish Studies: Twentieth Century*, 2 (1974), 3–19.

[21] For the *Anima Christi*, see p. 46. Changó, an Afro-Cuban deity, reappears later in *Juan sin Tierra* (p. 49), also in the context of a satire of Christianity.

integrating 'yo' pointing to an erosion of the notion of a unifying *cogito* at the centre of *Señas*. Despite the novel's subjective focus, the new identity that Álvaro desires is both inachievable and inexpressible, except as an aspiration implied by the dialogic discourse of 'tú'. This absent centre reflects an existentialist phenomenological view of the self as action, project, or process. It moves the focus from a coherent, conscious core towards a fragmented linguistic entity, something that *Don Julián* will develop further; yet, it does not remove entirely the notion of a self, nor does it erase identity as an impossibility. What it does is begin to refract these through the lens of a pronominal instability which, by the final chapter, begins to develop into more radical textual experimentation.

The ambiguities inherent in the dialogue of voices in *Señas* create the sense that life is a self-conscious, shifting narrative, but in this life-story the relationship between fiction and reality – between the life and the story – is seen in a positive, rather than a negative, light. Contrary to the structuralist collapsing of world and text into one another, *Señas* establishes a dialectic between life and narrative, which suggests that, although experience may be linguistically mediated, it is not pure or mere textuality.[22] There are, granted, brief allusions to linguistic play in the novel – for instance, words having 'intenciones huidizas y cambiantes' (p. 175) – but, despite this, *Señas* is a broadly existentialist novel in which language retains a referential function. It is only in the areas of pronominal instability, the limited use of intertextuality (such as the repetition of religious discourse and the allusions to children's books), and in the short final chapter that the work anticipates the radical experimentation of *Don Julián* and *Juan sin Tierra*. The concluding pages of *Señas* break with the (by the 1960s) rather conventional perspective of the rest of the novel by dividing the text into discursive sections and even brief phrases that move towards fragmentation rather than synthesis. Contrasting with the homogeneity of the main body of the text, with its use of natural description and circumscription of different discourses (such as the 'diario de vigilancia' or the voice of officialdom) within quotation marks, chapter 8 adopts the perspective of a tourist viewing the city of Barcelona through the lens of a telescope in order to turn this into a metaphorical shattering of unity and coherence. If Álvaro's identity is ultimately found to be mutable and

---

22 *Señas* has been interpreted by some critics as the first step in Goytisolo's move towards the idea that reality is textual, since it links the fictional and the autobiographical. In *Trilogy of Treason* Ugarte emphasizes the idea that Goytisolo's use of intertextuality in *Señas* – manifest in the overlaps between Goytisolo's earlier works and the film documentary of life in southern Spain that Álvaro makes – casts the relationship between Goytisolo and Álvaro not as one of author and character, but as a relationship between texts (p. 67). David Herzberger, on the other hand, is one of the few critics to note the dialectical relation of reality and fiction in *Señas*, in 'Language and Referentiality in *Señas de identidad*', *Revista Canadiense de Estudios Hispánicos*, 11 (1987), 611–21.

contested, then the novel seeks to reflect this textually at its close. Such textual experimentation gestures towards *Don Julián*, where the exploration of identity by means of an interrogation of the past and of memory is developed in the context of an exploration of Spain's historical and cultural past.

Language and Subversion in Reivindicación del Conde don Julián

Reivindicación del Conde don Julián radically develops the incipient textual experimentation of *Señas*, contrasting not just formally but even visually with that novel. Goytisolo now rejects standard chapter divisions and grammatical sentences, structuring *Don Julián* in four parts with no headings to guide the reader. He spurns grammatical sentences and normal punctuation in favour of colons that separate linguistic 'breath groups', thus impeding the conventional flow of written narrative and appealing more to the rhythms of speech.[23] This is entirely appropriate in a work presented as an inner or imagined dialogue, but the primary motivation behind such a narrative style is the disruption of sequential discourse and refusal to establish causal links between propositions. Instead, the author uses juxtaposition and the repetition of key images, ideas, and refrains in a poetic manner to create a web of suggestive associations and contrasts that the reader must piece together for himself. These techniques reveal, as noted above, the adoption of structuralist narrative devices, but they are underpinned not by a structuralist textual view of the world, but by a phenomenological vision of society and human agency as dialectically interconnected. The turn towards language in *Don Julián* thus serves to effect a contextualized interrogation of cultural memory.

The protagonist-narrator of *Don Julián* mischeviously declares the aim of the novel to be the creation of a 'palabra sin historia : orden verbal autónomo',[24] which concentrates on the medium rather than the content of communication yet still offers an effective mode of opposition to the Franco regime. Many critics have noted that the idea of an autonomous text that is politically subversive is a contradicion in terms, since the latter requires some element of semantic stability based on consensus in order to convey a political message.[25] Nevertheless, one should perhaps dissociate the protagonist-

---

[23] Goytisolo has not identified the inspiration for this approach to punctuation, but, given his position as a reader for the publishing house Gallimard, one can speculate that it originated in his familiarity with written French, where a space is left both before and after a colon in normal usage.

[24] *Don Julián*, p. 195. To preserve the punctuation of the original, full points are not inserted after indented quotations.

[25] For the most compelling version of this argument, see the introduction to Epps' *Significant Violence*, pp. 1–21. In practical terms, however, no work of literature can aspire to verbal autonomy since words inevitably carry meaning. That meanings are open to question, and that a work may deliberately cultivate linguistic ambiguity and obscurity,

narrator's statements from the intentions of the author and other evidence in the work. For one thing, *Don Julián* is an ironic novel in the sense that the circular structure of the text, the ending returning the reader to the beginning, casts doubt on the success of the protagonist's rebellion by exposing his need to enjoin battle on a daily basis. The novel concludes, 'el sueño agobia tus párpados y cierras los ojos : lo sabes, lo sabes : mañana será otro día, la invasión recomenzará' (p. 304). Furthermore, language is initially declared to be the 'vehículo necesario de la traición [. . .] esplendoroso y devastador a la vez' (p. 143), yet the efficacy of the written word as a form of rebellion is later rejected when the protagonist declares: 'la violencia es muda : para pillar, destruir, violar, traicionar no necesitarás las palabras' (p. 227). In order to resolve such contradictions, we must turn to aspects of the work other than the protagonist's overt pronouncements on language.

Don Julián articulates the utopian desire of its protagonist to forge a dissident identity for himself by rejecting the values of his family, his social class, and the established culture of the ruling oligarchy in Spain. The novel's discourse is grounded in a particular socio-political and cultural context, since Goytisolo seeks to create a dialectical interplay between the consciousness of his protagonist and the world he inhabits. The novel thus gestures towards a Merleau-Pontian intersubjectivity in which the protagonist, as an embodied agent, is partly determined by the cultural and historical horizon in which he finds himself, at the same time as he seeks to transform that horizon in the creation of a dissident identity. Fundamental to this project is a use of language which, far from appealing to a 'orden verbal autónomo', is necessarily grounded in a recognizable reality.

Goytisolo's use of language in *Don Julián* is, in fact, subtle, pivoting between literal and figurative meanings without giving precedence to either. The effect of this is to create an ambiguous relation between fiction and reality, a dialectic in which each spills over into and contaminates the realm of the other. Word and world are therefore not seen as separate entities, but are co-dependent aspects of an intersubjective world. As Merleau-Ponty argues in *Phenomenology of Perception* (pp. 388–9), 'It is true that communication presupposes a system of correspondences such as the dictionary provides, but it goes beyond these, and what gives its meaning to each word is the sentence. It is because it has been used in various contexts that the word gradually accumulates a significance which it is impossible to establish absolutely.' Language is not an abstract system, but a meaningful social practice, the means by which an embodied subject takes up a position in the social and symbolic order.[26] *Don Julián* illustrates this very point in its

does not free language from its semantic charge. Indeed, this is the very source of the richness and creativity of literature.

26 This view of language contrasts with Sartre's as outlined in *Qu'est-ce que la*

creation of a dialogue of voices through which the protagonist attempts to forge a new identity for himself against the cultural backdrop of Francoist Spain.

In a structuralist analysis of the novel, Martín Morán labels *Don Julián* a 'monólogo interior dialogado', since it consists of a dialogue that appears to take place solely in the mind of the protagonist.[27] Through this process of *desdoblamiento* the protagonist-narrator splits himself into two voices, a first-person 'yo' that appears in the opening lines of the novel, and a second-person 'tú' whom he addresses. Because neither pronoun stands for a clearly identifiable character in the traditional sense, Martín Morán concludes that the protagonist of the novel is reduced to an empty shifter 'que no tiene ningún referente externo' (p. 15), and that the real protagonist of the work is the discourse itself. Nevertheless, one can identify certain character-istics of *Don Julián* that suggest that these first- and second-person pronouns are not semantically vacuous. As we saw in chapter 1 in relation to Goytisolo's autobiographies, and above with respect to *Señas de identidad*, the author seeks in his writing to confer particular meanings on such suppos-edly 'empty' grammatical categories through the creation of a dissident iden-tity. To this end, the dual identity that the protagonist of *Don Julián* envisages for himself does carry specific semantic value that grounds it in external reference. The project of identity formation is, however, conceived in Sartrean terms as an existentialist choice between 'good' and 'bad', or authentic and inauthentic, options. For most of the novel, these options are not presented in terms of a struggle between an 'él' and a 'tú' in search of a 'yo', as they were in *Señas* – though, as we shall see, that paradigm does reappear in the novel's final epiphany of destruction and rebirth. Instead, Álvaro's identity is divided into his childhood and adult selves, the former representing the past to be destroyed and the latter the future to be forged. In this dialogue between past and present, pronouns no longer serve as markers of a particular identity – in this sense, their semantic value *is* fluid, serving to dramatize the battle that Álvaro is waging against both his own personal past and that of his mother country – yet, each usage of the pronouns contextualizes them, so that semantic fluidity and potential ambiguity repre-sents not a nihilistic absence of meaning but a potentially liberating surplus of signification.[28] Goytisolo's refusal, on the one hand, to fix meaning abso-

---

littérature? (Paris: Gallimard, 1948), where the language of prose fiction is seen as capable, transparently and unproblematically, of reflecting reality (p. 59).

[27] José Manuel Martín Morán, *Semiótica de una traición recuperada: génesis poética de 'Reivindicación del Conde don Julián'* (Barcelona: Anthropos, 1992), p. 21.

[28] As Merleau-Ponty argues in *Signs* (p. 81): 'Signs do not simply evoke other signs for us and so on without end, and language is not like a prison we are locked into or a guide we must blindly follow [. . .]. Language is not just the replacement of one meaning by another, but the substitution of equivalent meanings. The new structure is given as

lutely, and, on the other, to celebrate linguistic autonomy and non-meaning, signals a desire not to embrace the introverted, narcissistic approach of structuralism (despite using many of its textual devices) but an effort to tie his aesthetic practice to a definite ethical perspective.

Many critics have chosen to see the struggle of the protagonist in *Don Julián* as primarily textual, and have therefore sought to stress the respects in which *Don Julián* resembles a Barthesian texture of words.[29] Nevertheless, in the course of the novel, the protagonist's daily life in Tangiers is depicted as a Joycean odyssey around its streets. The sights and smells of the city are vividly portrayed. Its markets, its bars, a library, a visit to a clinic, encounters with tourists, beggars, and locals – all this serves to situate the protagonist in a particular time and place, and, while it may be the context for a mental struggle waged by the protagonist against his Spanish identity, it is not relegated to mere theatrical backdrop.[30] On many occasions, the life of the city becomes mixed with the protagonist's thoughts in a manner that blurs the boundaries between the physical and the mental, and, more importantly, between the literal and the figurative. The following quotation, for instance, conveys this sense of rootedness in the cityscape of Tangier at the same time as it offers an explanation of the dialogue in the protagonist-narrator's mind between conflicting aspects of his self. It also stresses the similarity between the profusion of streets of the city and the profusion of words of the text:

> mientras te internas por Chemaa Djedid y Chorfa en dirección a la calle del Baño : en la alternativa de subir hasta Nasería y la plazuela de la fuente o bajar hasta Cristianos y enfilar hacia Sebu : perdiéndote en dédalo de callejas de la Medina : trazando con tus pasos (sin previsores guijarros ni migajas caducas) un enrevesado dibujo que nadie (ni siquiera tú mismo) podrá interpretar : y desdoblándote al fin por seguirte mejor, como si fueras

already present in the old, the latter subsists in it.' This sense of the accumulation of latent meaning, which echoes Mikhail Bakhtin's idea of intertextuality, is, as we shall see, fundamental to Goytisolo's treatment of Spanish cultural memory in *Don Julián*, and it will emerge in our discussion of Ricoeur's view of metaphor in relation to *Las virtudes del pájaro solitario* in chapter 6.

29 See particularly the analytical approach adopted in Martín Morán, *Semiótica de una traición recuperada*; Black, *The Poetics of Contagion*; Epps, *Significant Violence*.

30 In fact, considerable reference is made in the novel to the economic boom of 1960s Spain. The country's enthusiastic development of tourism and consumerism is contrasted with the barter economy of Tangier's *Zoco Grande* on numerous occasions, and the Arabs' hostile attitude towards tourists is explicity related to the protagonist's own hostility towards his *madre patria* (p. 118). When the protagonist states that he wishes to free himself 'del devenir histórico' (p. 99), a phrase that echoes the famous desire of Joyce's hero, Stephen Dedalus in *Ulysses*, to awaken from the nightmare of history, the reference is in fact to the specific situation of capitalist development in Spain, since the text continues, 'del raudo progreso que, según testigos, juvenece la faz, ayer dormida y torva, hoy floreciente y dinámica del vetusto país'.

> otro : ángel de la guardia, amante celoso, detective particular : consciente
> de que el laberinto está en tí : que tú eres el laberinto : minotauro voraz,
> martir comestible : juntamente verdugo y víctima   (p. 126)[31]

Pivoting between the literal sense – the protagonist actually lost in the
Medina's labyrinthine streets, his path tracing an uninterpretable arabesque –
and a metaphorical one – the protagonist alienated from his true self, for
which he searches by internalizing the spatial labyrinth as an image of his
existential quest – Goytisolo seeks to blur the boundary between fiction and
fact, the text and the world. Indeed, he goes further than this, for the labyrinth
of words which the protagonist-narrator weaves as he seeks to interrogate his
old identity and forge a new one is also the 'selva' of words which the reader,
becoming himself a 'detective particular', is forced to decode. The novel thus
challenges the reader, seducing him into engaging in the same existential
self-analysis as its protagonist – all the more so because of the insistent use of
'tú', which places the reader in the position of addressee alongside the
protagonist himself.

However, such boundary-breaking – the transgressing of conventional
limits between fiction and reality – does not reach the ludic proportions of
structuralist and post-structuralist writing,[32] for Goytisolo sustains throughout
the three referents suggested by the metaphor of the textual labyrinth. Even as
the novel, by its fourth and final part, seems to be increasingly distanced from
reality, it still grounds itself in external reference. Certainly it is the case that
the narrator transforms the world around him into a fantasy realm in which
stories – treated as a kind of cultural patrimony – fuel his dream of destruction
and rebirth, yet each of the key elements of the final epiphany that enacts the
provisional creation of a new dissident identity are taken from the protagonist's physical encounter with the city of Tangier.

In depicting his protagonist's odyssey around Tangier, Goytisolo presents
the myriad details of daily life that besiege the character's mind but are not
initially sorted or categorized by him.[33] Hence, factual details from the material world combine with cultural recollections of both a popular and a literary

---

[31] The importance of trajectory and an awareness of movement through space might
be explored in relation to the protagonist's search for self in *Don Julián*. As Benson argues
in *The Cultural Psychology of Self*, the self is a 'locative system' (p. 3), and our perceptual
construction of space is rooted in the morphology of our bodies, composed of bounded
cells, which inherently have an 'inside' and an 'outside'. Notions of 'here' and 'there', self
and non-self, derive from this duality, so that 'the literal coexists with the metaphorical' (p.
5). ' "Here" means where I am, where I stand,' he argues (p. 25), 'and "there" is where I
might or might not want to be. Getting from here to there in social networks, as in physical
space, is a function of what I am and of where my current "here" lies in reference to the
desirable "there".' We shall return to this question in relation to *Makbara*.

[32] In *Postmodernist Fiction* (London: Routledge, 1987), Brian McHale identifies
boundary-breaking as a characteristic of such fiction, pp. 121–8.

[33] This recalls Merleau-Ponty's emphasis on a philosophy of perception in which 'the

and intellectual kind. For instance, in coming across a travelling knife-sharpener playing his shawm to attract business the protagonist presents him as an Arab Pan, the Greek god of shepherds, making his way through the city's 'selva urbanizada' (pp. 89–90). A few lines further on, the text incorporates the address of the estate agent selling a plot of land that the protagonist passes, without noting any qualitative distinction between the highly intellectual mytholological allusion and the mundane commercial advertisement. Another example occurs when the protagonist is seen scooping up the insects he has poisoned and will later use to defile the pages of works from the Spanish literary canon in the Tangier library. We are given a description of the picture postcard that he uses as if this were as important to his destructive task as the actual killing and collection of the insects:

> alguna abeja tal vez, alguna cucaracha : muertos [. . .] en la euforia del opulento banquete o en implicante y morosa conjunción copulativa [. . .] : mientras aflojas el cordón de la bolsita e introduces en ella las víctimas con ayuda de una añosa tarjeta postal : retrato de una jeunne fille Árabe muy comienzos de siglo, rabiosamente coloreado a posteriori : sin olvidar por eso el cómputo, el balance aproximativo del siniestro : muertos y más muertos   (p. 92)

This technique is sustained throughout the novel, creating the sense of an active mind initially perceiving and then beginning to order and process material. The protagonist-narrator himself refers to 'el arriesgado descifrar de los mensajes que la suerte interpone en tu camino' (p. 135), yet this process of selection is achieved primarily through the repetition of salient ideas rather than as the result of direct statement. The novel thus emphasizes – indeed, it dramatizes – not a flight from reality, but an initial encounter with it and its subsesquent moulding into an act of mental and cultural subversion. One should note that such moulding, rather than demonstrating a late structuralist and post-structuralist free-play of signification, indicates the creation of causal links of a non-grammatical kind and ultimately offers a new reading of Spanish cultural history. The Nationalist 'story of Spain' upon which a particular identity was built, is thus challenged by a new national narrative of dissidence and rebellion.

The Challenge to Cultural History

The dangers of a selective reading of what Jan Assmann terms 'fateful events' (p. 129) in a nation's cultural memory, are exposed deliberately by Goytisolo in *Don Julián*. In the novel he creates a dialogue that connects his

world is always "already there" before reflection begins' (*Phenomenology of Perception*, p. vii).

protagonist's personal past with Spain's cultural past, willing the destruction of the protagonist's childhood self through a deforming re-enactment of the children's tale of Little Red Riding Hood, and, in parallel, reinterpreting the legend of the fall of Spain to the Moors in 711, which resulted in almost eight centuries of Arab rule. An examination of each of these aspects of memory in the novel reveals the contextualized use of language that we have been exploring, and allies it to an appeal to the reader through emphasis on a shared, or intersubjective, symbolic order. However, rather than developing the implicit reciprocity in his Merleau-Pontian use of language into a depiction of the relations between the self and its projected other as mutually supporting, Goytisolo opts for a Sartrean antagonistic view in which the assertive gaze of the self desires the anihilation of the other. Taking issue with the Sartrean theory of the gaze, Merleau-Ponty argues in *Phenomenology of Perception* (pp. 360–1) that 'the other's gaze transforms me into an object, and mine him, only if [. . .] we both make ourselves into an inhuman gaze, if each of use feels his actions to be not taken up and understood [. . .]. The objectification of each by the other's gaze is felt as unbearable only because it takes the place of possible communication.' Such a reciprocal view is arguably not open to Goytisolo. In *Señas de identidad* and *Don Julián* he both illustrates and denounces the objectifying gaze to which the Franco regime subjects dissidents, and challenges its unwillingness to engage in dialogue with opposing interpretations of the nation's cultural memory. It is unfortunate, but possibly inevitable that, drawn into a Sartrean structure of reifying gaze and counter-gaze, Goytisolo ultimately finds himself trapped by the symbolic order he seeks to subvert.[34]

In *Don Julián* the protagonist's attempted destruction of his past self culminates, as noted above, in an imagined re-enactment of the children's tale of Little Red Riding Hood in which the wolf violates the child in a 'nueva versión psicoanalítica con mutilaciones, fetichismo, sangre' (p. 85). While this may seem a far cry from the vivid evocation of life in Tangier, each of the key elements in this final epiphany of destruction and renewal are drawn from the protagonist's perceptions as he wanders its streets. Many critics,

---

[34] In all fairness, one should note that, although Merleau-Ponty's dialectical view of history as both progress and regress, or *sens* and *non-sens*, offers an ethical perspective that is free from essentialism, it questions the very possibility of revolution – the ultimate goal of *Don Julián*. If human agency is partly determined by the social order, and if agents constitute themselves through the taking up, and then transformation, of rules and resources from that order, then social change is not possible through entirely free, intentional acts. In this respect, Merleau-Ponty diverges significantly from Sartre. On Merleau-Ponty's philosophy of history, see Nick Crossley, *The Politics of Subjectivity: Between Foucault and Merleau-Ponty* (Aldershot: Avebury, 1994), pp. 83–6; Richard Kearney, *Modern Movements in European Philosophy*, pp. 84–7; and James Schmidt, *Merleau-Ponty: Between Phenomenology and Structuralism* (Houndmills: Macmillan, 1985), pp. 147–8.

indeed, have noted the way in which Goytisolo reiterates central motifs throughout the novel, weaving a web of apparently disparate allusions, which gradually cohere in the new version of Red Riding Hood, although they have tended to interpret this as a gradual loss of contact with the material world.[35] One should stress, though, that despite the novel's descent into the mind of the protagonist, the material world is never completely lost from sight in *Don Julián*. The emphasis on the protagonist as a perceiving agent ensures that this is the case.

The use of elements from the perceptual world in the protagonist's fantasized destruction of his old self is most clearly evident in a comparison between the first and final parts of the novel. In part one, the section conventionally taken to be most closely rooted in the external world, the protagonist wakes up in his lodgings, leaves for a visit to a clinic where he receives an anti-syphilis injection, visits a library where he defiles the pages of certain books with dead insects, stops at a café to peruse the newspaper, visits the toilet and reads the graffiti there, and finally enters the public baths. Along the way, he meets the shawm-playing knife-sharpener, several beggars, a group of tourists watching a snake-charmer, and a local child who offers to act as a tourist guide for him. It is from these encounters, and certain personal and cultural recollections that they bring to mind, that he constructs his new version of Little Red Riding Hood, making it not just a symbolic rite of passage but the imagined destruction of his old self and rebirth as a dissident hero.[36]

The transformation of these elements into an imaginary scene of schizophrenic sodomy, in which the adult Álvaro anihilates his childhood self, is, of course, inexplicable without the symbolic charge that the author attaches to them in the intervening parts of the novel. Nevertheless, each and every aspect can – indeed, for the purposes of political and cultural subversion, must be – related to some identifiable stimulus beyond the protagonist's mind. That is to say, the raw material for the protagonist's rebellion is part of a shared cultural order and not chosen at random. And for the novel to have its full impact, the reader must be able to identify this raw material and the manner in which it has been transformed.

By part four of *Don Julián* it is true that the protagonist's direct physical encounter with Tangier seems largely to disappear from view, and it is only with difficulty that the reader can reconstruct aspects of the journey taken.

---

[35] Linda Gould Levine offers a comprehensive study of this aspect of the structure of the novel in *Juan Goytisolo: la destrucción creadora*, and Abigail E. Lee analyzes brilliantly Goytisolo's treatment of the childhood tale of Red Riding Hood in 'La paradigmática historia de Caperucita y el lobo feroz: Juan Goytisolo's use of "Little Red Riding Hood" in *Reivindicación del Conde don Julián'*, *Bulletin of Hispanic Studies*, 65 (1988), 141–51.

[36] Lee notes how the original children's tale can be read as a rite of passage from childhood to adulthood (p. 144).

The protagonist visits a building site and the *Zoco Grande*, of which he offers a vivid description. However, the final lines of the novel carefully and explicitly return to the setting of the opening pages as the protagonist returns to his room and recapitulates almost verbatim the initial very precise and rather theatrical description of it:[37]

> el habitual decorado te aguarde : dos sillas, el armario empotrado, la mesita de noche, la estufa de gas : el mapa de Imperio Jerifiano escala 1/1 000 000 impreso en Hallwag, Berna, Suiza : el grabado en colores con diferentes especies de hojas [. . .] : la lámpara de cabecera, el cenicero lleno de colillas, el cuaderno rojo con las cuatro tablas dibujadas detrás, el librillo de papel de fumar que utiliza Tariq para liar la hierba : nada más? : ah, la araña del techo   (p. 303)

It might be argued that this theatricality and the return to the opening serve to unsettle the concrete references in part one to a recognizable reality as much as they anchor part four in that recognizable world; yet, the specificity of the description, down to the scale of the map on the wall, does suggest a concern with physical setting. And even if the imaginary 'action' of part four occurs predominantly in the mind of the protagonist, this does not mean that the reader is subsumed into a subjective world the elements of which make little sense to him. On the contrary, throughout the course of his novel Goytisolo carefully weaves a network of suggestive allusions, which create a dialectical relationship between text and world.

In the fourth part of *Don Julián*, Red Riding Hood is presented as a boy – 'Caperucito Rojo' – whose mother sends him off with 'torrijas' for his ailing grandmother. The child, who is also referred to as Álvaro, encounters in granny's bed a wolf by the name of Ulbán who rapes him in a parody of the standard incantion from the tale:

> abuelita, qué bicha tan grande tienes!
> es para penetrarte mejor, so imbécil!   (p. 275)

Yet this imagined scene of violence does not satisfy Goytisolo's protagonist, and in the third sub-section of part four he re-creates the destruction of his childhood self in a different context, drawing together the outline of the Little Red Riding Hood tale with symbolism from another source, namely the legend of the fall of Spain to the Moors and the treachery of Conde don Julián, to which we shall presently return. It is at this point that key elements from the material world depicted in part one become stimuli in a perverse re-creation of this national foundational myth. But, lest the novel lose touch

---

[37] For the initial depiction of the room, which is introduced with the words, 'silencio, caballeros, se alza el telón, la representación empieza', see pp. 85–7.

with the particular context of Francoist Spain, Goytisolo inserts references to the socio-economic development of the country from the austerity of the 1940s to the boom of the 1960s. The scene merits close analysis for, as the central focus of the novel, it is the moment when the dialogue between the child and adult Álvaro should culminate in the forging of a new identity. Noticeably, the subtleties of the pronominal shifts that we saw in *Señas* recur. The moment is, however, less than decisive, as Goytisolo returns to the earlier dialogic use of 'tú' and 'él' in search of a provisional, dissident 'yo'.

The scene opens with a reference, concealed behind a Cervantine allusion, to 1940s Barcelona, as well as to the economic boom that would later affect the city:

> en un barrio olvidado de esa ciudad de cuyo nombre no quieres acordarte (calles silenciosas y pulcras [. . .] : verjas de hierro con rejas en forma de lanza, tapias erizadas de cristales y cascos de botella rotos [. . .] : villas recién recuperadas por sus dueños en aquellos dichosos años de racionamiento y Auxilio Social : sistema premonopolista y burgués, anterior a la invasión turística, al plan de desarrollo y a la apoteosis internacional del Ubicuo : mundo abolido hoy) has sido testigo y parte de la historia [. . .] : tú y tu fuerte compañera, la culebra : prolongación indispensable de ti mismo y de tu modo de ser   (p. 279)

This is the world in which the young Álvaro, in echo of Goytisolo himself, was raised, and the protagonist quickly offers a vision of himself as a child returning from school: 'el niño? : qué niño? : tú mismo un cuarto de siglo atrás' (p. 280). The relationship between the protagonist and this child has, however, already been foreshadowed in the first part of the novel in the figure of the child-guide that the protagonist meets and who he follows, rather ironically as it turns out, as a distraction from his 'perturbador soliloquio' (p. 135) against Spain. That child had evoked in him memories of himself and the connection will ultimately lead not to the protagonist's escape from his obsession with Spain, but to a moment of confrontation. The textual echo between the beginning and end of the novel is clear:

> su rostro evoca alguna imagen que inútilmente quisieras arrancar del olvido : algo remoto tal vez : recuerdo de la ciudad, del país de cuyo nombre no quieres acordarte [. . .] súbitamente, lo crees reconocer : un cuarto de siglo atrás : un barrio de calles recogidas y absortas, orilladas de umbrosos jardines y torres conventuales : verjas de hierro con rejas en forma de lanza, muros erizados de cristales y cascos de botella rotos   (pp. 144–5)

The *desdoblamiento* by which the protagonist is split into his child and adult selves is thus grounded in an encounter initially presented as part of the protagonist's perception of the external world of the city. Likewise, the setting for the final sodomy can be seen to have its origin in the child-guide's account of his visits to a snake-charmer who works as a watchman on a building site. In part one we read: 'tengo una cita [. . .] con un hombre, te dice : el guardián de unas obras que hay en mi barrio : vive con una culebra y, cuando voy, me la enseña [. . .] es un encantador' (p. 144). In part four, the protagonist has now assumed the role of the snake-charmer – 'tú, el hosco guardián de las obras' (p. 280) – and the snake is a rather conventional phallic symbol. Other elements also drawn from the world of part one include the grafitto from the public toilets, 'CON LOS NIÑOS EL LÁTIGO ES NECESARIO', suggesting the violence of the rape of the child, and the persistent recall of a natural science lesson in which a scorpion kills an insect.[38]

The pronominal instability that is a mark of *Señas* reappears in this section of *Don Julián*, as the protagonist simultaneously identifies with, and yet attempts to distance himself from, the child that he was and wishes to destroy. On the one hand, the child is referred to as 'el niño' and designated by the pronoun, 'él', while the adult narrator is clearly identified by the second person. On the other hand, the child is 'tu mismo un cuarto de siglo atrás', and adult and child share a 'suerte recíproca' (p. 282). This hesitation between the fusion of the protagonist and child, and their separation, is marked visually and grammatically in the text slightly later when the child is referred to as 'tú (él)' (p. 287). Their joint fate is then played out as a narrative. Both 'protagonistas', as they are specifically designated, are aware that they are still 'en el preámbulo de la historia' (p. 285), the dénouement of which will see the adult protagonist adopting the identity of Julián, the mythical traitor whom the novel sets out to vindicate, in order to anihilate the child. 'Soy Bulián, tu admirador y amigo : pobrecito guardián de infaustas, avarientas obras' (p. 285), he says in a significant slip into the first person.[39] In contrast to the formulaic appearance of a first-person voice in the mock religious incantation at the end of *Señas*, this use of the first person signals the protagonist's momentary achievement of a dissident identity through his metamorphosis into the legendary figure of Conde don Julián.

The achievement of this longed-for identity is, however, provisional, for at the very moment of destruction, when the novel seems most distanced from the external world, it in fact returns to that concrete reality and undermines the fulfilment of the protagonist's aims. Following the imagined rape of the

[38] The grafitto first appears on p. 133 and is evoked on many later occasions. The use of capitals in the phrase serves to mark it off from the rest of the text, thus emphasizing its importance. The natural science class is first described on pp. 103–4, and is also frequently recalled. Gould Levine masterfully traces the development of these initial ideas into the violent, sexually charged imagery of the final part of the novel.

[39] Taking Luis G. de Valdeavellano's *Historia de España* as one source of the legend of Julián, his name is spelt variously Julián, Bulián, Ulyan, Urbano and Ulbán. See *Don Julián*, p. 70, n. 1.

protagonist's childhood self, the text specifically recalls the original child-guide of part one, with his story of the licentious snake-charmer: 'mañana empezaremos otra vez [. . .] : llegada la hora, a su regreso del colegio, los pasos le encaminarán inexorablemente hacia la calle desierta en donde el prudente celador de las obras aguarda : el cielo es bajo y opaco [. . .]' (p. 286). This circularity serves to emphasize not the achievement of a dissident identity, but the process of rebellion that constitutes the quest for that identity. So, while *Don Julián* glorifies dissidence as a core principle, it refuses to fix a single, enduring identity for its protagonist, dramatizing instead a negotiation between different interpretations of personal and cultural memory.

Unfulfilled Potential: Latent Boundary-Crossings in Don Julián's *Depiction of National Identity*

The dissident identity to which Álvaro aspires in Goytisolo's text is that of Julián, the mythical traitor responsible for the fall of the Iberian peninsula to the Moors in 711. According to legend, Julián, seeking to avenge the rape of his daughter, La Cava, by King Rodrigo of Spain, led the Moors into the peninsula, initiating nearly eight centuries of Arab colonization. Rodrigo's sexual crime thus led to the loss of his kingdom, and his punishment, according to some versions of the tale, was to lie in his own grave where he would die from a poisonous snake-bite 'por do más pecado había'.[40] In seeking to vindicate Julián's betrayal, Goytisolo employs many of the same symbols as the legend, but reverses its paradigm of fall and redemption to offer an alternative reading of Spanish history. If Rodrigo's sexual misconduct led to the loss of the country, then Julián's will be its resurrection. And if the snake in the original legend represents punishment, in Goytisolo's new version it represents salvation. So, immediately after the protagonist identifies himself with Julián in the use of a first-person voice, he pleads with his child victim, almost as if he had now slipped into the role of Rodrigo instead: 'tu amor consentido puede todavía regenerarme : escúchame bien : confía en mí : un hada antipática, en los furores de la menopausia, me redujo a este triste estado y me encerró en lóbrega y cruel sepultura sin otra compañía que una culebra hambrienta' (p. 285).

---

[40] The Rodrigo legend was preserved in medieval ballads, and the story developed over time. Early versions recounted only the sexual crime and fall of the peninsula; later ones added the elements of penance and redemption. For examples, see Colin Smith (ed.), *Spanish Ballads* (Oxford: Pergamon Press, 1964), pp. 51–8. Alfonso el Sabio also recounted the story of Rodrigo in his *Primera crónica general de España*, from which Goytisolo takes an epigraph for his novel. Valdeavellano is, as we have noted, another source. The story is thus one of the foundational narratives of Spanish identity, and is preserved in accordance with Assman's definition of cultural memory.

Such deformation of the original legend signals Goytisolo's intention to subvert it through narrative restructuring, and this must necessarily occur within a specified historical context. The symbolic order with which Goytisolo establishes a dialogue is therefore that of the Francoist interpretation and manipulation of the myth of the fall of the peninsula in 711 to propagate a particular view of Spanish cultural and national identity.[41] The terms by which the Nationalist victors in the Civil War read the 'story of Spain' – which is to say, the narrative they constructed to justify the 1936 uprising – followed a religious paradigm of fall and redemption similar to the Rodrigo legend. Franco was presented as the saviour of the nation, who, in emulation of Isabel la Católica, the 'mother of the nation', centuries before, had purged Spain of alien elements during the Civil War and returned her to her 'true destiny' as a conservative, Catholic society. Of course, the 'alien elements' in each case were rather different – for Isabel it had been the Moors, for Franco it was a cocktail of liberalism, anarchism, communism, marxism, and separatism. In exploiting the legend, Goytisolo seeks to highlight these cultural connections and, by exposing Nationalist historiography as based on legend rather than fact, sabotage the regime's narrative of self-justification. In Goytioslo's version, Julián is vindicated as a hero whose actions led to a fertile period of *mestizaje* destroyed by the actions of Isabel, and emulated later by Franco. The *Reconquista* and Civil War, instead of being moments of purifying salvation, represent deviations from a desired cultural promiscuity, which draws upon all available influences to construct an open-minded society.

On one side of the equation, then, we find a series of values that Francoist Spain views negatively and Goytisolo positively – Julián, Moorish culture, *mestizaje*, openness to outside influence – and, on the other, a set of values associated with Francoist Spain that Goytisolo condemns through their negation – the *Reconquista* as a racial cleansing re-enacted symbolically during the Civil War, economic autarky, social and cultural isolationism. Each set of values is represented by one half of the divided Álvaro, his childhood self standing for the doctrines of Francoist Spain that formed the backdrop to his upbringing, and his adult self symbolizing the new, dissident identity he seeks to realize in destroying the former. Thus, the existential search for identity in *Don Julián* is also an ethical project grounded in contemporary political circumstance.

Numerous critics have argued that Goytisolo's reversal of the paradigm of fall and redemption leaves him a prisoner of that same paradigm and thus enslaved to the historical vision that he seeks to refute.[42] The above summary

---

[41] For an analysis of the Nationalist view of history and its relation to Spanish fiction of the 1960s and 1970s, see Jo Labanyi, *Myth and History*, and Robert Spires, *Narrating the Past: Fiction and Historiography in Postwar Spain* (Durham: Duke University Press, 1995).

[42] Labanyi states this case cogently in *Myth and History*, pp. 196–214.

would certainly seem to justify this position, yet this critical argument focuses purely on the mythical content of the novel in the context of Nationalist historiography and not in relation to the socio-economic backdrop of 1960s Spain as drawn by Goytisolo. We have already seen above the importance of Goytisolo's interweaving of myth and contemporary historical conditions, and this provides a new perspective on the actual functioning of countermythification, or demythification, in *Don Julián*. If nationhood is conceived of as a mythical discourse justifying the ideological apparatus of state power, and if resistance is the subversion of this myth either through an appeal to countermyths or verifiable historical fact, then criticism of Goytisolo's binary mythical scheme is perhaps inevitable. However, an approach to national identity that seeks to fracture the opposition between myth and countermyth, or between myth and history, throws up a different perspective.

As Homi Bhabha argues in *Nation and Narration*, there is a tendency to view the nation in very restricted terms as either a repressive ideological apparatus or as a utopian expression of popular sentiment preserved in shared memories. Bhabha seeks a more ambivalent approach, viewing not nationalism but 'nationness' as akin to a narrative process in which the establishment of cultural boundaries is not limiting, but rather results in the creation of 'thresholds of meaning that must be crossed, erased, and translated in the process of cultural production'.[43] Attempting to fracture the oppositional approach to national identity implicit in the self/other, or inside/outside, binary that is often used to explain national identity, Bhabha seeks, as he puts it, to uncover ways in which 'the "locality" of national culture is neither unified nor unitary in relation to itself, nor [simply] "other" in relation to what is outside or beyond it'. The 'other', concludes Bhabha (p. 4), 'is never outside or beyond us; it emerges forcefully, within cultural discourse, when we *think* we speak most intimately and indigenously "between ourselves".' For this reason, one should look not to fixed markers of national identity, but to the intersections and slippages between reified categories that blur and problematize the apparently clearly defined boundary dividing the inner sanctum of the nation's conceptual space from its external enemy. In order to do this, Bhabha postulates the existence of two opposed yet co-existing views of national narratives, a pedagogical one, arising out of the mythical and authoritative discourses of the state, and a performative one, deriving from the daily negotiations that turn the 'scraps, patches, and rags of daily life' into national culture.[44] From the split between the 'continuist, accumulative

---

43 Homi Bhabha, introduction to *Nation and Narration* (London: Routledge, 1990), pp. 1–7 (p. 4).

44 Bhabha develops the ideas of his introduction to *Nation and Narration* in an extensive essay in the same volume, 'DissemiNation: time, narrative, and the margins of the modern nation', pp. 291–322 (p. 297).

temporality' of the pedagogical and the 'repetitious, recursive strategy' of the performative emerges, according to Bhabha (p. 297), 'the cutting edge between the totalizing powers of the social and the forces that signify the more specific address to contentious, unequal interests and identities within the population'.[45]

If a productive view of nationness looks to slippages between discourses that point to hybridity and an overlap between self and other, then, as Richard Kearney argues, danger does not arise from myth itself, but from its use. We need, he argues, 'to keep our mythological memories in dialogue with history.' Every culture must unceasingly tell stories, he continues, 'inventing and reinventing its inherited imaginary, lest its history congeal into dogma'.[46] This is precisely what Goytisolo attempts in *Don Julián*, where the narrative of the nation is retold not simply as a countermyth, but as one possible countermyth set against the socio-economic backdrop of 1960s Spain. It is unfortunate that the novel's specific context is frequently overlooked, for it provides precisely the contextualized dialogue with history that Kearney regards as essential to an informed and ongoing negotiation of nationhood. Goytisolo writes his novel at a time when growing consumerism had obscured the mismatch between the ideological bases of the Franco regime – its appeal to a mythical or pedagogical legitimacy – and an economic policy that was bringing the country in line with captialist democracies.[47] The juxtaposition of myth and economic detail in *Don Julián* therefore serves to disrupt the easy forgetfulness of the late 1960s by juxtaposing Nationalist myths, Goytisolo's countermyths, and present historical conditions. This triadic negotiation throws into relief not two, but three, perspectives, thus fracturing the binaries that critics have concentrated on in their readings. However, Goytisolo could have gone further, revealing slippages between the reified categories of Spaniard and Moor, or self and other, that Bhabha calls for.

---

[45] In *Narrating the Past*, David Herzberger states (p. 2): 'In post-Civil War Spain, authority over history is bound up with restrictive narrative practices shaped and regulated by historians of the State. The absence of choices and alternatives for framing the past therefore begets a narrowly construed notion of historical truth.' Ideologically, this is certainly the case; yet, in order to establish its particular notion of historical truth, the Regime was forced to manipulate the details of history to suit its interpretation, thus engaging in complex and ever-changing negotiations concerning such issues as national foundational myths, the image of the Moorish other, and the legitimacy upon which the administration's rule was based. As we shall see below, a detailed analysis of these negotiations would reflect not clearly defined views of self and other, but shifting views dependent upon discursive context. A full study of the Regime's micro-manipulation of history has yet to be written.

[46] Richard Kearney, *On Stories* (London: Routledge, 2002), p. 90.

[47] The wave of nostalgia evident in the huge success of TVE's recent series, *Cuéntame como pasó*, suggests that Goytisolo's virulent attack on Spain's popular amnesia concerning its violent past is more necessary than ever.

In the opening essay of *Crónicas sarracinas*, 'Cara y cruz del moro en nuestra literatura', Goytisolo hints that the Moor has a more fragmented and contested cultural significance than is generally recognized. Although his epigraph to the volume, taken from Gertrude Stein, declares, 'Scratch a Spaniard and you find a Saracen', his essay in fact points to evidence of cultural influence moving in the opposite direction. Granted, he does make the conventional observation that the Moor is the Spaniard's other:

> Desde los primeros balbuceos de nuestro idioma, el muslime es siempre el espejo en el que de algún modo nos vemos reflejados, la imagen exterior de nosotros que nos interroga e inquieta. A menudo será nuestro negativo: proyección de cuanto censuramos en nuestro fuero interno, y objeto por tanto de aborrecimiento y envidia.[48]

But he goes on to note that Spain's arch rival is 'irreductible' and, most significantly, 'íntimo'. Although his image is usually presented as the mirror opposite of the qualities the nation values as its own, this is not exclusively the case in Spanish literature.

The Civil War era is a case in point, and Goytisolo recalls the propagandistic use of the sterotypical image of the Moor as violent and barbaric by both sides in the conflagration. He notes the tendency to 'confundir al rifeño explotado y manipulado por el colonizador con quienes interesadamente lo manipulan' (p. 10), thus reversing Stein's formulation to suggest that under a Rifeño one might perhaps find the barbarity of a Spaniard.[49] Indeed, Goytisolo recalls the infamous incident of a photograph of Spanish legionaries with the decapitated heads of several Rifeños published in the memoirs of Abd el Krim in 1927. 'Este salvajismo', Goytisolo comments (p. 22), 'era moneda corriente entre nuestros voluntarios africanos.' The picture was later credited by Nationalist propaganda in 1938 to their Republican enemy. The

---

[48] 'Cara y cruz del moro en nuestra literatura', in *Crónicas sarracinas*, pp. 7–25 (p. 8); epigraph, p. 5.

[49] The left argued during the War that it was the Spanish in Morocco who had brutalized the Moors, and not vice versa, thus countering the oft-cited view that Franco himself had been brutalized by his experiences there. On 9 January 1936, for example, the Communist newspaper *El Mundo Obrero* published an eye-witness account of rapes, atrocities, and shootings in Oviedo under the title, 'El terror blanco de Octubre: la obra negra del gobierno Lerroux-Gil Robles'. It concluded that 'Las tropas mercenarias moras copiaban los metodos de colonización que los habían ensenado los conquistadores españoles.' In a forthcoming article, Filipe Ribeiro de Meneses argues that modern historiography fails to appreciate a general hostility, following the First World War, to the use of African troops on European soil, and that it has also perpetuated the mythical dehumanization of the Moroccan troops by not 'seeking to inquire into their motivations or their reasons for being in the conflict, and their reaction to the orders they were given' ('Popularising Africanism: The Career of Victor Ruiz Albeniz, El Tebib Arrumi', forthcoming in *Journal of Iberian and Latin American Studies*).

legend of the barbarous Moor in contrast to the heroic Spaniard is thus reversed at critical times in Spanish history, revealing the slippages in meaning, or 'supplementarity', of the 'trasvases de símbolos e imágenes' ('Cara y cruz', p. 23), which Bhabha highlights as the 'the *in-between* spaces through which the meanings of cultural and political authority are negotiated' (p. 4). Sadly, although in *Don Julián* Goytisolo takes the first step in Bhabha and Kearney's approach to nationness, juxtaposing various mythical readings with contemporary circumstance, and thus establishing a dialogue between mythical memories and history, he does not follow through with a rigorous consideration of the image of the Moor in Spanish culture. Our author admits as much in *Crónicas sarracinas*, but this leaves *Don Julián* as a novel of unfulfilled possibilities. As we shall see in the next chapter, it is only a decade later, with the publication of *Makbara*, that a pluralist vision is finally articulated in a convincing manner.

4

MIGRATING SOUTH, WANDERING EAST:
JUAN SIN TIERRA AND *MAKBARA*

> *We might in all seriousness (and without arrogant or*
> *magnanimous defiance) call ourselves 'generous and*
> *mobile spirits' because we feel the pull towards freedom*
> *as our spirit's strongest drive, and, in contrast to*
> *the bound and firmly rooted intellects, might almost*
> *take a spiritual nomadism as our ideal, – to use a modest*
> *and almost disparaging expression.*
> Friedrich Nietzsche[1]

The Space of the Text and the Author as Authority

In *Juan sin Tierra* (1975) and *Makbara* (1980) Goytisolo develops a number of themes already outlined in *Don Julián*, but from a more international and less purely Spanish perspective. The author's search for a dissident literary identity, as the majority of critics have argued, is now subsumed into a wider political preoccupation with North–South and East–West relations.[2] Although certain autobiographical aspects of the earlier novels are retained – the opening allusion to a Cuban sugar plantation in *Juan sin Tierra*, for instance, deliberately recalls the manner in which Goytisolo's great-grandfather amassed the family fortune[3] – the focus broadens to a geographical contrast between the Orient and the Occident, which finds expression in an intensification of the parallel between the physical world and the world of the text. Dissidence is now given a spatial configuration, developing the comparison between the city and the text that underpinned *Don Julián* into a

[1]   Quoted in Douglas Smith, *Transvaluations: Nietzsche in France 1872–1972* (Oxford: Oxford University Press, 1996), p. 181.

[2]   See, for instance, Schaefer-Rodríguez, *Juan Goytisolo: del 'realismo crítico' a la utopía*; Gonzalo Navajas, '*Juan sin Tierra*: fin de un período novelístico', in *Teoría y práctica de la novela española posmoderna* (Barcelona: Mall, 1987), pp. 83–9; and Luce López-Baralt, 'Hacia una lectura "mudéjar" de *Makbara*', in *Huellas del Islam en la literatura española: de Juan Ruiz a Juan Goytisolo* (Madrid: Hiperión, 1985), pp. 181–209.

[3]   Part one of *Juan sin Tierra* alludes to the family 'pecado de origen' (p. 14) from which the narrator must seek redemption. It also refers to Goytisolo's great-grandfather's adultery with a slave (pp. 46–7) which the author discovered in a letter that he transcribed in the first volume of his autobiography (*Coto vedado*, pp. 12–13).

contrast between two manners of inhabiting space and two associated ways of writing fiction.

In *Juan sin Tierra*, Goytisolo sets out a comparison between nomadic and sedentary society that draws on the theories of Gilles Delueze and Félix Guattari to offer a 'nomadic text' that has no apparent narrative coherence in the traditional sense. *Makbara*, although seeming to appeal to this same notion of nomadism, in fact focuses on a circumscribed space. The novel is centred on the oral storytellers of Marrakesh's main square, Xemaá-el-Fná, but the notion of oral literature allows Goytisolo to explore other means of achieving textual fragmentation and flux. Both novels retain *Don Julián*'s emphasis on physical embodiment, though Goytisolo destroys even the notion of a protagonist which that novel had retained in order to decentre the narrative speaking voice and wage war on authority.

A primary preoccupation in these works continues to be the articulation of dissidence and its association with alterity. Superficially, both books appear to challenge the conventional notion of the author as the origin of the text's meaning, an attack on narrative authority that recalls Barthes' declaration of the 'death of the author' in his famous essay of 1968.[4] A closer reading, however, reveals that, while *Juan sin Tierra* offers a view of a decentred text-in-the-making, and *Makbara* appeals to an oral tradition in order to diffuse narrative authority into a shared cultural code and set of references, in each work the figure of the author is surreptitiously placed in a central position in the discursive structure. Goytisolo does not assassinate the author in these works; rather, in seeking to articulate a voice of alterity, he explores the implications of a depiction of discursive origins as, respectively, written and oral.

The Lure of the South and An Ethics of Nomadism

Juan sin Tierra constitutes a shift south and east in the thematics of Goytisolo's fiction. The novel's title inscribes it within a tradition of exiles who have sought alternative styles of life and values to those of their mother country. Blanco White's adoption of the pseudonym Juan Sintierra is, as we have seen, the closest Spanish example of the intellectual and cultural dislocation that Goytisolo seeks,[5] though his journey was northward to England and Ireland. More pertinent in the present context are the figures whom Goytisolo evokes directly in his 1975 novel: Lawrence of Arabia, Père de

---

[4] Barthes declares that 'writing is the destruction of every voice, of every point of origin' and is thus the 'oblique space' where 'all identity is lost' ('The Death of the Author', in *Image–Music–Text*, ed. and trans. Stephen Heath [New York: Hill & Wang, 1977], pp. 142–8 [p. 142]).

[5] See p. 49, n. 49.

Foucauld, Fra Anselm Turmeda, Cavafy, and Pierre Loti, all of whom represent the 'judíos errantes, herederos de Juan sin Tierra' (p. 77) that Goytisolo's writing glorifies.[6] And behind these cultural renegades is another, unmentioned figure who was a close friend of our author and whose presence towers over his mature writing, namely Jean Genet.

Genet's was a life spent celebrating rootlessness. His *Journal du Voleur*, from which Goytisolo took an epigraph for *Don Julián*, expresses an obsessive attraction to the South and lauds Tangier as a land of traitors, a place of cathartic escape from the France which Genet rejects and which has rejected him. It is as if the Frenchman, as Jérôme Neutres argues, desires to be literally captivated by the South – and, indeed, the men of the South – and so to betray the values of the society that incarcerated him for theft. The title of his final book, *Un captif amoureux*, expresses the paradox of this desired captivity, which is developed thematically in the author's passion for Palestine and the Palestinian political cause as an example of the criminal 'other' that he in life represented.[7] But the difficulties inherent in Genet's desire to adopt the identity of the other – for his commitment to Palestine amounts to more than a longing for the exotic according to the terms by which Edward

6 T. E. Lawrence famously chose to embrace Arab culture in a manner that was more than mere exotic fascination. He fought with King Faisal against the Turks in the First World War, recording his memoirs in *Seven Pillars of Wisdom*, a text to which Goytisolo alludes frequently in *Juan sin Tierra*. Fra Anselm Turmeda was a Mallorcan Franciscan monk who converted to Islam around 1386. He became the interpreter of the King of Tunis and wrote the *Disputa de l'ase contra frare Encelm Turmeda sobre la natura y noblessa dels animals*, a humorous treatise in which man's superiority to animals is questioned. Goytisolo includes him in the third part of *Juan sin Tierra*, in 'El falo de Ghardaïa' (pp. 116–27), where the narrator adopts his voice to recount the tale of his journey to Africa, and recalls him again in the 'Con Ibn Turmeda, de vuelta a la zanja' (pp. 132–6). Charles de Foucauld, a Trappist monk who was martyred for his Christian faith in 1916, seems an odd figure for Goytisolo to choose as a fellow traveller. However, his letters to his cousin, Madeleine de Bondy, describing his journey to Africa, are haunted by a fascination with the desert and with a desire for physical punishment as mystical purification. This latter sentiment is satirized by Goytisolo in his own desire for self-destruction and rebirth in *Don Julián* and *Juan sin Tierra*, but it also foreshadows the mystical turn in Goytisolo's later novels, and the attraction of the desert for the protagonist in *Telón de boca*. Constantine Cavafy, or Kavafis, was born in Alexandria, Egypt in 1863, of Constantinopolitan parents. The most original Greek poet of the past century, he had several homosexual affairs and treated homosexual themes in a frank manner that was at odds with his contemporaries. Pierre Loti, the pseudonym of Julien Viaud, was a French novelist who wrote sentimental fiction of a sensuous, impressionistic type, often set in the Orient. He also wrote travel literature arising from his career in the French navy.

7 Neutres demonstrates Genet's attraction to, and political engagement with, marginality as represented by the 'South' in his study, *Genet sur les routes du Sud* (Paris: Fayard, 2002), the first part of which is entitled 'Jean sans terre et les hommes du Sud'. He also details the initial critical reaction to *Un captif amoureux*, first published posthumously in 1986, which sought to read the book as an aesthetic expression of marginality and to ignore the political aspect that he so ably elucidates.

Said analyzes Western Orientalist discourse[8] – the difficulties involved in this are also enshrined in his book's title. Desiring to be be a prisoner of the Southern or Eastern other, he must always remain a prisoner of his original, Western identity. As Neutres puts it, Genet is 'captif de son identité et amoureux d'une autre' (p. 63).

Goytisolo, like Genet, seeks to adopt the voice and marginal position of the other in a deliberate gesture of subversion. 'El exilio', the narrator-cum-author figure of *Juan sin Tierra* comments, 'te ha convertido en un ser distinto, que nada tiene que ver con el que conocieron : su ley ya no es tu ley' (p. 55). The southern shift in the thematics of Goytisolo's work is thus a journey that is consciously undertaken. But, just as Genet's aspiration to transgress the coordinates of his Western identity proves to be utopian, so Goytisolo's desire to occupy the place of the other will ultimately prove to be impossible. This can be related to the comparison that Delueze and Guattari make between the migrant, whose journey is plotted according to a particular rationale, and the nomad, whose wandering life style (they claim) follows no such predetermined pattern. The present chapter seeks to explore this paradox at the heart of Goytisolo's work in the late 1970s, arguing that his journey South is a conscious act of migration that contains within it the desire for a nomadic wandering East, but finds this to be inachievable.[9]

The triad that Genet's work creates between captivity, freedom, and desire is echoed in *Juan sin Tierra*.[10] The novel opens with an unidentified narrator-author figure comparing the Hindu aspiration towards spiritual

---

[8] The fundamental thesis of Edward Said's ground-breaking book, *Orientalism* (reprinted with a new Afterword [Harmondsworth: Penguin, 1995], p. 3), is that Western discourses about the East constitute a 'style for dominating, restructuring, and having authority over the Orient'. Neutres discusses the issue of Orientalism in Genet's work, situating it in the same written tradition as Goytisolo by discussing such figures as Lawrence, Foucauld, Pierre Loti, Baudelaire and Nerval. However, Neutres contrasts Genet's identification with the South with his attempts to alienate himself from fellow Frenchmen at home, thus complicating any direct contrast between inside and outside, or self and other, by placing the other within. In private letters to Goytisolo, the originals of which were stolen from the Goytisolo archive in Almería but which exist in photocopies, Genet recounts his experiences of mundane life in the small town of Abbeville in order to reveal precisely the lack of profundity of 'la France profonde'. Neutres transcribes three of the letters, to which access is currently restricted, in his study (pp. 40–5). He also discusses their theft and Goytisolo's amused reaction to the pilfering of letters from a thief (p. 38).

[9] An awareness of the traveller's inability to become one with the people of the regions he visits is articulated in Goytisolo's travel writing from *Campos de Níjar* to the *Cuaderno de Sarajevo*. See Abigail Lee Six's excellent critical guide to the former (London: Grant & Cutler, 1996) and my article, 'Juan Goytisolo's *Cuaderno de Sarajevo*: The Dilemmas of a Committed War Journalist', *Journal of Iberian and Latin American Studies* (forthcoming, summer 2005).

[10] The theme of desire in *Juan sin Tierra* has been much discussed by critics, and I shall not rehearse their arguments here. For analyses of the theme, see Paul Julian Smith, *Laws of Desire*, pp. 31–42; and Epps, *Significant Violence*, pp. 137–9.

purity through meditation – 'según los gurús indostánicos, en la fase superior de la meditación, el cuerpo humano, purgado de apetitos y anhelos, se abandona con deleite a una existencia etérea, [. . .] desdeña, altivo, la irrisoria esclavitud de los placeres, puro, esbelto y sutil' (p. 11) – with the sensuality of slaves on a Cuban sugar plantation – 'es medianoche, la hora del diablo, y los esclavos se escurren a hurtadillas del barracón [. . .] : noche tropical de la canción de Elvira Ríos, cálida y sensual' (p. 38). The theme of enslavement is thus developed in a particular context and in two particular ways: first, it relates to the separation of body and soul, which underpins not only Western metaphysics but mystical thought in general; second, it evokes social and political oppression through direct reference to slavery. The narrator-author himself turns out, like the slaves, to be 'cuerpo tan sólo, despliegue de materia : hijo de la tierra y a la tierra unido' (p. 12). Interestingly, however, the divide between East and West is not a simple one, for the condemnation of sprituality with which *Juan sin Tierra* opens relates it to the Eastern religion of Hinduism. Goytisolo's reading of the cultural markers of 'South' and 'East' is, therefore, selective. As in *Don Julián*, it is not quite the case that he establishes two sets of terms, East and West, or North and South, and then seeks to reverse them – even though this is what the novel misleadingly suggests of itself in the narrator-author's remark, 'dividirás la imaginaria escena en dos partes : dicho mejor : en dos bloques opuestos de palabras' (p. 27). What Goytisolo does is single out *certain* features of Eastern and Western society for praise or condemnation and ignore others.

The particular, selected values that Goytisolo associates with the terms 'East' and 'West' have been much discussed in relation to *Juan sin Tierra*, and are generally agreed to be as follows: East and West represent respectively, Islam against Christianity; sexuality against spirituality; a healthy proximity to the land and to bodily functions against an unhealthy obsession with cleanliness and an aversion to the scatological;[11] and finally, in a rather large jump to literary matters, textual *jouissance* against simplistic realism.[12] Contrary to the prevailing critical view, however, I wish to move beyond the notion that there is an easy progression from a particular way of viewing man's physical

---

11 This is an aspect of the novel that has been much studied and I shall not cover it here. For details, see Susan F. Levine, ' "Cuerpo" y "no-cuerpo" – una conjunción entre Juan Goytisolo y Octavio Paz', *Journal of Spanish Studies: Twentieth Century*, 15 (1977), 123–35; Kessel Schwartz, 'Juan Goytisolo, *Juan sin Tierra* and the Anal Aesthetic', *Hispania*, 62 (1979), 9–19; Robert Spires, 'Latrines, Whirlpools, and Voids: the Metafictional Mode of *Juan sin Tierra*', *Hispanic Review*, 48 (1980), 151–69; Epps, *Significant Violence*, p. 167.

12 For further discussion of these contrasts, see Ugarte's *Trilogy of Treason*, pp. 129–45; and Lee Six's *Juan Goytisolo*, chapters 2–3. Paul Julian Smith criticizes Goytisolo's insensitivity to the persecution of homosexuality in certain Arab countries, in *Laws of Desire*, p. 41.

nature to a particular way of writing fiction.[13] Goytisolo's celebration of
corporeality and physical desire seeks not simply to relate them to a textual
freeplay of signifiers, but to a particular philosophy of man's being-in-the-
world which recalls Deleuze and Guattari's theory of nomadism as a form of
both social organization and textual structure.[14] Once again, the verbal weave
of Goytisolo's novel and the external reality with which it is apparently
contrasted exhibit a symbiotic relationship that prevents the complete disso-
ciation of the former from the latter.

In *Anti-Oedipus* and *A Thousand Plateaus*, Deleuze and Guattari relate
desire to subversion and freedom, not in its Lacanian sense of lack, but as a
desiring-production which is, in Nietzschean terms, active rather than reactive.[15] While Goytisolo's attitude towards Francoist Spain may ultimately be
judged to be reactive, in that, at base, he defines himself as dissident through
a contrast with that which he virulently opposes, and fails to develop fully
potential nuances in this oppositional view,[16] nevertheless, the spatial config-

---

[13] This link is forged by many critics, including Black, *The Poetics of Contagion*, p.
123. Jerome S. Bernstein argues that there is a contradiction between the apparently
self-contained nature of *Juan sin Tierra* and its thematics, in 'Body, Language and
Divinity in Goytisolo's *Juan sin Tierra*', *The Analysis of Hispanic Texts: Current Trends in
Methodology*, second York College colloquium, ed. Lisa E. Davis and Isabel C. Tarán
(New York: Bilingual Press, 1976), pp. 79–89. Epps gives a more nuanced reading of the
issue in *Significant Violence*, p. 157, suggesting that although the novel anticipates
possible critiques and tries to invalidate them, it ultimately offers a contradictory moral
certainty in its utopian faith in the possibilities of the written word to achieve liberation
through destruction.

[14] Opposing the tyranny of the signifier in structuralism and post-structuralism, since
it is, according to Deleuze in 'Nomad Thought' (*The New Nietzsche: Contemporary Styles
of Interpretation*, ed. David B. Allinson [Cambridge, Mass.: MIT Press, 1985], pp. 142–9
[p. 149]), 'the last philosophical metamorphosis of the despot', he and Guattari seek in
Anti-Oedipus: Capitalism and Schizophrenia (trans. Robert Hurley, Mark Seem, and
Helen R. Lane [New York: Viking Press, 1977]) to decentre the notion of structure itself
by offering a new view of the relationship between language, desire, thought, action, social
institutions, and material reality. Underpinning their argument, according to Ronald Bogue
in *Deleuze and Guattari* (London: Routledge, 1989), p. 150, is a Nietzschean conception
of the cosmos as 'the ceaseless becoming of a multiplicity of interconnected forces'. Their
desire to relate material reality, social institutions, desire, and language without privileging
one set of forces over another is interesting, if ultimately utopian.

[15] Deleuze's early work on Nietzsche is discussed by Douglas Smith, in *Transvaluations*, pp. 140–50, 164–84; and Bogue, in *Deleuze and Guattari*, chapter 1.

[16] Linda Ledford-Miller ('History as Myth, Myth as History: Juan Goytisolo's *Count
Julian*', *Revista Canadiense de Estudios Hispánicos*, 8 [1983], 21–30) reads *Don Julián* as
an affirmation of the Nietzschean suggestion that history can best serve life as a form of
art, and on one level this is the case. However, Goytisolo's treatment of Francoist Spain
disavows another Nietzschean argument that Deleuze and Guattari develop, namely their
re-reading of the Hegelian master–slave dialectic in terms of active and reactive forces.
According to Smith (p. 145), 'the ultimate goal of Nietzsche's philosophy is, for Deleuze,
the liberation of thought from nihilism as represented within the dialectic by the reactive
categories of identity and negation. Since traditional thought in philosophy and science is

uration that he gives to ontological questions in *Juan sin Tierra* evokes Deleuze and Guattari's argument that the structure of representational systems is directly related to forms of social and spatial organization. Comparing nomadic and sedentary social structures, Deleuze and Guattari argue that, although nomadism occupies a particular territory, it does not seek to 'parcel out a closed space', as occurs in sedentary organization. Instead, nomadism 'distributes people (or animals) in an open space' that is 'indefinite and noncommunicating'. In this sense, 'the life of the nomad is the intermezzo', that is, a liminal, in-between space.[17] In contrast, sedentary space is 'striated, by walls, enclosures, and roads between enclosures' (p. 381). The nomadic life also contrasts with migration, where the movement is determined by a particular goal. 'Whereas the migrant leaves behind a milieu that has become amorphous or hostile,' they write (p. 381), 'the nomad is one who does not depart, does not want to depart, who clings to the smooth space left by the receding forest, where the steppe or the desert advances, and who invents nomadism as a response to this challenge'.

Delueze and Guattari draw an intimate connection between man's response to the physical environment and the abstract concept of power, seeing the sedentary social order as repressive, as seeking to striate space in order to 'regulate circulation, relativize movement, and measure in detail the relative movements of subjects and objects' (p. 386). Nomadism, on the other hand, is subversive and resists such control, offering complete deterritorialization without the reterritorialization into sedentary organization that migration involves. This sense of the nomadic is, of course, utopian,[18] but it is an ethical view that extends beyond the mere analysis of social organization to embrace a mode of thought and of writing. Life, philosophy, and literature are not simply compared, but intimately connected. In the opening paragraphs of *A Thousand Plateaus*, Deleuze and Guattari self-consciously discuss books, and their method of composing them. 'In a book,' they say (p. 3), 'there are lines of articulation or segmentarity, strata and territories; but also lines of flight, movements of deterritorialization and destratification.' Thus their approach is rhizomatic, seeking a multiplicity that they compare to the func-

---

largely predicated upon nihilism, the primacy of identity and negation, this project implies the elaboration of a new way of thinking and enquiring which affirms difference and expels the negative. Nietzsche thus proposes an active science to replace the reactive tradition.' Goytisolo's approach, in Nietzschean terms, is clearly an example of reactive nihilism, as Epps acknowledges in *Significant Violence*, p. 141.

17 Deleuze and Guattari, *A Thousand Plateaus*, p. 380.

18 Utopian, not only in that it is a harsh life that is led constantly on the edge of survival, but also because the nomad is not entirely free to wander in the sense in which Deleuze and Guattari argue. His trajectory is determined by certain points – oases, for instance – where water and resources are available, and trading partners may be found. Economic reality striates nomad space just as it does sedentary space, and the consequence of 'wandering off the beaten track' may literally be death.

tion of an animal's burrow as 'shelter, supply, movment, evasion, and break-out' (p. 7). A rhizomatic text, then, like the nomad's life, is 'always in the middle, between things, interbeing, *intermezzo*' (p. 25). In this emphasis on in-between spaces, the rhizomatic text recalls Bhabha's focus on nationness as the active negotiation of liminality as outlined in chapter 2.

In his Postface to Neutres' study of Genet, Goytisolo compares the nomadic aspect of Genet's life to the structure – or apparent lack of structure – of *Le captif amoureux* (p. 332): 'Un large éventail de thèmes d'arguments se déploie dans les pages du livre avec cette même cohérence mystérieuse qui structura sa vie ; une vie constituée [. . .] d'un réseau complexe d'attractions, de répulsions, d'orbites, de cercles, de tensions, de ruptures : une espèce de système solaire avec ses astres fixes, ses satellites, ses planetès mortes, ses étoiles filantes.'[19] Genet's text is thus nomadic, or rhizomatic, in that it moves in various directions simultaneously, attracting and repelling, creating move-ment and rupture, offering fertile avenues of thought and dead-ends. It is also similar to the wandering textual form that Goytisolo seeks in *Juan sin Tierra*. Of the novel, Goytisolo commented to Julián Ríos, 'hay un paralelo evidente entre el paseo, el vagabundeo en busca de placer en la calle y en el espacio blanco de la página.'[20] Let us turn, then, to the interweaving of space, text, desire, and the subversion of authority in the novel itself.

Like a Moth round a Light: The Fragmentation of the Text and the Dethronment of the Author in Juan sin Tierra

Much more than in either *Señas de identidad* or *Don Julián*, Goytisolo flamboyantly exposes the process of textual construction in *Juan sin Tierra*. His unnamed narrator-cum-author self-consciously alludes to the existential act of writing on numerous occasions, equating, for instance, the silence that greets the religious fervour of one of his characters with a hiatus in the text of the novel: 'interrupción, oquedad, silencio : como cuando dejas de escribir' (p. 29). On another occasion, lauding the exuberant sexuality that the film icon

[19] In 'Thievish Subjectivity', pp. 163–81, Epps rightly notes that, for Genet, 'exuber-ance is [. . .] the stuff of the self and its writing' (p. 165), and that, although Goytioslo may emulate this in his fiction, his autobiographies retreat from such exuberance. The meta-phor of stellar constellation for textual structure is also used by Goytisolo in *Las virtudes del pájaro solitario*, a novel that pays homage to yet another literary 'Juan', namely the Christian mystic, San Juan de la Cruz. Indeed, the identification of the three writers is reinforced in one of the letters from Genet to Goytisolo that Neutres (p. 42) cites. Genet addresses Goytisolo as 'San Juan', having used the name Juan for himself in his *Journal du Voleur*.

[20] 'Desde *Juan sin Tierra*', *Juan sin Tierra*, Espiral/Revista no. 2 (Madrid: Fundamentos, 1977), pp. 7–25 (p. 15). In the same volume, Severo Sarduy notes the importance of Delueze and Guattari's theories for *Juan sin Tierra* in 'La desterritorializ-ación', pp. 175–83.

King Kong conventionally represents, he declares, 'glorificarás la potencia amorosa del simio : poniendo tu pluma al servicio de su desmesura magnífica, entronizando sus prendas con todos los recursos de la insidia verbal'. And he continues by viewing this subversive celebration of physical desire as textual *jouissance* (p. 67), 'mediante la sutil, empozoñada subversión de los sacrosantos valores lingüísticos : sacrificando el referente a la verdad del discurso y asumiendo a partir de ella las secuelas de tu delirante desvío'. The narrator-author's delirious *desvío* can be taken as either moral and sexual deviance, or as literary deviance, since the triad of desire, rebellion, and writing is maintained throughout the novel. One must question, however, whether the novel does, ultimately, sacrifice external reference for pure textuality – or, indeed, oppose them in the fashion that this quotation suggests. Quite to the contrary, I shall argue that, in evoking Deleuze and Guattari's theory of nomadism, Goytisolo attempts in *Juan sin Tierra* to retain external reference through an ethics of nomadism, although his use of nomadism fails to achieve the desired deterritorialization, and falls into a counter reterritorialization that is not provisional but essentialist. Goytisolo ultimately proves to be more migrant than nomad. This aspect of the novel can best be seen in the depiction of the figure of the narrator-author and the strategies employed to decentre the text in evocation of a Genettian exuberance.

The sixth section of *Juan sin Tierra* is perhaps the most blatantly metafictional part of the novel. It opens with a description of the narrator-author's working environment which, as we noted in chapter 2 in a different context, constitutes a spatial metaphor for the construction of the text itself. As in *Don Julián*, the mixing of literal and metaphorical language serves to a blur the boundaries between life and fiction (it is worth citing the passage again here):

> en el silencio del escritorio-cocina la mariposa nocturna ronda en turno a la lámpara : gira, planea, describe círculos obsesivos, se aleja cuando la espantas pero vuelve en seguida, una vez y otra vez y otra, hacia el fulgor que la fascina y atrae, absorta en su alucinada tarea, desdeñosa de tus manotadas : así, desde el instante en que regresas del baño, la idea fantasmal, reiterada surge y te acomete, se desvanece cuando la rechazas, porfía, tenaz y muda, con la certeza de su victoria paciente, sabedora de su inmediato cansancio : te resignas, pues, y la acoges : la soledad propicia su vuelo y el paralelo, a todas luces, se impone : por qué te resistirás aún a trazarlo? (p. 203)

The image of the moth circling the light in a paradoxical movement of attraction and repulsion recalls the manner in which Goytisolo describes Genet's *Captif amoureux* as a 'réseau complexe d'attractions, de répulsions, d'orbites, de cercles, de tensions, de ruptures'.[21] In this type of work, centripetal and

---

21 The notion of circularity in this image of the moth may have other sources,

centrifugal forces pull in opposite directions simultaneously, pushing the text towards an internal coherence located in a central logos – for Goytisolo, this is the figure of the narrator-author in his 'escritorio-cocina' – yet also fragmenting it through a celebration of multiplicity that disperses and disrupts univocal coherence.

Juan sin Tierra continues by linking sexual intercourse with the activity of writing, which is depicted as a purely male act in which the author '[empuña] la pluma y [deja] escurrir su licor filiforme, prolongando indefinidamente el orgasmo' (p. 203). Taking inspiration from T. E. Lawrence's *Seven Pillars of Wisdom*, a copy of which the narrator-author peruses as he writes, Goytisolo explicitly echoes Deleuze and Guattari's theory of nomadism – with its association of physical space and social order – in associating sexuality, writing, and the freedom of the empty desert. His narrator-author figure longs to be:

> independiente y libre también como un jeque beduino : dueño del aire, los vientos, la luz, el inmenso vacío : arriba, el cielo inodoro y sutil, y abajo la arena, inmaculada, como un refulgente glaciar : la siluetas de los camellos se perfilan en tierra conforme avanzas por la estepa jordana [. . .]   (p. 203)

Allusions to Bedouin society and the steppe recall the *intermezzo* life of the nomad, but Goytisolo's reference to a '*jeque* beduino' (my italics) indicates the paradoxical nature of his treatment of the theme of nomadism, for his perspective focuses on a tribal chief, a figure of authority, even as it desires to reject such authority. Likewise, his novel coalesces around the figure of the author while seeking to destroy his univocal power over the text.

One of the ways in which Goytisolo seeks to dethrone the figure of the author is to fragment his voice through a process that Lee Six has termed metamorphosis.[22] The narrator-author figure of *Juan sin Tierra*, as noted

including Guillermo Cabrera Infante's *Tres tristes tigres*, which Goytisolo analyzes in *Disidencias*. In 'Lectura cervantina de *Tres tristes tigres*' (pp. 233–67), Goytisolo compares Cabrera Infante's novel to *Don Quijote* and Sterne's *Tristram Shandy*, both texts that have been related by critics to *Juan sin Tierra* itself (see my 'En el principio de la literatura está el mito', and Abigail E. Lee, 'Sterne's Legacy to Juan Goytisolo: A Shandyian Reading of *Juan sin Tierra*', *Modern Language Review*, 84 [1989], 351–7). However, *Tres tristes tigres* is more comical and Joycean than *Juan sin Tierra*, which is written, as the author himself declared to Julián Ríos, in 'una forma más ensayística que propiamente narrativa' ('Desde *Juan sin Tierra*', p. 14). The notion of a circular structure is parodied, for example, in Cabrera Infante's novel when a character states (*Tres tristes tigres*, 7th edn [Barcelona: Seix Barral, 1998], p. 288): '¿La vida es un caos concéntrico? No sé, yo solamente sé que mi vida era un caos nocturno con un solo centro que era Las Vegas y en el centro del centro un vaso con ron y agua o ron y hielo o ron y soda.'

[22] See *Juan Goytisolo*, chapter 5. Lee Six discusses not only character metamorphoses in Goytisolo's work, which she interprets as evidence of a longing to transcend the limits of the self and the human condition, but also textual and linguistic metamorphoses, which testify to a search for the 'ceaseless flux' of chaos (p. 166) that she opposes to order and authority in her reading of Goytisolo's work.

earlier, seeks to locate himself within a tradition of wanderers who have written favourably about their experiences of the Orient, and he does so not only by alluding to them but by arrogating their voices and assuming their identities. Hence, in a similar fashion to the technique adopted by Goytisolo in his literary criticism, the narrator-author of *Juan sin Tierra* desires, in the unconstrained space of the virgin page, to actually become Lawrence of Arabia, Père de Foucauld, Fra Anselm Turmeda, etcetera. Ugarte (*Trilogy of Treason*, pp. 121–7) demonstrates how the text of *Juan sin Tierra* meshes with the words of these figures, colonizing them and subsuming them into its own discourse. The manoeuvre is achieved textually through an ambiguous use of pronouns, which the novel explains as follows:

> YO/TÚ
> pronombres apersonales, moldes substantivos vacíos! : vuestra escueta realidad es el acto del habla mediante el que os apropiáis del lenguaje y los sometéis al dominio engañoso de vuestra subjetividad reductible [. . .] quién se expresa en yo/tú? : Ebeh, Foucauld, Anselm Turmeda, Cavafís, Lawrence de Arabia? : mudan las sombras errantes en vuestra imprescindible norma huera, y hábilmente podrás jugar con los signos sin que el lector ingenuo lo advierta : sumergiéndole en un mundo fluyente, sometido a un proceso continuo de destrucción : distribuyendo entre tus egos dispersos los distintos papeles del coro y orquestándolos a continuación conforme al vuelo inspirado de la batuta : el leve correr de la pluma en el espacio rectangular de la página   (p. 124)

If pronouns are empty moulds to be filled with whatever identity the speaker wishes, then the narrator-author is free to adopt the voices of the exiles and marginals he admires and whose rebellion he seeks to emulate. These figures thus come to represent for the him 'los tuyos' (p. 76). Yet, as we saw in relation to *Don Julián*, pronouns can only ever be empty shifters in grammar-book discussions. As soon as they are placed in the context of a speech-act like that referred to in the above passage, they acquire quite precise significance and this undermines the nomadic lack of fixity that Goytisolo's novel lauds.

In *Juan sin Tierra*, heroic renegades are transformed from 'sombras errantes' into 'textos errantes', their names standing as short-hand for the ethical identification with the South and East that the narrator-author – and, by extension, Goytisolo himself – seeks. It is as if both wish to emulate Nietzsche's effort to become 'all the names of history'.[23] Deleuze interprets Nietzsche's comment as a perpetual displacement that is evidence of his revolutionary nomadic approach to philosophy, and in *Anti-Oedipus* the idea is developed into a destruction of the notion of the unified subject:

---

23 Cited by Delueze in 'Nomad Thought', p. 146, and discussed by Smith, pp. 22–6.

> We pass from one field to another by crossing thresholds: we never stop migrating, we become other individuals as well as other sexes, and departing becomes as easy as being born or dying. Along the way, we struggle against other races, we destroy civilizations, in the manner of the great migrants in whose wake noting is left standing once they have passed through.   (p. 85)

In chosing particular figures who stand for Dissidence (with a capital 'D'), Goytisolo, however, fails to follow the logic of Delueze and Guattari's notion of the nomadic self. If, for Nietzsche, becoming all the names of history is not a question of 'identifying oneself with personages [but with] fields of intensity on the body without organs' (*Anti-Oedipus*, p. 86), for Goytisolo, 'all the names of history' refer back to 'the name of the father' (*Anti-Oedipus*, p. 86) in the symbolic sense of designating an original meaning behind the act of writing. The 'names' thus become 'Names' with a capital, the source of authority for the ethical journey that Goytisolo undertakes. They identify – or name – not simply an undefined space, but a defined set of coordinates marking a place or point of transgression. Goytisolo's gesture towards nomadism thus ends up circumscribing the narrative space in precisely the way in which Deleuze and Guattari describe the striated space of sedentary society. In chosing certain figures to symbolize his ethical move South and East, Goytisolo valorizes a particular *direction* of movement that is anti-nomadic and thus gives his text 'constant directions [which] are oriented in relation to one another, divisible by boundaries' (*A Thousand Plateaus*, p. 382).[24]

The search for fragmentation and the attempt to dethrone the author as controlling figure of authority and single source of meaning in *Juan sin Tierra* is thus frustrated. Furthermore, the transformation of the protagonist of a more traditional novel into a narrator-author figure who is clearly male (adjectival endings in the text indicate as much), and is presented as sitting in a clearly defined place (an 'escritorio-cocina') where he reflects on the existential act of writing, brings the author all the more clearly to the fore. A gesture intended to signal an end to narrative authority thus reinscribes it as the potent centre of an apparently decentred novel. In a further paradoxical twist, Goytisolo's identification of his own working environment as an 'escritorio-cocina' in his autobiography reinforces this crowning of the author as a source of authority, since it implicitly places him within the text of his own novel.[25]

---

[24] Though Deleuze and Guattari themselves seem aware of the impossibly utopian nature of their nomadic enterprise in using the term 'migration' in the above passage.

[25] *En los reinos de Taifa*, p. 229. As Bernstein notes in 'Body, Language and Divinity', the novel 'has behind it a design and a plan invented by its creator, however great a role randomness may have played in the elaboration of the design' (p. 86). Douglas Smith also argues that, despite Deleuze's philosophical sophistication, his reading of Nietzsche

This has implications for Goytisolo's desire to become the marginalized 'other' through the articulation of his (rarely her) voice. In order to reverse Western colonial discourse on the Orient, Goytisolo must shift from being the observer to become the observed, so that his appropriation of the voice of the repressed other does not constitute a new form of oppression. In *Juan sin Tierra* the initial reversal of colonizing and colonized perspectives in the narrator-author's awareness of being 'other' – of being watched by a Hindu mystic 'desde la cubierta coloreada del high fidelity' (p. 11) – is not borne out in the main body of the novel. Instead, the Names chosen are *Western* travellers, despite the utopian aspiration to cross the threshold from West to East that the novel's final pages in Arabic signal. Unlike Genet's attempt to become the 'other' within France, Goytisolo seems to transgress a clearly defined boundary in order to embrace otherness without. But it still remains to be seen if he has truly thrown off his Spanish and Western identity, leaving himself 'extrañado para siempre de la fauna nativa', if 'las fórmulas de urbanidad que ocasionalmente cruzas con ella' are really, in echo of *Señas de identidad*, 'algo tan mecánico y huero como la sonrisa desvaída de la abuela el día memorable en que le desconoció' (*Juan sin Tierra*, p. 257).

Not Space but Place: 'Lectura del espacio en Xemaá-el-Fná'

In *Makbara*, Goytisolo rejects the configuration of dissidence as textual nomadism in favour of a new spatial metaphor, that of the market square in Marrakesh. Dissidence is now located in the circumscribed, economically and culturally specific location of Xemaá-el-Fná. This is, of course, paradoxical, for the enclosed space of the square is used to represent textual fluidity and human freedom from authority. In a further paradox, the square is also the home of oral storytellers whose art the novel deliberately evokes, thus playing off oral narrative against the written text. Finally, the narrator of *Makbara* is termed a *halaquí nesraní* – an oral teller of tales, but one who is also a foreigner. Does this, then, mean that the novel is self-defeating? Most critics have argued that the use of irony and parody are the work's salvation.[26] To a certain extent this it true, but I wish to suggest here that behind these still

in terms of decoding and re-coding – and, indeed, by implication the contrast between nomadic and sedentary society – contains a residual essentialism in its creation of oppositions. 'Direct Opposition', he argues (*Transvaluations*, p. 184), 'consolidates what it attacks, while oblique opposition through the operations of displacement/reversal can bring about a much more fundamental de-stabilization.'

26 See, for instance, Luce López-Baralt, 'Juan Goytisolo aprende a reír: los contextos caribeños de *Makbara* y *Paisajes después de la batalla*', *Ínsula*, 468 (1985), 3–4; John Macklin, 'Modernity and Postmodernity: Personal and Textual Identities in Juan Goytisolo's *Makbara*', in Ruth Christie, Judith Drinkwater, and John Macklin (eds), *The*

lies a belief in the possibility of articulating an authentic ethical response that undercuts *Makbara*'s apparent celebration of performance as postmodern superficiality. We shall return to this point in the next section, after considering *Makbara*'s depiction of Xemaá-el-Fná, the market square in Marrakesh.

In order to adopt the voice of the other, Goytisolo must, as noted above, adopt the position of the other, turning the gaze of the Western colonizer into that of the Oriental colonized. To achieve this, he now locates the narrative origin of his text in a particular place, rejecting the unlimited space of nomadism for the defined coordinates of Xemaá-el-Fná. Indeed, the significance of this development can be seen in the difference between the terms 'space' and 'place'. Place, according to the psychologist Ciarán Benson, is 'humanised, personalised space'. It is a 'subjectification of space and time' that has its roots in 'collective cultural achievements' and is intimately rooted in the 'morphology of our bodies'.[27] Place is fundamental to an individual's understanding of self, for, again quoting Benson (p. 10), 'location is the ontological condition for all human being. Not to be in a place is to be nowhere, and to be nowhere is to be nothing.' As we noted in chapter 3, such contrasts as 'here' and 'there', or 'inside' and 'outside', structure human life even in its most basic elements.[28] The adoption of a place from which to actually speak as the other, rather than simply the creation of a space that might represent alterity, and the embodiment of this voice in the figure of the oral storyteller, are fundamental for Goytisolo's attempt in *Makbara* to reverse the Western gaze on the Orient – the 'here' and 'there', or 'us' and 'them', paradigm requires place not space in order to signify division and difference. Two key features of the novel contribute to this reversal: the 'lectura del espacio' of the final section, and the use of oral narrative techniques and literary antecedents.

Makbara seems, superficially, to evoke the sense of nomadism outlined in *Juan sin Tierra*. The section entitled 'Dar Debbagh' celebrates an idea of freedom as the Angel, the novel's female protagonist, longs for 'nomadismo, pastoreo, erranza, leyendas escuchadas al calor de la jaima'.[29] Later, in 'Como el viento en la red', the connection between freedom and oral stories is reinforced as the Pariah, the male protagonist of the book, desires to imitate

---

Scripted Self: Textual Identities in Contemporary Spanish Narrative (Warminster: Aris & Phillips, 1995), pp. 117–33.

[27] *The Cultural Psychology of Self*, pp. 6–7.

[28] See p. 78, n. 31, on Benson's comment that the inside/outside, or here/there contrast extends even to cell structure.

[29] *Makbara*, revised edn (Barcelona: Mondadori, 1995), p. 58. This is the edition used here, since Goytisolo revised the novel, including a reference to Juan Ruiz's *Libro de buen amor* in the final section by replacing the original 'en homenaje a Prévert' (4th edn [Barcelona: Seix Barral, 1988], p. 208) with 'en homenaje a Juan Ruiz' (p. 203).

the 'juglar de áurea, centelleante sonrisa con talentos de bufón, de alfaquí y de poeta' (p. 177). These references are, however, only a prelude to a more coherent development of notions of liberty, nomadic society, and wandering oral narrative in the final section of the novel, 'Lectura del espacio en Xemaá-el-Fná'. It offers a textual depiction of the market square in Marrakesh as an 'espacio abierto y plural' where one can wander with a 'gracioso y feraz nomadismo' (pp. 199–200). Aware of his Western gaze, Goytisolo seeks not to disguise it, but to highlight it by recalling previous depictions of the square in tourist guides. Just as *Juan sin Tierra* sets itself within a tradition of writing about the Orient, so *Makbara* evokes the Guide Bleu, Fodor, Baedeker, et al. They each offer recommendations as to the best time and angle from which to view the activity of the square, yet all defraud the traveller by failing to capture its true alterity, settling ultimately for 'couleur locale' (p. 199). The square, then, is the unrepresentable, at least in conventional discourse. An 'ágora', it resists the fixity of textual inscription just as it refutes the order of settled society in favour of nomadism. A socially level realm, it stands as a 'desquite de lo espontáneo, abigarrado, prolífero contra la universal regulación clasista : tierra de nadie donde el cuerpo es rey' (p. 201). With a strong tinge of nostalgia, Goytisolo views the square as a 'supervivencia del ideal nómada en términos de utopía' (p. 201).

The equation of social and economic order with both textual organization and creativity more generally is clear in the terms by which Goytisolo refers to Xemaá-el-Fná. In calling it a 'vasto ejido' (p. 199) – 'ejido' translates loosely as a village common or shared area of land – in which there is 'libre circulación de personas y bienes' (p. 201), he expresses an abhorrence of property ownership that recalls Delueze and Guattari's condemnation of settled land as striated by power structures that seek to control and limit movement.[30] And the textual connection is made by the fact that Xemaá-el-Fná is also a realm of intellectual freedom – an 'ejido de ideas' – in which the conventional rules of intellectual property are inoperable. Socio-economic nomadism is thus equated with a particularly postmodern conception of creativity, that of intertextuality or cultural pilfering, which will be developed in relation to the tradition of oral narrative within both Spanish and Arab culture.[31]

---

[30] The recent racial conflict between Spaniards and North African immigrants in the area of El Ejido makes this term all the more pertinent for Goytisolo's campaign against the persecution of the socially excluded. He has written about racial tensions in this Andalusian area in 'España y sus Ejidos', *El País*, 20 March 2000, collected with other essays on Spanish–Moroccan links in *España y sus Ejidos* (Madrid: Hijos de Muley-Rubio, 2003), pp. 32–9.

[31] Interestingly, in 'What was an author?', *Yale French Studies*, 73 (1987), 229–57, Molly Nesbit argues that Barthes' declaration of the death of the author was partly inspired by the modernization of French copyright law in 1957, which sought to regulate 'the

Nevertheless, despite this appeal to nomadism, there is an underlying geometry, or set of rules, at work in the depiction of Xemaá-el-Fná, which is less open space than settled, striated place. That is to say, the square is laden with a particular cultural and intellectual significance, which, following Benson, humanizes and personalizes it. It may, as *Makbara* declares, be a 'polígono irregular' (p. 63), but it still physically circumscribed, in that its walls and boundaries create a relationship of inside and outside. It is intellectually circumscribed, too, by virtue of the particular values that Goytisolo associates with it. The square, as he depicts it, is a realm of utopian freedom and non-capitalist economic activity through which one may wander aimlessly and in which one may barter for the useless objects that are on sale amid its 'proliferación demencial de inútil mercancía' (p. 206). This lack of economic purposefulness is contrasted with the capitalist West, most notably the United States, with its preoccupation with industrial production and socio-economic progress – hence the satire of Pittsburgh in the 'Sightseeing tour' and 'Radio Liberty' sections of the novel. A binary structure of 'here/there' thus complements the 'inside/outside' contrast implicit in the bounded nature of the square, and recalls the contrast between East and West that informs *Juan sin Tierra*.

There is, though, an important respect in which *Makbara* can be said to complicate any simple opposition between 'here' and 'there'. The interplay between the bounded square, and the freedom from restriction that Goytisolo associates with it, does suggest that, rather than seeing the restricted area of the square as a place *from* which to escape – as the narrator-author of *Juan sin Tierra* does in his mental flights of fancy that liberate him from the confines of his 'escritorio-cocina' – the square becomes a place *into* which to escape. It offers momentary respite from the poverty and harshness of life, being an 'antídoto necesario de la vida pobre y descalza, el hambre insatisfecha, la realidad inicua' (p. 215). Freedom thus lies not beyond the square, or beyond the confines of place, but within it. This paradoxical fusion of opposites is also evident in other textual metaphors employed in *Makbara*. Although, in demanding a 'lectura paralela de los astros' (p. 202), *Makbara* does suggest a stellar image for the rhizomatic lack of structure to which Goytisolo aspires, it also offers the reader other images of textual structure that convey more accurately a dialectic between restriction and freedom, inside and outside, here and there.

Annie Perrin compares the text simultaneously to a labyrinth and a network, seeing it as 'the labyrinthine configuration of a spider's web structured on the schema of the one and the multiple, the quest and the meeting'.[32]

---

market economy for culture at the same time that it set it apart from the regular economy' (p. 235).

[32] '*Makbara*: The Space of Phantasm', *Review of Contemporary Fiction*, 4 (1984), 157–75 (159).

She regards the square, quite rightly, as a place where dualities converge and centripetal forces are balanced by centrifugal ones. The image of the labyrinth is suggested by the novel itself in the opening words of the 'Aposentos de invierno' section, yet it is an image whose applicability is questioned. The novel reads, 'laberinto cretense? estructura elaborada por Dédalo? posible residencia de algún resucitado, fabuloso Minotauro?' (p. 87) Goytisolo's omission of inverted question marks here serves to emphasize the dubiousness of the mythological reference. Another suggested image for textual structure, in 'Sic transit gloria mundi', is that of queen bee at the centre of her hive. She attracts worker bees who swarm to her, just like listeners who form an 'anillo mágico' (p. 53) around an oral storyteller. There is, though, something paradoxical about these comparisons, and Goytisolo is correct to raise doubts about them. A labyrinth is not free from spatial divisions; on the contrary, it works precisely by having too many. And a queen bee in her hive – or, indeed, a spider at the centre of a web – is far from being an image of randomness and disorder. In each case, the metaphor chosen focuses on a central point, whether it be the sought-after core of the labyrinth, the reproductive centre of a carefully constructed hive, or the deadly point at which the spider patiently awaits its prey. *Makbara*, likewise, constructs a textual centre or core, despite depicting Xemaá-el-Fná as both circumscribed space and the place of liberation. This is most evident in relation to the novel's equation of writing with reading, signalled in the title and opening lines of the concluding section, 'Lectura del espacio de Xemaá-el-Fná', and in the celebration of oral narrative. All this should not surprise us, for what Goytisolo ultimately seeks is not to destroy any notion of origins, but to create a narrative logos – a place of origin – from which to articulate alterity.

From Writer to Reader . . . to Oral Storyteller

In declaring his intention to offer a *reading* of space in Xemaá-el-Fná, Goytisolo suggests that writing is akin to interpretation, thus anticipating the criticism that his depiction of the square is a personal one, determined by his particular Western cultural perspective. More interestingly, however, in equating writing with reading, he collapses two activities which, in the Barthesian theory of the death of the author, were rigorously separated. Barthes declared that, since a text's unity lies 'not in its origin but in its destination' (p. 148), the death of the author results in the birth of the reader. This reader, though, is devoid of history, biography, and psychology, being 'simply that *someone* who holds together in a single field all the traces by which the written text is constituted' (p. 148). Despite their divergent perspectives on writing and reading, however, Barthes' description of a figure drawing together the threads of the text into a coherent interpretation seems to anticipate the role that Goytisolo envisages for the oral storyteller in *Makbara*.

The *halaiquí* is an embodied, but unidentified voice, who recounts the tale of the Pariah and the Angel, 'asumiendo por turno voces y papeles' (p. 195), and drawing attention to the fact that his story permits the listener to wander far and wide without leaving the physical confines of the square.[33] As a mere reciter of pre-existing stories, rather than a originator of a new narrative, the oral storyteller has no biography. He is described at the end of the section, 'Noticias del más allá', as simply the weaver of one version among various possibilities. Refusing to confirm the truth of any of the extant versions of his story, he arbitrarily chooses a happy ending as this is, he says, most likely to please his listeners. Creativity is here presented not in its Romantic sense as individual inspiration, but as intertextual dialogue with an existing oral tradition in which a retelling of the story is a re-reading, or interpretation, of it. This again seems to fit with Barthes' reader-oriented theory of the text as made up of 'multiple writings, drawn from many cultures and entering into mutual relations of dialogue, parody, contestation' (p. 148). Indeed, *Makbara* mimicks such a notion of creative originality in the intertextual links that it draws with both European and Arab culture. The legendary twelfth-century correspondence between Abélard and Héloïse, alongside Juan Ruiz's fourteenth-century *Libro de buen amor* and the *Thousand and One Nights*, all feature in the novel. The presence of allusions to these latter two are highly significant, since both works, although now existing in written form, relate to oral literary traditions in their respective cultures.

In *Makbara*, as we noted in chapter 2, Goytisolo imagines a recital of the *Libro de buen amor* in the *zoco*, thus linking Western and Eastern culture through oral performance. His new work – a contemporary reading of a medieval text – seeks to reveal an underlying coherence beneath distant literary epochs, albeit a coherence that he associates with fragmented, experimental narrative. Thus, despite the *Libro*'s current written form, its oral characteristics and possible oral origins – evident in the use of formulaic structures, dependence upon easily recognizable religious and legal discourses, and ritualistic repetitiveness – are valorized as the source of yet more Genet-style textual 'quiebras, desniveles, rupturas, tensiones centrífugas, transmutaciones de voces'.[34] In appealing to previous texts from both oral and written traditions – including biblical and religious sources, Latin antecedents, and even perhaps an Arab connection[35] – the *Libro*, whose author exists only as a name

---

[33] Though the Pariah does celebrate the storyteller's life of literal wandering from place to place in 'Como el viento en la red', p. 177.

[34] 'Vicisitudes del mudejarismo', p. 54.

[35] On the intertextual connections evident in the *Libro*, see Félix Lecoy, *Recherches sur le 'Libro de buen amor' de Juan Ruiz*, ed. Alan Deyermond (Farnborough: Gregg International, 1974). The work's oral features are examined by Jeremy Lawrance in 'The Audience of the *Libro de buen amor*', *Comparative Literature*, 36 (1984), 220–37. An alternative reading that places the *Libro* squarely in a written tradition is given by John

recorded in the text, seems to disperse textual authority among a series of co-existing origins and offer itself as a Barthesian 'tissue of quotations' (p. 146). The *Thousand and One Nights*, likewise, consists of a diverse collection of stories, and stories within stories. It includes fairy-tales and fables, heroic epics, mystical devotional tales, and scatological and pornographic jokes. Robert Irwin labels it a 'cultural amphibian', in that it seems to derive from both oral and written literary traditions. Not only is the narrative generated by Scheherazade's desire to stave off death by telling innumerable and unending tales, it also draws upon pre-existing written material and, in its present form, it exhibits evidence of the careful literary shaping that is usually associated with written reworkings of a text.[36] Thus the *Nights*, even more than the *Libro de buen amor*, dissolves narrative authority to the point of associating it with an oral recounting of material from pre-existing oral and written literary traditions.

Makbara establishes a similarly complex relationship between oral and written narrative. As a book, it is, of course, part of the written tradition, but it appeals to orality both indirectly, through the intertextual allusions cited above, and directly, in dramatizing the love story of the Pariah and Angel as told by a *halaiquí* in Xemaá-el-Fná. The novel's opening words, 'al principio fue el grito' (p. 15), stress its imitation of oral narrative, and the characters' desire to 'usar del carisma de la palabra' in order to achieve a state of 'libertad de albedrío, voz recuperada' (pp. 38–9) reinforces the emphasis on speech rather than writing as a privileged mode of communication. The shout with which the novel begins is meant as a gesture of recuperation, signalling the intention of giving voice to the socially marginalized and silenced other. Oral narrative thus becomes, in Goytisolo's novel, the means by which exclusion can be reversed, and literature is equated with the spoken word. This connection is, of course, not new, but Goytisolo presents a particularly complex inflection of the speech-act theory of literary discourse, which he links to his conception of narrative creativity as discursive dialogue.[37]

In developing J. L. Austin's analytical philosophy of language, John Searle argues that literary works are a special case in which the illocutionary act is pretended, but the utterance itself is real.[38] In mimicking oral narrative, *Makbara* adds the further complication of pretending to be a pretend illocutionary act, and of existing as written utterance. One might choose to see in

Dagenais in *The Ethics of Reading in Manuscript Culture: Glossing the 'Libro de buen amor'* (Princeton: Princeton University Press, 1994).

36 See *The Arabian Nights: A Companion* (Harmondsworth: Penguin, 1994), p. 114.

37 On orality in *Makbara*, see Annie Perrin, 'Pour une écriture–lecture–audition: *Makbara* ou la voix retrouvée', in *Cotextes*, 5 (1983), 41–57; Stanley Black, 'Orality in *Makbara*: A Postmodern Paradox?', *Neophilologus*, 78 (1994), 585–98.

38 John Searle, 'The Logical Status of Fictional Discourse', in *Expression and Meaning: Studies in the Theory of Speech Acts* (Cambridge: Cambridge University Press, 1979), pp. 58–75.

this a source of irony, by which – in a postmodernist never-ending series of regressive mirrors – the novel undercuts its own pretence to orality and thus defies its claim to offer a place in which the marginalized voice may be recuperated.[39] However, an examination of two particular aspects of the novel – the use of the metaphor of the *theatrum mundi*, and the articulation of dissidence through the voices of the Pariah and Angel – when taken in the context of Paul Ricoeur's development of speech-act theory into a theory of hermeneutics, suggests a more nuanced view.

In *Interpretation Theory: Discourse and the Surplus of Meaning*, Ricoeur approaches all discourse, whether spoken or written, as an event. By refusing to divide language into the standard Saussurian categories of *langue* and *parole*, he avoids the divisiveness of the Derridean attack of phonocentrism and offers, instead, a dialectical view of discourse as, simultaneously, a 'vanishing event' and 'understood meaning'.[40] Each instance of discourse is a vanishing event in that the performance is singular and unrepeatable; yet its 'propositional content' is capable of being retained, reiterated, even translated (Ricoeur, p. 9).[41] In this view, 'meaning' implies two interpretations, which establish a dialectical movement between the public and the private – or, by extension, the 'interior' and the 'exterior', the 'here' and the 'there'. 'To mean,' writes Ricoeur (p. 12), 'is both what the speaker means, i.e. what he intends to say, and what the sentence means, i.e. what the conjunction between the identification function and the predicative function [of the sentence] yields.' The inner structure of the sentence refers back to the speaker through a system of grammatical shifters, such as pronouns and deictics, creating what Ricoeur terms the 'self-reference' of discourse. But discourse also moves beyond itself, since its essential nature is dialogue (p. 16): 'Because the sense of a sentence is, so to speak, "external" to the sentence it can be transferred; this exteriority of discourse to itself – which is synonymous with the self-transcendence of the event in its meaning – *opens* discourse to the other.' And Ricoeur goes on to clarify how a message contains the grounds of its communicability in the structure of its meaning:

> By speaking to somebody we point towards the unique thing that we mean, thanks to the public devices of proper names, demonstratives, and definite

---

[39] Black argues as much in *Juan Goytisolo: The Poetics of Contagion*, chapter 5.

[40] In *Interpretation Theory: Discourse and the Surplus of Meaning* (Fort Worth: The Texas Christian University Press, 1976), Ricoeur states apropos of Derrida (pp. 25–6): 'Writing is the full manifestation of discourse. To hold, as Jacques Derrida does, that writing has a root distinct from speech and that this foundation has been misunderstood due to our having paid excessive attention to speech, its voice, and its *logos*, is to overlook the grounding of both modes of the actualization of discourse in the dialectical constitution of discourse.'

[41] The possibility of translation as cultural mediation based on a 'hermeneutic of trust' is similarly examined in a positive light by George Steiner in *After Babel: Aspects of Language and Translation*, 2nd edn (Oxford: Oxford University Press, 1992), p. 319.

descriptions. I help the other to identify the same item that I myself am pointing to, thanks to the grammatical devices which provide a singular experience with a public dimension.   (p. 16)

The consequences of this intersubjective view of discourse are profound. It regards communication as an opening up of the private to the public, and, indeed, the recuperation of the public in the private. The interior, so to speak, connects with the exterior, giving language reference – but only when it is used. From this results the nature of discourse as a dialectic of event and meaning (Ricoeur, p. 20): 'to refer is what the sentence does in a certain situation and according to a certain use.' Or, putting it the other way around, sense 'is traversed by the referring intention of the speaker'. Ricoeur's argument is complex, but salutatory. It combines the structuralist insights of semiotics with an appreciation of intentionality, without falling prey to a psychologically based view of human agency. And, in viewing inter-subjectivity as a result of the dialogic nature of discourse, it overcomes the 'radical non-communicability of the lived experience' (p. 16) in order to offer a theory of discourse that both embraces and seeks to articulate alterity.[42]

One of the most important ways in which *Makbara* seeks to overcome the limits of private experience and embrace a voice of alterity is by literally giving a voice to the socially marginalized, represented by the figure of the Pariah. If the novel's opening words seek to inscribe the text within an oral tradition in their reference to a shout – albeit an ironic one, in that the cries of alarm may be said to come from passersby who exclude the Pariah from their number as too dirty and disease-ridden to be socially acceptable – this reference to the shout is merely an opening gambit. More telling is a deliberately ambiguous use of pronouns that can be seen, for instance, in the main body of the section, 'Del más acá venido'. There, the overlap between the public and private, or interior and exterior, reference of language that Ricoeur indicates in relation to pronominal shifters becomes evident as the text slips in and out

---

[42] Ricoeur's debt to the phenomenological tradition, to which, as Richard Kearney puts it, he gives a 'hermeneutic turn', is evident in his appeal to intersubjectivity and his emphsis on intentionality. This brief survey of his work is therefore intended to supplement the argument of chapter 3, which drew upon Merleau-Ponty's philosophy. Ricoeur's hermeneutical innovation begins with the text but, instead of focusing on it as an objective structure or as the result of an authorial consciousness, seeks to reveal language's capacity to open up possible worlds. This is highly relevant to our present concern with the articulation of a voice of alterity. As Kearney argues in *Poetics of Imagining: Modern to Post-modern*, new edn (Edinburgh: Edinburgh University Press, 1998), p. 142, 'for Ricoeur, the hermeneutic circle precludes any short cut to immediate self-understanding. The human subject can only come to know itself through the hermeneutic detour of inter-preting signs – that is, by deciphering the meanings contained in myths, symbols and dreams produced by the human imagination. The shortest route from the self to itself is through the images of others.'

of the voices of the unidentified *halaiquí*, the Pariah, and the passersby whom he meets.

Beginning with the oral storyteller – whose role as collator of different versions of the tale we only know with hindsight, but whose presence is evidenced by generalized comments concerning the Pariah's 'compostura insólita, transgresora : radical negación del orden existente' (p. 15) – the text moves on to adopt first the perspective of the Pariah, and then that of the passersby. Even in this very gesture, Goytisolo attempts a discursive rapprochement by giving voice to both the socially acceptable and the marginalized, but the manner in which he achieves these shifts of perspective reveals an even more profound search to embrace otherness within an intersubjective context. The following extract illustrates the point (the italics are mine):

> avanza, sí, avanza, no *te* pares, no hagas caso, actúa como un ciego, no cruces jamás su vista, el leproso que anda, el monstruo, el apestado, eres *tú*, eres *tú* : [. . .] pies sombríos, descalzos, insensibles a la dureza de la estación : pantalones harapientos, de urdimbre gastada e improvisados tragaluces a la altura de las rodillas : abrigo de espantapájaros con solapas alzadas sobre una doble ausencia : *yo* mismo : imagen venida del más acá : aparentemente incapaz de objectivar *su* situatión fuera del flus, daimen el flus que continuamente *repito* : inmune contra las reflexiones malignas del gentío desparramado en la acera : un fou probablement, qu'est-ce qui peut se passer dans la tête? : rompiendo a reír para *sus* adentros : como si no lo supieran! como si no supieran lo que discurre en *mi* cabeza!   (p. 17)

This passage relies for its effect upon the ironic contrast between the depiction of the social exclusion of the Pariah and certain discursive strategies that Goytisolo uses to overcome this. The text shifts arbitrarily between first-, second-, and third-person pronominal positions, beginning with the Pariah speaking to himself as 'tú', and moving on to a description of his attire that could only be furnished by the *halaiquí*, thus implying a third-person narratorial view. It then oscillates between the first-person perspective of 'yo mismo' and 'repito', and the narratorial third person of 'su situación', before expressing in French the views of the passersby. The final two lines again waver between the Pariah's thoughts in the first person and the narrator's apparently omniscient description of him laughing secretly at the reactions he provokes.

The overlap between the public and private reference of language is evident in these easily achieved shifts between 'yo', 'tú', and 'él', creating a dialogue of perspectives that supplement rather than exclude one another. The most significant oscillation is perhaps the final movement between a position of omniscient narration ('rompiendo a reír para sus adentros') and first-person experience ('lo que discurre en mi cabeza'). The event of discourse – the oral recitation of a tale by the *halaiquí* – is here collapsed into the meaning – the reference of what may be going on in the Pariah's head. This results in the articulation of a perspective of alterity that constitutes neither an existentialist quest for identity, as we saw in the use of pronouns in Goytisolo's autobiographies and in *Señas de identidad*, nor an oppositional discourse that relies upon the reversal of a mutually exclusive set of binaries, as is frequently, but not always, the case in *Don Julián* and *Juan sin Tierra*.

Goytisolo thus celebrates dialogue as communication in *Makbara* not only in appealing to an oral literary tradition but in employing a form of discourse that is shot through with a dialectic of public and private, interior and exterior, here and there. By dramatizing storytelling as a dialogue – between distinct cultural periods in drawing upon medieval texts, between Western and Eastern cultures in imagining a recital of the *Libro* in Xemaá-el-Fná, and between discursive perspectives in attempting to bridge social exclusion – he ultimately appeals to the metaphor of the *theatrum mundi*, but in terms rather different than the usual postmodern sense of performance as all surface and no depth. Admittedly, *Makbara* does refer to the *halaiquí*'s story as a 'representación teatral' in which play-acting is a means of escape through the adoption of others' roles. Thus, one can 'ser, por espacio de horas, nabab, peregrino, rey : ofrecerse en espectáculo a uno mismo y a los demás' (p. 205). However, the story that provides such refuge is delivered, quite specifically, in Xemaá-el-Fná, and the symbolic importance that Goytisolo attaches to this place (as opposed to regarding it as mere space) marks the oral performance that *Makbara* envokes as an authentic ethical response to alterity – as a true articulation of the voice of the other. Furthermore, it is not a transitory articulation, for, following Ricoeur's argument, it consists of a repetition, or re-reading, of pre-existing narrative material. Through careful discursive dialogue and intertextual allusion, *Makbara* achieves what *Juan sin Tierra* set out to find and failed to achieve, and it does it by reversing expectations. Instead of fleeing from a centre of authority, and paradoxically finding this impossible, it looks directly to the oral storyteller as author or origin, but manages to evade the prescription of authority that this might normally involve.

PART III

DIVERGENCES AND CONVERGENCES

5

THE AUTHOR AS VOYEUR:
PAISAJES DESPUÉS DE LA BATALLA, LA SAGA DE LOS MARX, AND EL SITIO DE LOS SITIOS

Adrift in a sea of symbols, we find ourselves,
voyeurs all, products of the cinematic gaze.
Norman Denzin[1]

Voyeurism and the Postmodern Cinematic Gaze

A turn to the pictoral seems to characterize contemporary literary studies.[2] The late twentieth-century privileging of discourse, with its trend to read pictures and images as texts, seems now to have turned back upon itself, seeking the visual in the verbal, as well as vice versa.[3] The roots of this might be traced to Foucault's work on the panoptic gaze, but that, for him, was purely a surveillance act, and thus more restricted than the broad view of the visual that I wish to adopt here.[4] Vision implies both to see and to be seen, but not necessarily in an aggressive act of political, economic, or social domination. To look on a scene, in a voyeuristic sense, is, of course, associated with sexual deviance; but one may also look on a scene with sympathy, or horror, or detachment, or mere curiosity. It is this broader conception of seeing, not only as voyeuristic, but also as evidence of an interest in the other, that is the focus of the present chapter.

---

1 *The Cinematic Society: The Voyeur's Gaze* (London: Sage, 1995), p. 2.

2 W. J. T. Mitchell coined the phrase 'the pictoral turn' in *Picture Theory: Essays on Verbal and Visual Representation* (Chicago: University of Chicago Press, 1994). An important example of a preoccupation with the visual is Martin Jay's ground-breaking study, *Downcast Eyes: The Denigration of Vision in Twentieth-Century French Thought* (Berkeley: University of California Press, 1994), which proposes that, despite its strong tradition in the visual arts and cinema, French thought of the last century was consistently 'ocularphobic' (p. 15). Within Hispanic studies, María Silvina Persino's *Hacia una poética de la mirada* is an important survey.

3 Claude Gandelman's book, *Reading Pictures, Viewing Texts* (Bloomington: Indiana University Press, 1991) anticipated the trend by demonstrating the intertwining of the visual and the textual.

4 The panopticon as an image of the disciplinary society is developed in Foucault's *Discipline and Punish: The Birth of the Prison*, trans. Alan Sheridan (New York: Pantheon, 1977).

The postmodernist gaze, as understood here, arises out of theories surrounding that most characteristically contemporary of visual media, the cinema.[5] According to Norman Denzin in *The Cinematic Society*, the voyeur is the iconic, postmodern self. Denzin regards the camera as a kind of voyeuristic 'knowing eye', which exposes the illusory structures of truth fabricated by contemporary society, thus broadening the concept of illicit viewing to embrace both social criticism and a form of cultural self-reflexivity in which the questions of who gazes, on whom, from where, for what motiviation, and with whose permission are paramount. The postmodern cinematic voyeur has adopted characteristics of the classic peeping-tom. He or she is socially abnormal, even paranoid, and is marginalized by the society upon which he or she casts an eye. But these features are fused with a social conscience that gives the contemporary watcher a particular insight denied to society at large. The classic voyeur has thus developed into a professional onlooker – the detective and the spy are the most obvious examples from popular culture, but there is also the psychoanalyst, the journalist, the photographer, the tourist, the anthropologist, even the modern writer. In a self-reflexive mode, the traditional gaze of the voyeur is now reversed: he or she who had conventionally been depicted as an illicit watcher, invading private spaces and rendering them public, now turns society's gaze back on itself, providing a reflective mirror in which it can examine its own nature and premises.[6]

Thus, the contemporary turn to the visual, having heeded the lessons of theory's so-called 'linguistic turn',[7] involves a self-reflexive movement in which viewing is at least double, and frequently triple. There is the seer, the seen, and often also the recording of this act of the seer seeing and being seen. The cinematic structure that juxtaposes a particular shot with a reverse-angle shot, creating two looks but – it is generally agreed – concealing the camera

5   Cinema, as Patrick Fuery argues in the introduction to *New Developments in Film Theory* (Houndmills: Macmillan, 2000), has become an essential component in postmodernism, not simply through the illustration of certain ideas but by throwing up theoretical preoccupations in the first place. One of these is the concept of the gaze, which, he notes (p. 6), is no longer simply a term for perception but now includes such issues as subjectivity, culture, ideology, gender, race, and interpretation.

6   Denzin builds on, but subtly adapts, Foucault's use of the panopticon, noting the shift from a system of discipline to one of deterrence 'where the person gazed upon is the person doing the gazing; the voyeur as newsmaker, tourist, travelling ethnographer' (p. 9). He also builds, of course, on the psychoanalytical tradition within film criticism, exemplified by Christian Metz, who argued in *Psychoanalysis and Cinema: The Imaginary Signifier* (trans. Celia Britton, Annwyl Williams, Ben Brewster and Alfred Guzzetti [London: Macmillan, 1982]), that cinema turned the spectator into a voyeur. Recent examples of the investigator as social commentator in Spanish cinema include Alejandro Amenábar's *Tesis* (1996) and David Trueba's adaptation of Javier Cercas' novel, *Soldados de Salamina* (2001).

7   The phrase is Richard Rorty's, from *The Linguistic Turn: Recent Essays in Philosophical Method* (Chicago: University of Chicago Press, 1967).

and the film-maker's role, has thus been complicated by the addition of a further gaze that explores the fabricated nature of the scene and implicates the spectator in the activity of seeing.[8] This late twentieth-century cinematic gaze is, according to Furey, a psychoanalytic one. 'When we analyze the gaze,' he notes (p. 8), 'we are also examining the structures, functions, and operations of ourselves as subjects (both conscious and unconscious beings) within socio-cultural and historical contexts.'[9]

In Goytisolo's late novels, as we shall see, the multiple foci of the cinematic gaze are assimilated to metafictional narrative devices that deliberately flaunt the process of the texts' construction. The figure of the onlooker or voyeur permits a blurring of boundaries, especially between the public and private domains, not in order to remove limits altogether, but, ultimately, to question where those limits might legitimately and morally be drawn. And the background presence of psychoanalytic theory allows the author simultaneously to present a vision of society and analyze the unconscious premises upon which that vision is predicated. In a sense, Goytisolo both continues to put forward his anti-Western, anti-capitalist agenda and attempts to query the position from which he, as a Westerner, does so.

I have, of course, already touched on the issue of the gaze in Goytisolo's work. It is evident in the antagonistic configuration of the Sartrean *regard* in the discussion of self and identity in *Coto vedado*, *En los reinos de Taifa*, and *Señas de identidad*. It reappears as a paradigm of self–other relations in *Don Julián* and *Juan sin Tierra*. However, it first emerges in an exclusively visual form, rather than as a philosophical metaphor, in Goytisolo's 1982 novel, *Paisajes después de la batalla*; it is developed in the context of the exploration of the biographical investigation of a life in *La saga de los Marx*, of 1993; and it finally becomes a central motif, aimed at articulating an ethical response to contemporary political and humanitarian dilemmas, in *El sitio de los sitios*, from 1995. The focus on the gaze highlights a paradoxical feature of Goytisolo's writing from the mid-1980s on, namely the fact that it is concerned with expressing a sense of solidarity with marginalized and perse-

---

8   Denzin discusses the apparent realism of the shot/reverse-angle shot format, and the manner in which it is now exposed as an illusion (p. 31), particulary by feminist cinema criticism's exposure of a 'third look' implicit in the male gaze directed towards the female on screen. However, the notion of the third gaze has been supplemented by Paul Willerman, in 'Voyeurism, The Look, and Dwoskin', in *Narrative, Apparatus, Ideology: A Film Theory Reader*, ed. Philip Rosen (New York: Columbia University Press, 1986), pp. 210–18, with the notion of a 'fourth look', by which he means the implication of the spectator as precisely that, a spectator or voyeur included in the cinematic simulacrum.

9   In arguing this, he draws on Freud's *On Metapsychology: The Theory of Psychoanalysis*, trans. J. Strachey (Harmondsworth: Penguin, 1987). Furey argues that the interplay between the antitheses of seeing and being seen, or scopophilia and exhibitionism, in Freud's work is often ignored, particulary by the feminist critical tradition stemming from Laura Mulvey's highly influential essay, 'Visual Pleasure and Narrative Cinema' (in *Visual and Other Pleasures* [Bloomington: Indiana University Press, 1989], pp. 14–26).

cuted groups, at the same time as it privileges the figure of the author (in various guises) and, ultimately, represents an increasing textual introversion. The groundedness of Goytisolo's writing in historical circumstance, and his desire to use self-conscious and metafictional modes of writing to explore issues, thus continue as apparently contradictory impulses that his novels seek to unite in a single, socially and politically committed discourse of dissidence and marginality.

The Protagonist as Voyeur: Paisajes después de la batalla

Paisajes después de la batalla has as its protagonist a 'personaje sospechoso', a morally reprehensible admirer of Charles Lutwidge Dodgson, better known as Lewis Carroll, the author of *Alice in Wonderland* and *Alice Through the Looking Glass*.[10] 'Nuestro mirón' (p. 34), as the protagonist is frequently dubbed, lives in a small flat close to a cinema in the Sentier district of Paris, and enjoys enticing there young girls to whom he is sexually attracted. He is also a sower of discord, a socially disruptive figure who, as the text begins, has just replaced local French street signs and advertisements with ones in Arabic. Paradoxically, however, this voyeur is physically unable to see the results of his handiwork, since his flat overlooks an inner patio and not the street, although he does listen carefully to the noisy chaos that he has caused while self-consciously filing his nails in the safety of his home. Just as the outside world has been turned upside down by the appearance of Arabic, which, appropriately, reads 'todo de revés' (p. 11), so the classic image of the voyeur as onlooker is initially turned on its head too. The 'autor de la tropelía', instead of taking delight in witnessing the hecatomb he has created, is perverse in quite the opposite respect (p. 16): 'el cercano bulevar podía ser escenario de un drama inesperado y terrible y él, instigador y causante del mismo, sentado en el sofá-cama, lima que lima, sumido en la contemplación egoísta de sus manos, con una indiferencia rayana a la perversidad'. Playing god, like some industrial magnate who manages his business without a thought for the welfare of his workers, this 'monstruo' (p. 19) is utterly indifferent to the effects of his actions, which, nevertheless he finally decides to see for himself. He is thus, in a double movement, simultaneously fascinated by, and detached from, the consequences of his recent subversive activities.

The protagonist of *Paisajes* embodies three key features of the contemporary voyeur. First, he takes pleasure in the secret observation of others. Second, he is socially dysfunctional, both because of his sexual attraction to young girls and his general life style. He communicates with his wife only

---

[10] The second section of *Paisajes después de la batalla* (Barcelona: Montesinos, 1982) is entitled 'Un personaje sospechoso' (pp. 16–19), and the ninth 'Tras las huellas de Charles Lutwidge Dodgson' (pp. 33–6).

through translations of Arab mystic poetry, which he pushes under her door, and takes delight in such acts as urinating in the sink instead of the toilet. Third, he becomes a social observer, sufficiently detached from society to offer an outside view of it – although not, of course, an unbiased view. Aping Flaubert's social satirists, Bouvard and Pécuchet, he aims to call into doubt 'le bon sens du peuple' through the ridicule of *idées reçues*.[11] Crucially, however, he is also ridiculed himself, as the insistence upon the self-regarding activity of filing his nails indicates.

Goytisolo's voyeur certainly gazes upon others, but he is also, as we shall see, gazed upon by them, in a replication of the cinematic shot/reverse-shot format. Moreover, the use of metafictional techniques in *Paisajes* indicates that the voyeur is the object of the gaze of both Goytisolo, author of the book, and we, its readers. This interplay between the various gazes is further complicated by the fact that Goytisolo blurs the boundaries between life and fiction with apparent autobiographical references that suggest that his protagonist is a caricature of his own literary persona. The consequence of this fusion of fiction and autobiography in *Paisajes* is a double self-reflexiveness, albeit a playful one. If Goytisolo, as author, casts his gaze upon the protagonist, and if this protagonist recalls Goytisolo, then the novel seems to acquire a psychoanalytical dimension – Goytisolo caught in the Lacanian mirror, gazing at himself. But if Goytisolo is drawn into the text, are we as readers also confronted with an image of ourselves? I shall argue that this is indeed the case, and that in a much later novel, *El sitio de los sitios*, such voyeuristic textual practice is put to ethical ends. Now, however, let us examine more closely the visual qualities of *Paisajes*.

Popular visual media are almost ubiquitous in this novel. Aside the pictoral appeal of the depiction of the Sentier as layered like a puff-pasty cake (pp. 19–23), and the visual allusions in such section titles as 'Verlo para creerlo', 'En la penumbra', and 'Algunas rectificaciones al cuadro', the novel contains a plethora of references to cinema, television, and advertising. Newspapers are evoked in one ironically titled section, 'Ojos claros, serenos', to suggest that late twentieth-century Western culture is a voyeuristic one in which what most appeals to 'Monsieur Tout le Monde' are tittilating stories of the type, 'El romance de Julio Iglesias con Margaret Thatcher' or 'Violada por su propio padre el día de su Primera Comunión' (pp. 23–4). If the protagonist is an unsavoury character, gleefully watching a local funeral, for instance, then so too, implies Goytisolo in his exposition of *idées reçues*, is contemporary society. It is a society that is content to view only what tickles its fancy, closing its eyes to the horror of death in the 'Justicia revolucionaria' section,[12]

---

11 Epigraph to *Paisajes* (p. 5).
12 This seems to anticipate the opening of *Tesis*, in which the female protagonist almost witnesses a death in the metro system, but is herded back by the authorities at the last moment. The scene conveys the protagonist's ambivalence towards viewing violence

and seeing no more than stereotypical images of other cultures 'en carteles de propaganda' in 'Come Back, África'. These may either take the form of idyllic 'paisajes africanos de pacotilla, mar teñido de anil', or horror-film images of 'cádaveres mutilados, cuerpos desnudos, una muchachita cosida a cuchillazos con la sangre reseca de su doncellez' (pp. 32–3). It is a society obsessed with the technology of vigilance, in which the private and public realms are increasingly becoming confused ('Espacio en movimiento'), and in which truth does not matter, so long as plausibility reigns ('Lo dijo ya Platón').

In this 'mundo al revés', it is left to the protagonist, as perverse onlooker, to rectify the malaise. The text playfully declares, 'nuestro héroe no es un simple mirón' (p. 36). In conventional terms, of course, he is worse. We see him, in 'El modelo de Rodin', viewing Dodgson's pictures of young girls and collecting erotic adverts from the personals column of the newspaper. Para-doxically, however, he is presented as more perceptive than the rest of society to the world's injustices, a point drawn out through the blurring of the bound-aries between autobiography and fiction and the intertextual links that *Paisajes* makes to Goytisolo's own journalistic output. Not only is the protag-onist a writer who lives in the same street in Paris as Goytisolo at the time of writing, and shares his birthday of 5 January,[13] he is referred to as the 'autor' of the invasion of the Sentier with Arabic script (p. 16). While these connec-tions should clearly not be interpreted on a literal level, they are striking from a metaphorical point of view. Goytisolo has consitently sought in his fiction to shock by giving expression to sexual and moral taboos, and one might see this as echoed in the sexually motivated letters his protagonist writes. Goytisolo has also deliberately peppered his works with Arabic script, notably in *Juan sin Tierra* and *Makbara*, where the language is used to unsettle the European reader though the visually alienating quality of the text.

An author's note at the beginning of *Paisajes* thanks 'su presunto homónimo, el remoto e invisible escritor «Juan Goytisolo», la reproducción de sus dudosas fantasías científicas aparecidas en el diario *El País*' (p. 7). The reference is to the article, 'Apuntes de historia contemporánea', which appeared in *El País* on 10 September 1981. Two sections from it, 'Justicia revolucionaria' and 'Manifesto', are included verbatim in *Paisajes* (pp. 30–1). The newspaper article, initially a satirical attack on Western indiffer-

---

and death, and encapsulates Aménabar's main 'thesis', that ours is a society simulta-neously fascinated with, and repulsed by, visual violence. Of course, *Tesis* can be said to satify this voyeuristic desire just as much as it exposes it.

[13] The novels reads (p. 102): 'El estrafalario vecino de la Rue Poissonnière vino al mundo hace medio siglo un día cinco de enero a última hora de la tarde: es, por consiguiente, un capricornio.' Commenting on this aspect of the novel, Francisco Javier Blasco calls it an 'autobiografía deliberadamente grotesca', in 'El palimpsesto urbano de *Paisajes después de la batalla*', *Anales de la Literatura Española Contemporánea*, 10 (1985), 11–30 (13).

ence to oppressed nations in Africa and, by implication, elsewhere in the world, ends with a series of jibes at Spain's own political class following the *Tejerazo* earlier that year.[14] Its conclusion, *plus ça change . . .*, is intended as an indictment of Spain's lack of progress in the area of social justice and equality in the years since the end of the Franco regime. What is most interesting about the inclusion of sections of this article in *Paisajes*, however, is the manner in which the mixing of journalism (albeit satirical) and fiction colours the playful exploration of authorship in the latter genre. The clear intention is to blur and fuse the identities of the novel's protagonist, an unidentified narrator who is declared unreliable (p. 177), the unnamed 'author' implicit in the note at the beginning of the novel, and Goytisolo himself.

The confusions begin with the protagonist of the novel being labelled on several occasions a scribe, or amanuensis, emulating medieval monks by collating 'la enciclopedia de conocimientos de su época' in his 'celdilla de la Rue Poissonnière' (p. 82). Elsewhere, he is a 'copista, recopilador, corresponsal o autor capucero de fantasías científicas' (p. 86), and 'el polifacético memorialista y redactor del Sentier' (p. 90).[15] This depiction of authorship as a collective enterprise is a reprise of the view presented in *Makbara*, where, with each new recital, the oral storyteller weaves together a provisional and constantly changing version of an old tale. The notion of creativity that lies behind it is, of course, radically different from the Romantic one prevalent today,[16] and in *Paisajes* ambiguity arises concerning the protagonist's authority over his collage-like creation. 'Su vocación de amanuense,' we read (p. 181), 'le ha llevado a asumir la paternidad de la copia e, insidiosamente, confundirse con el autor.' He thus becomes an

---

14 On 23 February 1981 Lieutenant Colonel Antonio Tejero Molina threatened Spain's young democracy by leading an attempted coup. The puppet of more senior army officers, he marched into the Cortes with a select band of *Guardias Civiles* and held its members at gunpoint for almost twenty-four hours. King Juan Carlos I's direct appeal to the army to remain loyal to him is widely credited as being instrumental in ensuring the coup's failure.

15 Both Lucille V. Braun ('Inside and Outside: Topology and Intertextuality in Juan Goytisolo's *Paisajes después de la batalla*', *Revista Canadiense de Estudios Hispánicos*, 14 [1989], 15–34) and Kessel Schwartz ('Themes, Écriture, and Authorship in *Paisajes después de la batalla*', *Hispanic Review*, 52 [1984], 477–90) stress a structuralist angle on the novel, distancing Goytisolo from his author/scribe figure by viewing him as a 'producer of texts' (Braun, p. 16) and a combined 'author-hero-narrator-performer' (Schwartz, p. 482). However, the latter notes the ambiguous overlap between this figure and Goytisolo himself, and concludes that 'Goytisolo always writes about himself and his rebellion against society and thus his novel is not, strictly, self-contained literary discourse' (p. 490). While I agree with Schwartz's conclusion, I disagree that Goytisolo is aiming at creating self-contained *écriture*.

16 Even the recent theoretical interest in intertextuality denotes an obsession with authorship and intellectual property, since it implies the delimiting of creativity as much as it does the promiscuous attribution of it to all and sundry.

author. The text then adds a further level of authorial confusion by drawing Goytisolo himself into the equation:

> las elucubraciones científico-grotescas sobre la humanidad futura, ¿son obra de su musa o de ese escritor huraño y a todas luces antipático que las divulgó en El País?; la dificultad de vivir, comunicar con los demás, adaptarse a las normas y actuar conforme al llamado sentido común, ¿es propia del narrador o corresponde simplemente al personaje?   (p. 181)

Clearly, the suggested overlap of identity between the protagonist, an unreliable narrator, the supposed author of *Paisajes*, and Goytisolo himself creates a smoke-screen which, echoing the myriad authors, editors, and translators in one of Goytisolo's constant literary references, the *Quixote*, seems to hinder the reader's identification of a single voice of authority in the text. The ambiguous use of pronouns to which we have become used in Goytisolo's work reappears once again in this respect. The apparently clear distinction between such terms as 'nuestro héroe' or 'nuestro protagonista', and second-person pronouns that seem to designate a narrator – or is it the implied author? – in, for instance, the 'Palimpsesto urbano' section, is rendered more complex by the occasional use of first-person pronouns – used, for example, to express the ideas of an abusive dictator in 'Ni Stalin ni Trujillo ni Pol Pot: Bela Lugosi'.[17]

This is further complicated by the creation of a series of gazes structured in infinite regress. The 'Palimpsesto urbano' section develops the metaphor of the city of Paris as a text in which the roving eye of a Baudelarian *flanêur*, an anonymous 'ninguneado', becomes a 'cámara cinematográfica que registra fríamente, con curiosidad neutra, el extraordinario crisol que le ciñe' (p. 73).[18] Following him through the streeets is a figure who is presumably either the narrator or implied author of *Paisajes*: 'agitación y efervescencia sobrepuestas te acompañan cuando caminas tras él por callejas cercanas al Bazar Egipcio' (p. 74). In 'Desdoblamientos' we find a similar voyeuristic scene, in which it is the protagonist who watches a 'personaje grotesco [. . .] tocado con una boina y con una escarapela tricolor en la solapa del impermeable' (p. 77). He appears in the street on Sundays and holidays, and furtively graffitis French slogans over Arab ones that upset his sensibilities. However, the relationship between viewer and viewed in this case is a complex one, revealing the psychoanalytic theme at the heart of *Paisajes*. 'Asomado al

---

[17] The use of pronouns in *Paisajes* appears to be deliberately obscurantist and does not follow the existentialist pattern of previous texts, in which each voice plays a clear role within the articulation of a dissident identity.

[18] The metaphor of the city as text, and vice versa, of course recalls *Don Julián*, although the protagonist in that novel can hardly be said to cast a cold eye on Tangier. Epps discusses the Baudelarian echoes of *Paisajes*, and relates them to Walter Benjamin's interpretation of the city, in *Significant Violence*, pp. 317–21.

balcón del piso de su mujer,' we read (p. 78), 'nuestro héroe espía desde las alturas las manipulaciones de su alter ego.' The shot/reverse-shot structure of cinema is replicated here as if the camera were a mirror, so that, as the person in the street feels the eyes of the protagonist upon him, he turns nervously and 'te descubrirá, se descubrirá a sí mismo, mofándose de él, mofándose de ti, apuntando hacia él, hacia ti, la rosada y procaz extremidad de la lengua' (p. 79). The first of these two examples of voyeurism suggests the objectivity of a distanced, excluded gaze, which merely records the world around; the second that of an involved, compromised gaze. It is the second gaze which, because of the identification of the protagonist with Goytisolo, is more interesting. In rather simplistic terms, it must be admitted, it recalls psychoanalytic theory, since the same figure is both viewer and viewed, 'discovering' himself and, in a parody of the supposed moment of identity formation in the Lacanian 'mirror stage', also poking fun at himself.[19] To this point I shall return, but let us first turn to the metafictional features of *Paisajes* that reinforce the association between the protagonist as author and Goytisolo, and thus affirm his controlling authority over this highly introverted text.

Metafictional Games and Authorial Control in Paisajes

The self-reflexiveness of the voyeuristic gaze in *Paisajes* is underlined by the apparent suggestion that the fragmentary, disconnected texts compiled by the protagonist are akin to the text of *Paisajes* itself. This standard metafictional technique is explained in the 'Su vida es sueño' section, in which the protagonist reads his own work and realizes that:

> un repaso a las ciento setenta páginas de su manuscrito descubre la existencia de un ser fragmentado: ideas, sentimientos, líbido tiran por diferentes caminos, el desdichado cronista de su vida ha sido incapaz de aglutinarlos. Hojear su relato acuciado por la premura del tiempo es un lancinante ejercicio de irrealidad: al final, ya no sabe si es el remoto individuo que usurpa su nombre o ese goytisolo lo está creando a él.
>
> (p. 182)

On the face of it, the reference to a 170-page manuscript would appear significant, even if it appears on page 182. Other editions of the novel do change

---

19 In brief, the Lacanian notion of the mirror stage is a crucial step in the formation of the subject. According to Lacan, at about 18 months of age a child develops a concept of self through awareness of itself as other – as if seen in a mirror – before it enters the linguistic domain that supplies the term 'I'. This quasi-mythical moment, however, establishes the subject as fundamentally split, for the self as seen in the mirror is always more stable than the actual self, thus providing the subject with an illusory sense of fixity and continuity. For a useful summary of Lacan's ideas, see Elizabeth Wright, 'Modern Psychoanalytic Criticism', in Ann Jefferson and David Robey (eds), *Modern Literary Theory: A Comparative Introduction*, 2nd edn (London: Batsford, 1986), pp. 145–65.

this figure in accordance with their pagination. The Espasa-Calpe edition, for instance, mentions a manuscript of 248 pages, although the actual reference occurs on page 221.[20] However, given that there is no coincidence between the number of pages in the protagonist's manuscript and the actual page on which the reference occurs in either of these editions,[21] one can only conclude that Goytisolo is teasing his reader to search for a hidden meaning that does not exist. The protagonist's manuscript, despite what a reader well-schooled in self-reflexive writing may expect, cannot be said to coincide exactly with Goytisolo's book.

In that case, can either the protagonist or the implied author figures of *Paisajes* be equated with Goytisolo? Given the ambiguities that Goytisolo has suggested in this regard, the answer must be both yes and no. No, since narratological criticism has demonstrated the fallacy of assuming the flesh-and-blood author of a fictional work can be located within his text,[22] and Goytisolo goes to great lengths to stress the shifting narratological responsibilities in his novel. However, authorial games are one thing, and the incorporation of texts by Goytisolo quite another, especially given their journalistic origins. The press cuttings that the protagonist of *Paisajes* collects recall Goytisolo's frequent journalism, an example of which, 'Apuntes de historia contemporánea', as we have already noted, is included in the novel. There is also an allusion to another essay, 'De vuelta a Merimée', originally published in *El País* in 1981 and later anthologized in *Contracorrientes*.[23] The inclusion in *Paisajes* of press cuttings – which, incidentally, also include pieces by journalists from *Libération*, who are thanked at the beginning of the book – is evidently meant to question conventional generic boundaries. Surprisingly, however, the effect of this is not to broaden discursive horizons, but to limit them.

Goytisolo's newspaper essays, particulary those dealing with current affairs, are often impassioned and generally committed to the revelation of some perceived injustice. Frequently published in the Madrid daily, *El País*, they derive their authority from two sources. First, the newspaper in which they appear is a serious publication, committed to the norms of international journalistic good practice.[24] This context determines the manner in which

---

[20] *Paisajes después de la batalla*, ed. Andrés Sánchez Robayna (Madrid: Espasa-Calpe, 1990).

[21] As occurs, for instance, in Carmen Martín Gaite's *El cuarto de átras*, ed. Lluís Izquierdo (Barcelona: Destino, 1997), p. 181, where the same metafictional device is used.

[22] The argument was cogently made by Wayne Booth in *The Rhetoric of Fiction* (Chicago: University of Chicago Press, 1961).

[23] 'De vuelta a Merimée', *El País*, 31 March 1981; *Contracorrientes* (Barcelona: Montesinos, 1985), pp. 107–11. Sánchez Robayna draws attention to the echo of this article on the *Tejerazo* in his edition of the novel, p. 142.

[24] The paper currently defines itself as a 'diario independiente, de calidad, de vocación europea y defensor de la democracia pluralista'. Its commitment to professional

Goytisolo's essays might normally be read. Although the short piece, 'Apuntes de historia contemporánea', is satirical, it was printed in the 'Tribuna' section of *El País*, one of the paper's regular opinion pages.[25] A reader would not, therefore, view it as fiction, but as a satirical comment on the contemporary world intended to highlight a need for change. Satirical writing of this kind is necessarily connected to an external world with which readers can readily identify.

The second source of authority for Goytisolo's essays derives from his own name and reknown as a successful writer and dissident intellectual. The by-line under which he publishes – 'Juan Goytisolo' – does not just identify its author as a flesh-and-blood individual, but also operates as a culturally significant signature. It actually becomes self-authenticating, justifying the premises upon which Goytisolo's social and political comments are based simply by the fact that he utters them. Andrew Wernick stresses how the author's name has become 'an identification tag, which [. . .] functions at once as the signatured assertion of a property right, and as a vehicle for whatever significance, reputation, or myth [. . .] that name has come to acquire'.[26] Of course, an authorial signature operates rather differently in fiction – where, as Goytisolo himself noted in *Juan sin Tierra*, 'todo es posible en la página' (p. 96) – than it does in journalism – where the validity of the argument and the writer's credentials in making it are paramount. Given the pressing, often life-or-death, nature of the topics that Goytisolo generally addresses in journalism, the combination of the two types of signature in *Paisajes* results in a greater contamination of fiction with the serious matters of journalism than vice versa. The idea of reducing such issues as the siege of Sarajevo, the Palestinian *Intifada*, or illegal immigrants arriving in El Ejido in southern Spain from North Africa, to mere narrative games is morally repre-

journalism is highlighted in its 'adopción de usos periodísticos como el Libro de Estilo, la figura del defensor del lector y el Estatuto de la Redacción que [. . .] regula las relaciones profesionales entre la redacción, la dirección del periódico y la sociedad editora'. See http://el.pais.es/corporativos/elpais/elpais.html [accessed 9 December 2003].

25 The majority of Goytisolo's journalism appears on the opinion pages. An exception are the two series of essays on violence and political turmoil in Algeria and Chechnya, both of which appeared in the international news section. The former were published 27 March–3 April 1994, and later collected as *Argelia en el vendaval* (Madrid: El País/Aguilar, 1994); the latter came out 1–7 July 1996, and were collected as *Paisajes de guerra con Chechenia al fondo* (Madrid: El País/Aguilar, 1996). Interestingly, an earlier series of reports, from besieged Sarajevo, 23–31 August 1993, appeared on the opinion pages and were collected as *Cuaderno de Sarajevo: anotaciones de un viaje a la barbarie* (Madrid: El País/Aguilar, 1993). All three series of articles have since been published, along with reports from Palestine, in *Paisajes de guerra: Sarajevo, Argelia, Palestina, Chechenia* (Madrid: Aguilar, 2001).

26 See 'Authorship, and the Supplement of Promotion', in *What Is An Author?*, ed. Maurice Biriotti and Nicola Miller (Manchester: Manchester University Press, 1993), pp. 85–103 (p. 87).

hensible. The games that *Paisajes* seems to play with authorial responsibility are therefore recast, becoming little more than a smoke-screen that seems to – but ultimately does not – conceal the extrinsic author of the novel. As in the *Quixote*, where Cervantes' similar games apparently fudge the issue of authorship through the creation of a plethora of authors, narrators, and stories within stories, the effect is to reinforce that which is meant to be hidden. Cervantes may *seem* to disguise his presence, but he does so in order to assert his authority over the text, rebuff Avellaneda's spurious sequel, and affirm his genius as a writer.[27] Goytisolo, likewise, simply draws attention to his own authority over his fictional discourse by attempting to disguise it. As we saw in chapter 2, the refraction of dissidence through the lens of the writings of others merely serves to affirm the centrality of the notion of dissidence in Goytisolo's writing. Likewise, the emphasis placed on several author-figures in *Paisajes* does not remove from view the central preoccupations of Juan Goytisolo, the extrinsic author of the novel, whose presence is increasingly strong in his works of the 1980s and 1990s.[28]

In the light of this, the psychoanalytic resonances in the use of voyeurism in *Paisajes* become more significant. Superficially, a voyeuristic scene in which the protagonist – already, as we have seen, associated with Goytisolo through autobiographical references – views his alter ego in the street suggests that the novel itself is a textual mirror in which Goytisolo can view himself as a writer. Indeed, the parody of the mirror stage as the formative moment of identity in 'Desdoblamientos' suggests that Goytisolo is in fact making fun of himself and his personal preoccupations, for the Lacanian parallel obviously does not stand up to scrutiny. For one thing, the protagonist who spies on his alter ego in the street is an adult, and not an infant. He can hardly be said to be 'sunk in his motor incapacity and nursling dependence',[29] and, as a writer, he certainly no longer inhabits a pre-linguistic realm.

The reason for the Lacanian parody would seem to be to deflect potential criticism by anticipating it. In making fun of his obsessions, the author prevents the reader from doing precisely that – yet another technique that is

---

[27] Nesbit's argument that Barthes' declaration of the death of the author is a response to revisions in French copyright law is interesting in the light of the case of the *Quixote*. The latter was, of course, written in a culture in which copyright, as we understand it today, did not exist. As William Byron notes in *Cervantes: A Biography* (London: Cassell, 1978), p. 498, 'art was largely thought of as common property, not, to be sure, to be stolen outright, but to be modified, adapted, imitated at will'. Confronted with Avellaneda's spurious sequel to *Don Quixote*, Cervantes was outraged, not at the fact of being imitated, but at being imitated so badly and with such little respect for both his skills as an author and his attempt to present more psychologically rounded, engaging characters.

[28] Inger Enkvist argues likewise in 'Ética, estética y política en *Paisajes después de la batalla* y *El sitio de los sitios* de Juan Goytisolo', *Un círculo de relectores: jornadas sobre Juan Goytisolo* (Almería: Instituto de Estudios Almerienses, 1999), pp. 29–55.

[29] Lacan, 'The Mirror Stage', from *Écrits*, quoted in Wright, p. 155.

anticipated by Cervantes in the *Quixote*. There, in order to avoid complaints about the loose structure of the narrative, Cervantes gives voice to them through his characters' frequent discussions of the art of storytelling. Both Cervantes and Goytisolo draw the reader into their texts by seeming to make him or her complicit in the creative development of the narrative. Goytisolo achieves this, most obviously, in labelling the protagonist of his novel 'nuestro héroe', a pronominal usage that places the reader in the position of a voyeur viewing, in his or her mind's eye, the scene presented. But the reader is also explicitly drawn into the novel, for instance, in the section '¡Eso no puede seguir así!', voicing certain concerns about what he or she is permitted to know and seeming to challenge the hegemony of the author. 'El sufrido lector de esta narración confusa y alimbicada,' we are told (p. 145), 'tiene perfecta razón en plantearse una serie de preguntas sobre sus silencios, ambigüedades y escamoteos y, según nos tememos, se las está planteando ya.' To take just one example, this reader figure in *Paisajes* complains at the lack of a physical description of the protagonist's wife, and demands to see her (p. 146). The voyeuristic echoes here are unmistakable. Goytisolo's 'sufrido lector' is male, and his request to see the protagonist's wife, supposedly in the name of feminist equality, amounts to no more than an invasive desire to '¡meter su curiosa nariz en el arcano de una vida escondida y remota en la que, a pesar del misterio en que él la encierra, intuye y adivina la existencia de un auténtico toro enchiquerado!' (p. 146)

Goytisolo's imaginary reader, though, favours a particular type of writing, the existence of which in literary terms is very doubtful. From *Juan sin Tierra* on, our author has consistently attacked a particular formulation of the realist novel in which naïve description predominates and there is no awareness of the complexities of narrative point of view.[30] Goytisolo's vision of the realist novel is of a text in which language is a transparent medium, faithfully reflecting reality without questioning underlying cultural and ideological assumptions. This is, of course, a distorted view of realism pressed into service to highlight the innovations of the author's own experimental narrative.[31] That his style of writing, by the end of the twentieth century, might no longer be at all innovative is not broached. Furthermore, the somewhat insulting and rather gratuitous nature of Goytisolo's depiction of the reader in *Paisajes* is left unexplored.[32] On the one hand, it might be argued that the

[30] In particular, see the comments made by the character, Vosk, in the sixth section of *Juan sin Tierra*.

[31] Recent criticism, such as Jo Labanyi's *Gender and Modernization in the Nineteenth-Century Spanish Novel* (Oxford: Oxford University Press, 2000), eloquently demonstrates the erroneous lack of subtlety in Goytisolo's definition of realism.

[32] For an impassioned critique of Goytisolo's depiction of readers in his late fiction, see Enkvist's 'Ética, estética y política', where it is argued that 'el afirmar que su meta [i.e the protagonist's, but by extension Goytisolo's] es provocar la antipatía del lector equivale a una declaración de guerra contra el lector' (p. 35).

figure of the reader in *Paisajes* is as much as caricature as the protagonist, and therefore not to be taken seriously. On the other, however, this is the only reader figure whom Goytisolo offers. Hence, a reader who fails to sympathize with his particular preoccupations is likely find him or herself alientated by their satricial depiction, and judge them to be simplistic, naïve, narrow-minded, dysfunctional, and even morally reprehensible.

One might argue, as is proposed in *Paisajes*, that the inclusion of a reader figure in a text challenges the author's authority, at least at the writing stage, but this is a fallacy. The only point at which a reader can intervene in the 'construction' of a text is at the moment of interpretation, as we have seen with Barthes' theory of the 'death of the author' and resultant 'birth of the reader'. So, while *Paisajes* claims to leave the reader free to reassemble the novel's fragments as he or she pleases in its final section, 'El orden de los factores no altera el producto', the fact that the textual order is immaterial totally undermines this freedom. The conclusion to the previous section, 'La ciudad de los muertos', is a rather more telling affirmation of the central role of the figure of the author – and of Goytisolo himself as controlling authority – in the novel, and it articulates a certain scorn for the contemporary society of which his readers are almost certainly members:

> Contemplar desde túmulo o fosa la brillante farándula de ruiseñores congregada en la Ópera: cogidos de la mano haciendo reverencias y pasos de baile robándose luz frente a las cámaras saludando alborozadamente al público: reír reírte de ellos: escribir escribirme: tú yo mi texto el libro
> yo: el escritor
> yo: lo escrito   (p. 193)

Voyeurism and a Cinematic Idiom in La saga de los Marx

Although *La saga de los Marx* is a rather weak and graceless book,[33] it develops the voyeuristic theme set out in *Paisajes* and points, through its references to Eastern Europe after communism, to the last work we shall discuss in this chapter, *El sitio de los sitios*. As a pivotal work, it therefore merits a brief analysis. *Saga* is a highly visual novel, not in the sense that it could easily be transferred to the silver screen, but because it relies heavily on cinema references and plays with concepts from film theory. The text begins with a list of *dramatis personae*, which gives brief descriptions of the main characters and includes personal details, such as nicknames, to offer an insight into their private world. It moves on to describe, with allusions to the

---

[33] Randolph D. Pope is of quite the opposite opinion in *Understanding Juan Goytisolo* (Columbia: University of South Carolina Press, 1995). He calls *Saga* 'arguably one of Goytisolo's best novels, brisk, humorous, inventive, compassionate, and ultimately profound' (p. 157).

Italian film-maker, Federico Fellini, the arrival in southwest Italy of refugees from Albania.[34] This event both opens and closes the text, framing it as a cinematic reprise and bringing to the fore one of Goytisolo's favourite topoi: the invasion of the West by, in this case, not the Orient but refugees from Eastern Europe following the fall of the Berlin wall. What links the arrival of refugees in Italy with the story of the Marx family is a re-examination of Marx's philosophical legacy in the light of the collapse of communism at the end of the twentieth century.

Saga is, however, a novel for the specialist reader of Marxist theory, as Marco Kunz's comprehensive notes to the text make clear.[35] The book is riddled with citations and paraphrases of works by Marx and Engels, with material taken from the Marx family's personal correspondence, and with quotations from later Marxist theorists, biographers, and scholars. It makes few concessions to the uninitiated reader, questioning the reception and inter-pretation of Marx's ideas not through explicit intertextuality, but by weaving a web of Marxist writings that is framed within a metafictional structure that parodies the traditional biographer's search for the 'truth' about a person's life.

Saga, as it title suggests, initially seems to offer the reader just such a biographical sketch of Marx. As the novel progresses, however, it turns his life and that of his family into a visual spectacle, depicting the making of a film about them and peppering the narrative with cinematic elements. In the third part, for instance, we encounter a director giving the 'actors' playing Marx and his family instructions for scene performances.[36] This use of filmic language serves as rather more than a gratuitous blurring of the boundaries between literature and cinema, however. Goytisolo's particular purpose is to reveal the invasive, voyeuristic quality of both scholars' and the public's interest in the Marx family's personal life. Thus he creates yet another of his ubiquitous author figures, in this case a biographer who is supposedly writing

[34] The novel's references to Fellini's *E la nave va* (1983) are discussed by Julià Guillamon in 'Fellini por Goytisolo: *La saga de los Marx*', *Quimera*, 121 (1993), 46–53. Guillamon notes that *Saga* can be understood as the direct consequence of *Paisajes* because of its 'composición fragmentaria, pero a la vez sintética' (p. 46), and she goes on to stress the novel's visual qualities and its aim to 'revelar los filtros a través de los cuales se forma la imagen de lo real' (p. 51).

[35] Marco Knuz, *La saga de los Marx: notas al texto* (Basel: Acta Romanica Basiliensia, 1997). Kunz also stresses the connection between *Saga* and *Paisajes*, indi-cating, for example, how the former novel imagines Marx in the Sentier district where the action of the latter is set (Kunz, p. 40, note to *Saga*, pp. 50–60). *Saga* also alludes to the 'En brazos de Josif Visarionovich' section of *Paisajes* (Kunz, p. 180, note to *Saga*, pp. 198–9). Finally, continuing the mixing of fiction and journalism in *Paisajes*, *Saga* contains several references to Goytisolo's own journalism (Kunz, pp. 35, 94, 150, 187).

[36] There are many illustrations of this, but see, for instance, *La saga de los Marx* (Barcelona: Mondadori, 1993), p. 146, which reads, 'ACCIÓN!! la script: *La Baronne Rouge*, secuencia primera, toma dos!'

a 'saga' about the Marx family, and then presents him as a peeping-tom investigating their domestic situtation. In the fourth section of part three, this biographer-voyeur is depicted gazing through various windows (a far from incidental metaphor), which give access to scenes from the family's private lives, such as Marx's daughter Laura's marriage to Paul Lafargue, and the birth of her children (pp. 150–1). A reference to a photograph of Laura taken just after her marriage (p. 152), in which she insistently stares at the camera, even allows her to symbolically return the intrusive biographer's gaze. The voyeuristic quality of his investigations into the Marx family's is further confirmed by his insistent practice of quoting their personal correspondence.

As he did in *Paisajes*, Goytisolo also creates a reader figure in *Saga*, and attempts to place him in the position of voyeur peeking in on Marx's life. This is partly achieved through the complicity between author and reader (whether fictional or real) that a phrase such as 'nuestro héroe' (p. 62) creates. It is reinforced, in the second part of *Saga*, in the altercations between the biographer and his editor, who requests certain realistic details that recall the reader's demands for a description of the protagonist's wife in *Paisajes*. The editor, anticipating the preferences of prospective readers of the biography-cum-saga in preparation, wants to see:

> surgir de sus páginas como personajes de carne y hueso a Moro y su familia, embeberse en las vicisitudes de su vida revolucionaria, etapas de miseria, luchas políticas, cambios de fortuna, elaboración del cuerpo doctrinal que trastornaría al mundo durante un siglo, en suma, una novela real como la vida misma   (p. 83)

Disagreeing radically with his editor, the biographer in *Saga* refuses to placate his potential readership and declares the aim of his book on Marx to be the 'contaminación cervantina del espectador' (p. 200). Waging war on his readers in this fashion is also what Goytisolo intends by the opening, Fellini-esque scene of *Saga*, and, as we shall see, by the self-reflexive narrative of the siege of Sarajevo in *El sitio de los sitios*. In his analysis of postcommunist Europe in both novels, Goytisolo turns the conventional meaning of voyeurism as illicit looking into a means of articulating his own political concerns. He will also attempt to saddle his reader with guilt for the – in his eyes – unjust way in which the Western world dealt with the collapse of communism and rise of ethno-nationalism.

The arrival off the coast of southern Italy of a ship laden with Albanian refugees is described by Goytisolo in *Saga* in a strongly cinematic idiom. The refugees, who until now have only been able to glimpse their 'Tierra Prometida' from afar, through the lens of a spyglass referred to as 'el ojo del cíclope' (p. 14),[37] find themselves being watched by Italian bathers 'con

---

[37] The mention of the Cyclops' eye is a clear echo of *Don Julián*, in which Góngora's *Polifemo* is a recurrent intertext. Polifemo's single eye is mentioned in the seventh stanza

ayuda de prismáticos' (p. 15). This exchange of gazes is a hostile one, depicting not communication and understanding, but a vision of otherness and a lack of empathy. The refugees' image of the West is a televisual one, based on fictional series such as *Dallas* (p. 18); the West's view of the Albanians as dirty and animalistic is equally stereotypical, echoing a centuries-long fear of alterity (p. 22). Neither, in Goytisolo's opinion, sees the other for what they really are. The East is duped by a Western myth of progress and a hope of finding sympathy and justice there; the West exalts justice but denies it to those most vulnerable and most in need.

Goytisolo uses this exchange of quasi-cinematic gazes for two purposes. First, he reveals the misleading view that East and West have of each other by stressing the divide between them. Second, he attempts to implicate his reader directly in the scene by self-reflexively drawing attention to the gazes as cinematic, and therefore constructed. The supposed naturalism of the classic Hollywood exchange of glances that occurs, for instance, during a conversation, and suggests communication, even intimacy, between the speakers,[38] is deliberately undermined by Goytisolo in the opening sequence of *Saga*. The narrative frame widens from the beach scene itself to depict Marx's daughter, Tussy, zapping between Fellini's film, *E la nave va*, and images of the arrival of the refugees on television:

> Vaya confusión! Secuencias entreveradas de un filme de Fellini y el reportaje en directo, desde el puerto de Bari, de un ferry atestado de fugitivos albaneses!
> el zapeo convulsivo de Tussy, su inveterada manía de teclear el programador a distancia, mezclaba imágenes, barajaba planos, pasaba del sofisticado transatlántico reconstruido en los estudios de Cinecittà al herrumbroso y maltrecho transbordador de jubilosa y exultante carga humana   (p. 20)

Goytisolo's reader, seeming initially to read or witness the arrival of the refugees *en directo*, as it were, suddenly discovers that the images are, in fact, *en deferido*, that is to say, mediated through a televisual format. He or she is thus placed, like Tussy, in the position of voyeur, aware of him or herself watching a series of images. And the televison presenter who introduces the footage from Bari functions as the voice of the disinterested West, with which the

---

of Góngora's poem. As we noted in chapter 3, *Don Julián* opens with a panoramic view of Spain across the Straits of Gibraltar, although Spain is certainly not a Promised Land in that context.

38 In *How to Read a Film: Movies, Media, Multimedia*, 3rd edn (New York: Oxford University Press, 2000), James Monaco explains thus the naturalism of the format (p. 211): 'the rhythms of this insistent shot–countershot technique are often intoxicating: we surround the conversation. This is the ultimate omniscient style, since it allows us to see everything from the ideal perspective.'

reader is associated: 'a quién diablos le importaba las lágrimas de un albanés y su retorno forzado a los escombros de su demencial utopía?' (p. 23) By attempting to implicate his reader in events, Goytisolo, whose ethical concerns filter clearly through the text of *Saga*, hopes to awaken a sense of sympathy for the plight of Eastern Europeans in the post-communist era. It is a strategy that he develops more consistently in *El sitio de los sitios*, where the figure of the voyeur, battling against injustice, is presented as the ethical conscience of his age.

The Voyeur as Ethical Conscience of his Age: El sitio de los sitios

El sitio de los sitios, like *Saga*, is clumsy and rather heavy-handed, but it does open and close with one of the most haunting and finely drawn scenes in Goytisolo's entire *obra*: the image of a woman attempting to make her way home along the infamous 'Sniper Alley' during the siege of Sarajevo in the early 1990s. This 'visión de invierno' is framed as a voyeuristic scene in which a mysterious traveller, recently arrived in Sarajevo, spies on the woman through a hole in the plastic covering the windows of the Holiday Inn. The motive for the man's spying is empathy rather than personal pleasure. Violence and death unite the two figures, 'como si ambos formaron un solo cuerpo'.[39] One watches from the confines of the room, described as a tomb, in which he will be killed by a mortar attack, while the other risks death in simply trying to cross the street below. Depicted as a 'cíclope inerme, viudo de un ojo', this voyeur is 'consumido de angustia' (p. 17) by the danger the woman faces. Identifying almost totally with her as he notes her progress, he ponders,

> Qué clase de tesoro protegía amorosamente en el bolso? Leña, comida, regalos para sus cuatro hijos? Caía la nieve en ráfagas oblicuas, chocaba contra el plástico, le humedecía el párpado. Una cifra revoloteaba en su mente como un copo voluble, insensato. Cuatro, había escrito cuatro? Qué vínculo secreto había establecido con aquella silueta huérfana en la desolación invernal?   (p. 18)

The close of the novel returns to the scene:

> El balazo le ha atravesado el cuello, su sangre se escurre y tiñe de rojo la nieve. Se repite el pasado y reimprime en presente: nadie escapa al destino y su natural crueldad. Las manos delicadas asidas al bolso no existen sino en tu mente. No necesitas abrirlo para saber qué contiene.   (p. 182)

---

[39] *El sitio de los sitios* (Madrid: Alfaguara, 1995), p. 17.

These passages reveal Goytisolo's creation, once again, of various author and editor figures. In the first quotation, reference is made to the voyeur *writing* that the woman he watches has four children. In the second, a figure, apparently the 'compilador' (p. 87) who organizes the fragments that make up *Sitio*, is either omniscient, since he knows what the woman has in her bag, or an all-powerful authorial presence whose imagination simply determines what she carries. Such blurring of narrative authority and responsibility is, of course, familiar to readers of Goytisolo. Also familiar will be the inclusion of a possible autobiographical echo, in this case the death of Goytisolo's mother in a Nationalist air-raid on Barcelona during the Civil War. In *Coto vedado* the author recounts that his mother was returning with toys for her four children when she died (p. 63). While the overlap between autobiography and fiction here is vague and ambiguous – and perhaps this is deliberate – it gives Goytisolo's depiction of the siege of Sarajevo an intensely moving quality.

Rather less subtle, however, is the suggestion that the voyeur in the opening scene is a fictional alter ego of Goytisolo himself. The title of the first part of *Sitio*, 'Hipótesis en torno a «J.G.»', echoes *Paisajes* in this respect. Where *Paisajes* makes reference to a certain 'Juan Goytisolo', whose journalism turns up in the text, *Sitio* narrates the arrival, violent death, and disappearance of the body of «J.G.», author of a notebook of homosexual love poetry that is appended at the end of *Sitio*. These events are investigated by a Spanish *Comandante* posted to Sarajevo as part of the 'Fuerza Internacional de Interposición', thus turning the novel partly into a detective story, though the investigator will learn as much about himself and his family history as he does about «J.G.» in the course of his search. The voyeur of *Sitio*'s opening scene is thus not the only intrusive onlooker in the book. Voyeurism, indeed, becomes central to Goytisolo's approach to the depiction of besieged Sarajevo, and to his attempt to seduce his readers into identifying with the city's victimized inhabitants.

There are numerous allusions in *Sitio* to Goytisolo's other writings, both fictional and non-fictional. The imaginary transfer of the siege of Sarajevo to a district in Paris in 'Prolegómenos a un asedio' and 'Distrito sitiado' evokes the apocalyptic opening of *Paisajes*, as does the reference in the same section to 'nuestro héroe' (p. 33). And the same figure's earlier denomination as 'el señor mayor' (p. 33) recalls a character in *Las virtudes del pájaro solitario*, a novel to which we shall shortly turn. There is also the description of the hotel's receptionist as having 'ojos serenos y claros' (p. 158), in echo of *Paisajes*. However, as in that novel, it is the non-fictional references in *Sitio* that are most interesting in the present context. Allusions to an essay by Goytisolo on Sir Richard Burton lie behind the title of the notebook of poems, 'Zona Sotádica', found in «J.G.»'s room after his death. As declared in *Sitio* (p. 43), 'El título de «Zona Sotádica» debe leerse como un guiño de complicidad al célebre explorador y erotómano inglés sir Richard Burton, cuya vida y milagros divulgó en nuestra patria el autor de

Coto vedado.'[40] And explicit reference to sexual matters, as is customary in Goytisolo's writing, is linked to the scatological, here through the figure of the 'Defecador', who recalls an anecdote about the poet and satirist Quevedo that Goytisolo recounts in an essay in *Disidencias*. There, the author remembers how his nursemaid, Eulalia, unabashed at scatological matters, delighted in telling the joke of Quevedo caught defecating in public by an Italian gentleman, who exclaimed, '¡Oh, *Qué vedo!*' The poet is supposed to have replied, 'Anda, ¡hasta por el culo me conocen!'[41] The 'Defecador' in *Sitio* thus evokes the strong Spanish tradition of socially corrective satire, and he is given the symbolic role of undermining, through ideological contamination, the moral and ethical norms of Western society. This is an aim which, as we have seen, he shares with the author figure in *Saga*.

The non-fictional work by Goytisolo that is most closely connected to *Sitio*, however, is the *Cuaderno de Sarajevo*, a collection of journalistic essays initally published in the opinion pages of *El País*. Arguably, this intertextual link is not flaunted in quite the same way as, for instance, the piece on Burton. Nevertheless, significant echoes of the essays can be found. The city of Sarajevo is imagined in *Sitio* as a tortured, broken body, the windows of its bombed-out buildings resembling empty eye sockets. When he arrives, the voyeur «J.G.» views 'la faz torturada de la ciudad' (p. 14) where the 'inmeubles lisiados, de órbitas oculares vacías, callaban' (p. 18). In the *Cuaderno de Sarajevo*, the city is similarly depicted as a wounded body, crumbling and decaying while the so-called civilized world looks on. It is 'lleno de heridas, mutilaciones, vísceras, llagas aún supurantes, sobrecogedoras cicatrices'.[42] But, anticipating his desire to 'contaminate' the reader of *Sitio* with his own sense of the injustice of the West's reaction to the Bosnian war, Goytisolo goes on, in *Cuaderno*, to suggest that Sarajevo is

---

[40] The essay, 'Sir Richard Burton, peregrino y sexólogo', is included in *Crónicas sarracinas*, pp. 147–72.

[41] 'Quevedo; la obsesión excremental', in *Disidencias*, pp. 143–82 (p. 143). In this essay, Goytisolo lambasts critics for failing to reconcile the apparently contradictory scatological and metaphysical aspects of Quevedo's vast body of writings. He takes this as illustrative of Spain's repression of corporeality, arising out of the particular Catholic, anti-Moorish values that he sees as having underpinned the *Reconquista*. Against this background, Goytisolo considers the case of Quevedo to be doubly interesting: traditional criticism of him reflects a general fear of the body and bodily functions that characterizes Spanish cultural life; but Quevedo's own work, with its dual image of woman as both the desired ideal and the scorned, degenerate body, also expresses the trauma of his society. Working from the Freudian premise that the repression of something is a means of dealing with it, or perhaps even controlling it, Quevedo's difficulty in presenting a unified picture of woman is, paradoxically, evidence of a healthy mind attempting to grapple with the relationship between mind and body. Thus, Goytisolo concludes (p. 147), 'la coprofilia de Quevedo, en vez de ser reflejo de una mente enferma, es, paradójicamente, un síntoma de buena salud'.

[42] *Cuaderno de Sarajevo*, p. 24.

metaphorically contagious, with its 'carreteras *plagadas* de hoyuelos de *viruela*' (p. 23, my italics). The experience of living with its inhabitants for even a few days wounds the traveller to the very quick. 'Nadie puede salir indemne de un descenso al infierno de Sarajevo,' he says. 'La tragedia de la ciudad se convierte al corazón, y tal vez al cuerpo entero de quien la presencia, en una bomba presta a estallar en las *zonas de seguridad moral* de los directa o indirectamente culpables, allí donde pueda causar mayor daño' (p. 106). The intention is that the *Cuaderno de Sarajevo* should 'wound' its readers, exploding like an incendiary device in their hearts and souls and moving them to ethical action.[43]

The unreality of life in besieged Sarajevo, which Goytisolo presents in the differing discourses of journalism and fiction, paradoxically leads him to what he perceives to be an enlightened moral clarity. A voyeur in the postmodern sense, the visitor to Sarajevo – whether the Juan Goytisolo of the *Cuaderno de Sarajevo*, or the myriad authors, narrators, editors, and vanishing characters of *El sitio de los sitios* – believes himself to be in possession of certain moral truths: the Bosnian cause is a wholly just one, and Serbian aggression against the city is unqualifiably wrong; history is to be appealed to only in a partisan fashion, to condemn Serbian ethno-nationalism, and not to uncover a prior web of complex ethnic strife in the former Yugoslavia; Bosnian government officials cannot possibly be accused of courting Western aid by either shooting their own people or luring Serbians into attacking high-yield sympathy targets, such as hospitals. The authority with which these assertions are made in the *Cuaderno* derives, as we saw earlier in relation Goytisolo's other journalism, from the reputation that his name carries.[44] For some readers, this will imply a certain cultural baggage, and even political bias; for others, it acts as a guarantee of moral truth. The author of the *Cuaderno* – and there is, as Prout notes (p. 94), no attempt to disentangle this figure from the flesh-and-blood Goytisolo – clearly believes in the authenticity of the ethical stance that he adopts. The case of *Sitio*, on the other hand, is rather different, for there is a clear attempt in that book to explore the issue of narrative perspective and to question the authority with which ethical judgements are made.

---

[43] Other echoes of the *Cuaderno* include allusions to the unreality of life in Sarajevo (*Sitio*, pp. 30, 52–3; *Cuaderno*, p. 84), references to the city as a 'ratonera' (*Sitio*, p. 74; *Cuaderno*, p. 21), the use of the term 'memoricidio' (*Sitio*, p. 77; *Cuaderno*, p. 53), references to the burning by Serbs of the library as an attempt to destroy the city's collective past (*Sitio*, p. 109; *Cuaderno*, p. 55), the staging of Beckett's *Waiting for Godot* (*Sitio*, p. 137; *Cuaderno*, p. 97), a reiterated quotation from Antonio Machado (*Sitio*, p. 173; *Cuaderno*, p. 9), the comparison of the siege of Sarajevo to that of Madrid during the Civil War (*Sitio*, pp. 173–4; *Cuaderno*, pp. 97–8), and, finally, the 'Nota del autor' at the end of *Sitio* (p. 183) revealing that the author visited the city on two occasions, at least one of which, of course, gave rise to the original essays in the *Cuaderno*.

[44] Ryan Prout makes the same point in relation to the *Cuaderno*, in *Fear and Gendering*, p. 104, n. 18.

The creation of a plethora of narrators, authors, and editors can, as we have seen, act as a smoke-screen, partly concealing, but not entirely removing, the controlling hand of authority in a text. *Sitio* certainly contains a variety such figures, drawing attention to the metafictional aspects of the narrative and undermining its claim to truth. The doubts that the text raises concerning the identity of «J.G.», the investigation of the circumstances surrounding the disappearance of his body and the *Comandante*'s various official *Informes*, the questionable authorship of two manuscripts included at the end of *Sitio* (the one, the 'Zona Sotádica' notebook of love poems, apparently written by the *Comandante*; the other, a series of mystical poems apparently drawing on both Spanish Christian and Islamic Sufi traditions) and the intertextual links that are established in *Sitio* with other works by Goytisolo only serve to muddy the textual waters. *Sitio* even seeks to question the premises upon which a visitor to Sarajevo might attempt to depict life there, having the *Comandante* from the 'Fuerza International de Interposición' remark that 'por este país desgarrado merodean numerosos samaritanos con credenciales de periodista que, so capa de humanitarismo y solidaridad con las víctimas, aprovechan cualquier fallo para denunciar nuestra acción' (p. 44). One of the features of the opening essay of the *Cuaderno de Sarajevo* is Goytisolo's attempt to distance himself from what he terms adventure tourists, motivated by the voyeuristic desire to witness war and suffering (p. 13). The author of *Sitio* is clearly also concerned with this question, which he attempts to deflect, first, by mentioning it, and, second, by accepting the status of a voyeur and turning this figure into a voice of moral authority, even into a symbol of the ethical conscience of his age.

Goytisolo attempts to do this by ambushing the reader. Just as he aspires, in the *Cuaderno de Sarajevo*, to turn his text into a moral incendiary device, so he endeavours, in *Sitio*, to entrap the reader through a form of emotive literary terrorism. There are various examples of this. The first – bearing in mind that the primary audience of *Sitio* will be Spanish, and the immediate wider audience Western – is to draw extended parallels between the contemporary situation in Bosnia and events from Spain's recent and more remote past. The siege of Sarajevo is thus repeatedly compared to that of Madrid during the Spanish Civil War, the burning of its library is related to the destruction of books by the Spanish Inquisition, and, in the fictional realm, the Spanish *Comandante* is revealed as the descendent of a certain Eusebio who was arrested by Francoist forces for subversive sexual practices on the outbreak of the *contienda* in July 1936. The West's apparent indifference to events in Bosnia is condemned as being on a par with the Allies' non-intervention policy during the Spanish Civil War, and both these historical responses are seen as a total abnegation of moral responsibility.[45]

---

[45] These are highly emotive issues. As I argue in 'Juan Goytisolo's *Cuaderno de Sarajevo*', the comparison between Bosnia and Spain is far from satisfactory. In particular,

The second means by which Goytisolo can be said to ambush the reader is in creating an exchange of voyeuristic glances which, echoing both *Paisajes* and *Saga*, attempts to implicate the reader in the events that the novel narrates. It is suggested, in the section 'El enemigo mortal', that each person is born into the world with an 'enemigo virtual' (p. 88). The notion is dramatized in an exchange of hostile gazes between victims and persecutors in the imaginary transferral of the siege of Sarajevo to a district of Paris:

> El individuo con la ceja apoyada en el alza del arma le había escogido por víctima. Entonces surgió del fondo de la memoria la lectura infantil: se trataba sin duda de su enemigo mortal. La amenaza virtual se había concretizado: ahora estaba a cien metros de él. El sitio de la ciudad les había puesto en contacto. (p. 91)

Ethnic conflict in Sarajevo is thus universalized – and arguably trivialized – by this appeal to the workings of fate, as it is also by the imaginary relocation of the siege to a district of Paris. Sniper and victim are united by a thread similar to that which linked the voyeur and woman in the opening scene – the weak thread of life perched on the edge of death:

> A momentos, creía ser víctima del autoengaño: vivir una escena producto de su esquizofrenia. Pero los disparos con los que el emboscado al otro lado del río le recordaba con regularidad su presencia disipaban al punto las dudas. Con una temeridad rayana en la irreflexión, corría por el pasillo hasta el escondrijo desde el que podía espiarle con los prismáticos y respiraba aliviado: seguía allí. El frágil hilillo de vida que les unía a través del frente y el río era su última y mejor garantía de continuidad. (p. 94)

The section ends with the depiction of the victim watching his sniper enemy, and losing touch with his own sense of identity, in quasi-psychoanalytical terms that recall *Paisajes*:

> Permaneció allí varias semanas, sin escribir ni casi alimentarse, con toda la mente centrada en el misterio del implacable enemigo. Envejeció, perdió peso, dejó de lavarse. Su rostro empezó a resultarle extraño en el espejo, aquel espejo de mano en el que una mañana, finalmente, vio reflejado de pronto a lo lejos el bloque de casas del otro lado del río, la madriguera del francotirador, el brillante y diminuto cañón del arma, la cabeza apoyada

---

the political parallels that Goytisolo draws there between the Holocaust and Serbian ethnic cleansing are, at the very least, misleading, and possibly disturbing. Furthermore, the author's attempt to engage his Spanish reader emotionally in the Sarajevan conflict by interviewing David Kahmi, a member of its Sephardic population, is rather mischevous. Kahmi remarks, 'soy bosnio, soy judío y soy español' (p. 60), although his family was expelled from the peninsula in 1492 and settled permanently in Sarajevo in 1551!

como siempre en el alza segundos antes de su disparo, esta vez mortal y definitivo. (p. 95)

Sitio, as its title suggests, uses the siege of Sarajevo as a metaphor for all sieges, thus attempting to bring it ever closer to the world of Western readers.[46] The novel is intended as a mirror in which the reader, like this imaginary victim in Paris, can realize that he or she is complicit in the persecution of Sarajevans through indifference and inaction. The strategy by which the reader is brought to this anagnorisis – a word used in the 'Enemigo mortal' section itself (p. 93) – is recognized in the novel as underhand and devious. Its narrator, we are informed, is unreliable, laying a series of traps for the reader 'en las que inevitablemente cae antes de advertir que ha mordido el anzuelo y sido arrastrado al punto adonde le querían llevar' (p. 86). While this figure cannot be simplistically related to Goytisolo, the same dismissive and controlling attitude towards the reader that this comment displays can indeed be ascribed to the author of *Cuaderno*.

Sitio turns the conventional meaning of voyeurism on its head, depicting not illicit sexual scenes, but a different kind of forbidden viewing – the almost unspeakably violent, silenced, ignored persecution of a city. Authors in this novel become snipers, as one imaginary writer demonstrates in 'La tertulia políglota', when he stares at a literary enemy 'con el ojo seguro del tirador que apunta directamente al blanco' (p. 161). In depicting a society in which voyeurism amounts to snipers watching their victims through gun sights, and victims watching their enemies through spyglasses, and then raising this to a metafictional level, with authors as voyeurs looking on the forbidden (because silenced) scene of besieged Sarajevo, Goytisolo turns the voyeuristic metaphor so often used to describe contemporary society into a mirror by which he can accuse that society of ethical irresponsibility. The lesson of the *Comandante* is meant to be instructive. Posted to Sarajevo, he became entrapped by his past (p. 172): 'allí me atrapó el pasado en forma de una muerte sin cadáver'. Ultimately, however, this results in a state of moral enlightenment in which he is forced to take a stand. 'Cuanto calló y tragó mi madre,' he says (p. 175), 'asciente hoy como una marea que amenaza ahogarme: mi afán de sobrevivencia moral me fuerza a tomar partido por la dignidad.' The reader, like the *compliador* of the final part of the novel, is exhorted to do the same, for the one thing that Goytiolo is unable to accept is his own society's and country's indifference to the Bosnian cause. It is a cause that he accepts unapologetically, flaunting the bias of his reading of the

---

[46] The back cover of the first edition of *Sitio* calls the book 'una metáfora de todos los asedios'. I am not in a position to speculate here on the reaction of non-Westerners to the symbolic terrorism that Goytisolo's writing wages against the capitalist West and its predominant values. However, in a post-9/11 world, and given the ethical concerns that Goytisolo's writing consistently raises, such an issue is far from irrelevant.

situation in 'Último sueño'. There, echoing the ending of *Señas*, he imagines
a city viewed from above through binoculars (p. 180): 'Has ascendido a unas
cimas nevadas, cuajadas de abedules y abetos, y abarcas impotente desde el
miradero la remota ciudad.' There is one question on his mind (p. 181):
'Únicamente tú vives, palpitas, tiemblas en esta ciudad de aparencia muerta y
machacada no obstante con saña?' The hope is that the answer is no, and that,
metaphorically, the reader is there too.

6

THE AUTHOR AS MYSTIC:
LAS VIRTUDES DEL PÁJARO SOLITARIO AND
LA CUARENTENA

This discord in the pact of things,
This endless war 'twixt truth and truth,
That singly held, yet give the lie
To him who who seeks to hold them both.
Boethius[1]

A Surprising Choice of Theme

When *Las virtudes del pájaro solitario* first appeared in 1988 the novel caused a certain sensation, its mystical theme taking readers by surprise. Research by Javier Escudero Rodríguez has since shown that this reaction was somewhat misplaced, given that an obsession with death and an emergent interest in mysticism can be traced in Goytisolo's fiction to at least the time of *Makbara*.[2] Indeed, looking back even further, we might recall from the discussion above (pp. 94–5) that *Juan sin Tierra* opens with an allusion to Eastern mysticism, though, admittedly, a pejorative one. The appearance of a religious theme is not, then, an anomaly in Goytisolo's work, although the exclusively positive light in which he came to view religious mysticism in the late 1980s is an unexpected turn in his career.

Mysticism has popular currency today, although less as a religious teaching or experience than as an interest in personal spirituality and growth.[3] But this is not what motivates Goytisolo to read and write about it. His

---

[1] Boethius, quoted in F. C. Happold, *Mysticism: A Study and An Anthology* (Harmondsworth: Penguin, 1990), p. 21.

[2] Javier Escudero Rodríguez, *Eros, mística y muerte en Juan Goytisolo (1982–1992)* (Almería: Instituto de Estudios Almerienses, 1994). In his first chapter, Escudero surveys the pervasive presence of cemetery locations in Goytisolo's work from *Campos de Níjar*, through *Señas de identidad*, to *Makbara*.

[3] As Colin Thompson notes in his recent study, *St John of the Cross: Songs in the Night* ([Washington: Catholic University of America Press, 2003], p. 17): 'at the start of the new millennium, the secular materialism of the West [. . .] seems open to ideas of personal growth and individual spirituality, though suspicious of the formal practice of religion.'

interest is both personal and intellectual – personal, in that he identifies closely with the writing of several mystics from the Christian and Islamic traditions; intellectual, in that he creates from his readings of them a vision of cultural *mestizaje* that is ethically motivated. Mysticism is thus harnessed by Goytisolo to further more general principles in his writing, namely a celebration of dissidence, pluralism, and intercultural dialogue. The relevance of mysticism to this task is not immediately apparent. Indeed, at first it may seem more of a hindrance than a help, for its appearance in Goytisolo's work creates a series of contradictions: whereas the form of mysticism that Goytisolo enlists is profoundly religious, he professes no faith of his own;[4] whereas mysticism is a highly personal experience, Goytisolo uses it to explore universal ethical preoccupations; and whereas, in certain forms, mysticism may imply a certain loss of a sense of self, as the goal of the mystic is spiritual marriage with the Divine, Goytisolo's fiction, as we have seen, consistently celebrates selfhood as dissidence. But mysticism does offer Goytisolo a new idiom through which to explore his enduring concern with cultural heterodoxy and intellectual intolerance. This is evident in two respects: in his use of intertextuality and his exploration of language as ambiguous, overflowing with meaning, and containing significant visual qualities. We shall consider each of these in relation to *Las virtudes del pájaro solitario*, before tracing the convergence of the mystical trend with the voyeuristic one outlined in the above chapter, in *La cuarentena*, which was first published in 1991.

San Juan de la Cruz as Dissident Hero: Intertextuality in Las virtudes del pájaro solitario

It might be supposed that Goytisolo's mature novels do not have heroes in the conventional sense of the term, yet *Las virtudes del pájaro solitario* explicitly celebrates the life and writings of one man: Juan de la Cruz, the Carmelite reformer, and nowadays 'santo y doctor de la Iglesia', whose poetry 'vertebrea la estructura de la novela', and whose arrest and imprisonment at the hands of fellow Carmelites is vividly described by Goytisolo in the third part of his novel.[5] The scene of the Saint's detention gives a flavour of the novel's highly poetic nature:

> a la profundas cavernas del sentido, que estaba oscura y ciego, irrumpían con lámparas de fuego un grupo de Calzados, docenas de seglares, gente de

---

4 In interview with María Luisa Blanco, 'En Marrakech puedo escribir y vivir', *Cambio16*, 20 April 1992, pp. 76–9, Goytisolo commented (p. 78), 'no simpatizo con ninguna religión'.

5 *Las virtudes del pájaro solitario*, pp. 87, 171 respectively.

armas, voces que se elevaban hirientes y acentuaban el timbre amenazador
según se aproximaban, habían descerrado el pasador clavija a clavija en
vista de que no abrían dándole tiempo de rasgar sus papeles y engullir los
de mayor peligro, ya voy, ya voy, luego, luego, mientras los frailes se
agolpaban a la puerta y conseguían forzarla, se abalanzaban a él y su
compañero, les arrastraban a un convento maniatados con hierros,
exponían su presa en el coro y la hacían flagelar por los guardias   (p. 79)

Traditional mystical images of light and dark, flames, pain and anguish, are
employed by Goytisolo to depict the frightening experience of violent arrest
and torture. It is as if he were imitating San Juan's own poems in an attempt
to convey an almost mystical identification with the persecuted Saint. The
apparent illogicality of certain aspects of the description – the irruption of
flaming torches into the deep caverns of the senses, the physically wounding
voices of the approaching Carmelites – result from Goytisolo's intertextual
reworking of San Juan's poetry. So, the opening two lines of the above
description come from third stanza of San Juan's poem, 'Llama de amor
vivo':

> ¡Oh lámparas de fuego,
> En cuyos resplandores
> Las profundas cavernas del sentido,
> Que estaba oscuro y ciego,
> Con extraños primores
> Calor y luz dan junto a su querido![6]

And the allusion to 'voces hirientes' is reminiscent of the wounding of the
flame in the first stanza of that poem –

> ¡Oh llama de amor viva,
> Qué tiernamente hieres
> De mi alma en el más profundo centro!   (p. 415)

– as well as of the wound caused by the absence of the Loved One at the
beginning of the 'Cántico espiritual':

> ¿A dónde te escondiste,
> Amado, y me dejaste con gemido?
> Como el ciervo huiste,
> Habiéndome herido;
> Salí tras ti clamando, y eras ido.   (p. 402)

---

[6] *Vida y obras de San Juan de la Cruz*, ed. Crisógono de Jesús, Matías del Niño
Jesús, and Lucinio Ruano, 9th edn (Madrid: Biblioteca de Autores Cristianos, 1975), p.
415.

Goytisolo, however, adds certain elements to the mystical idiom he borrows. Rather than depict a state of ecstasy through 'dislates', the phrase San Juan himself used to describe the illogicality of his writing,[7] Goytisolo uses the confusion of sensory stimuli to stress a state of fear and persecution.[8] He also alludes to the possibly apocryphal story of San Juan's having eaten potentially incriminating papers at the time of his detention,[9] thus emphasizing, in this instance, a negative reading of the images of light and dark. In Goytisolo's novel, the mystical celebration of suffering as a metaphorical transition leading to ecstatic joy is returned to its literal sense, becoming simply suffering at the hands of others. But this is in keeping with one of the reasons for Goytisolo's interest in San Juan, namely the respect in which he might be regarded as a dissident figure within Spanish culture and literature.

San Juan is, though, more than simply a persecuted figure to Goytisolo. He is also the author of a series of hauntingly beautiful, esoteric love poems, which are accompanied by commentaries that seem to open out the already ambiguous use of language in the poetry to even greater, strikingly modern, horizons of semantic charge. And his work achieves something which, according to Goytisolo, few other Spanish writers before the twentieth century have: a harmonious union between body and soul, between the corporeal and the spiritual aspects of human life.[10] Thus, Goytisolo's identification with the Saint in the *Pájaro solitario* arises out of the logic of his own poetics and is more than mere empathy at the mystic's suffering in life. When he claims that San Juan's poetry is the skeleton of his novel – 'vertebrea' is his word for this – he alludes to the vibrant intertextual dialogue that he creates between his own writing and that of his predecessor. This intertextuality is of two types. The first relates to a particular, Muslim-oriented interpretation of San Juan advanced by Luce López-Baralt; the second to Goytisolo's own imaginary re-creation of an apparently lost work by San Juan, the *Tratado de las propiedades del pájaro solitario*.

In *San Juan de la Cruz y el Islam* López-Baralt investigates the literary

---

7   In the preface to his commentary on the poem, also entitled *Cántico espiritual*, San Juan explained the illogicality of his poetry as a consequence of the mystical experience (*Vida y obras*, p. 703): 'por que ésta es la causa por que con figuras, comparaciones y semejanzas, antes rebosan algo de lo que sienten y de la abundancia del espíritu de amor et inteligencia que las llevan, antes parecen dislates que dichos puestos en razón'.

8   In *St John of the Cross*, Thompson remarks that 'Goytisolo's version of San Juan is an idiosyncratic construct, rewriting his imprisonment, for example, as the consequence of repressive Inquisitorial forces rather than of ecclesiastical politics and internal disputes within the Carmelite Order' (pp. 14–15). For a balanced account of San Juan's arrest and imprisonment, see Thompson, pp. 45–8.

9   See Crisógono de Jesús, *Vida y obras completas de San Juan de la Cruz*, 5th edn (Madrid: Biblioteca de Autores Cristianos, 1964), pp. 117–18; the story is rejected by José María Javierre, in *Juan de la Cruz: un caso límite* (Salamanca: Sígueme, 1992), p. 539.

10   Goytisolo lambasts Spanish canonical writers for eliding the body from their work in 'El mundo erótico de María de Zayas', in *Disidencias*, pp. 77–141.

similarities between the imagery and dislocated syntax of San Juan's poetry and that of Sufi mystics such as Ibn al-Farid, Farid ud-Din Attar, and Jalal al-Din Rumi.[11] Goytisolo draws upon López-Baralt's thesis by creating a *mestizo* text in which both the Christian and Islamic mystical traditions are perceived as having a common font of images and a shared literary praxis. López-Baralt's argument arises out of the illogicality of San Juan's use of language and his reluctance to pin down images to a single or particular meaning. 'San Juan', she writes, 'tiene que desconceptualizar el lenguaje y desmentir su natural capacidad de alusión. Las palabras quedan derrotadas: si los vocablos pueden significar todo, en el fondo no significan nada.'[12] There is, she argues, no Western precedent for the extreme dislocations of San Juan's poetry, thus leading her to other possible sources, of which the Sufis are the most intriguing.

The suggestion of a relationship of influence between San Juan and Sufism is problematic, given that, as López-Baralt freely admits, no concrete proof of the Spaniard's knowledge of the Sufis can be adduced. It may be a case of parallel development, the imagery upon which these Christian and Islamic mystics drew having a common origin that is now lost to us.[13] Never-theless, what matters most to Goytisolo is the possibility of an Islamic connection in the most unexpected of places, the work of a Christian mystic.[14] Extending the creative exploration of a potential literary overlap between Moorish and Christian Spain that underpinned the reading of Juan Ruiz's *Libro de buen amor* in *Makbara*, Goytisolo now brings together San Juan's poetry and that of several Sufi mystics by exploring shared imagery and placing it within a late twentieth-century context. His emphasis is on the Christian and Sufi mystics as intellectuals writing on the margins of their respective societies. Out of this he creates a new text – his own novel, the *Pájaro solitario* – at the same time as he simultaneously re-creates a personal version of what San Juan's lost *Tratado de las propiedades del pájaro solitario* might have been like.

In his 'reconstrucción intuitiva' (p. 73) of San Juan's lost work, Goytisolo

[11] For a more detailed discussion, see my 'Mystical Paradoxes and Moorish Reso-nances: A Solution to Juan Goytisolo's Problematic Aesthetic', *Journal of Iberian and Latin American Studies*, 4 (1998), 109–19 (published as Alison Kennedy).

[12] Luce López-Baralt, *San Juan de la Cruz y el Islam* (Mexico City: Colegio de México, 1985), p. 84. Goytisolo picks up on this aspect of López-Baralt's analysis in 'San Juan de la Cruz y el pájaro sufí', in *Cogitus interruptus*, pp. 170–6 (p. 173).

[13] For instance, Colin Thompson usefully summarizes various possible Christian origins of the image of the solitary bird, the closest connection that López-Baralt finds between San Juan and Sufism, in *St John of the Cross*, pp. 184–5, n. 37.

[14] In interview with Juan Carlos Herrera, 'La originalidad es volver a los orígenes', *La Nación*, 24 May 1992, Goytisolo admits that San Juan probably had no knowledge of Sufism, but that there is a 'convergencia sorprendente' between his poetry and that of Islamic mystics (p. 6).

echoes the Saint's description of the mystical symbol of the solitary bird – 'las condiciones del pájaro solitario son cinco: la primera, que se va a lo más alto; la segunda, que no sufre compañía, aunque sea de su naturaleza; la tercera, que pone el pico al aire; la cuarta, que no tiene determinado color; la quinta, que canta suavemente' (*Vida y obras*, p. 424) – and connects this with a Sufi defintion of the same image by paraphrasing the twelfth-century Iranian mystic, Suhrawardi, who wrote of 'el ave sútil e incolora, perfilada con inocente esbeltez en el cielo [que] parece volar sin dejar de estar inmóvil, suspendida con graciosa ingravidez' (*Pájaro*, p. 44).[15] The implications of such multi-layered intertextuality for questions of authorship and authority are significant: on the one hand, Goytisolo's unorthodox connection of Christian and Sufi mysticism serves to place his stamp of authority upon the text; on the other, the attempt to re-create an earlier text, and, indeed, the use of textual echoes from earlier authors, at the very least dilutes, and possibly even negates, this authority. At the end of the *Pájaro solitario*, with regard to the question, 'quién y cómo era yo?', the narrator replies, 'mi sobriedad, adustez y tonos apagados eran los del pajarillo en el *Tratado*' (p. 168). Such blurring of authorship and authority is, of course, a potential paradox of the practice of intertextuality, and one that Bakhtin signalled in his concept of heteroglossia. If one takes the words of others and adapts them, the presence of the other may nevertheless remain, as we saw in chapter 2.[16]

In his novel, Goytisolo thus seeks to unite the old and the new, shifting from a Romantic conception of textual originality as individual creativity to a collective or intersubjective view of it as a process of reading, re-reading, and transformation. He evokes San Juan's lost work but he also, to borrow the terms of Terence Cave's discussion of imitation theory, dismembers and reconstructs both it and the Sufi poetry he includes.[17] While Cave is at pains to point out the difference between this and the contemporary notion of intertextuality, in that the latter, at least in its Kristevan version, seeks to

---

15 Harry Corbin gives Suhrawardi's text in French translation: *L'Archange empourpré* (Paris: Fayard, 1976), p. 450.

16 Arguably, contemporary intertextuality brings about a dissolution of authorship, which incidentally follows Barthes' declaration of the death of the author, as the focus shifts from the figure of the writer as creative origin to the text itself, which becomes, in Julia Kristeva's words ('Work, Dialogue, Novel', in *The Kristeva Reader*, ed. Toril Moi [Oxford: Blackwell, 1986], pp. 34–61 [p. 36]), the 'intersection of textual surfaces'. However, intertextuality covers a broad spectrum from parody and imitation, in which origins and their reworkings are necessarily highlighted, through to more radical forms of dialogue, in which textual authority does seem to disappear.

17 In *The Cornucopian Text* Cave discusses Renaissance imitation theory, noting that (p. 76) 'it recognizes the extent to which the production of any discourse is conditioned by pre-existing instances of discourse; the writer is always a rewriter, the problem being to differentiate and authenticate the rewriting. This is executed not by the addition of something wholly new, but by the dismembering and reconstruction of what has already been written.'

avoid the image of an author who 'creatively determines his own text' (p. 76), Goytisolo's practice relies upon the reader's recognition of his dissident authorial voice at the same time as it strives to give a voice to a lost, or silenced text. This ambiguous interplay is reinforced by the choice of a mystical subject, and emerges most forcefully in the *Pájaro solitario* in certain textual strategies, particularly with regard to pronominal usage, to which we now turn.

Pronominal Shifts in the Pájaro solitario

The theme of mysticism poses some interesting questions in relation to the matter of self and identity, for the goal of the mystic is, of course, union with the godhead, whether conceived in a monistic or theistic manner.[18] Thus the mystic may seek either a total loss of self in complete union, or a transmutation in which the self remains distinct but is transformed by spiritual marriage. There are inherent differences between Christian and Islamic mysticism in this regard. San Juan, for instance, adopts a theistic position in which the identity of man and God are separate but the soul becomes transformed through union.[19] On the other hand, as Happold notes, Sufism tends toward a monism in which 'the union must be complete, the self must die absolutely' (p. 96). Given the textual union of Christian and Sufi mysticism that Goytisolo attempts in the *Pájaro solitario*, this point is not insignificant. The matter can be extended to Goytiolo's own identification with San Juan and the Sufis as persecuted figures, and his apparent renouncing of narrative authority through strategies that give voice to these writers.

Las virtudes del pájaro solitario begins with the use of a first-person plural narrative voice – 'se nos había aparecido' (p. 9) – which strikes a note of collective solidarity in the face of the tumultuous arrival of a figure symbolizing AIDS – the 'maldita de las dos sílabas' (p. 157), as the text later describes her. This quickly switches to a parenthetical first-person singular – '(no, no me vengáis ahora con fechas [. . .])' (p. 9) – which effectively draws the reader into the text by creating a dialogue between first- and second-person voices that echoes the technique of *Don Julián*. In that novel the addressee had been singular and had primarily designated part of the narra-

---

[18] I do not intend to engage here in a theological discussion concerning the nature of the self within mystical thought. The reader is referred to R. C. Zaehner, *Mysticism: Sacred and Profane: An Inquiry into some Varieties of Praeternatural Experience* (London: Oxford University Press, 1957), W. T. Stace, *Mysticism and Philosophy* (Philadelphia: Lippincott, 1960), and F. C. Happold, *Mysticism*.

[19] Colin Thompson discusses the point in *The Poet and the Mystic: A Study of the 'Cántico espiritual' of San Juan de la Cruz* (Oxford: Oxford University Press, 1977), chapter 1.

tor's split ego, but had indirectly implicated the reader as well; now, however, the addressees (in the plural) are both the narrator's fellow sufferers and the text's readers. This is an important new inflection in Goytisolo's support for alterity. It reflects his ethical commitment, in the *Pájaro solitario*, not just to an abstract conception of otherness, but to Paul Ricoeur's argument that ethical action – the self's achievement of the 'good life' – depends upon a dialectic of selfhood and otherness.[20] Such a nuanced view of solidarity as a dialogic relationship between the individual and the collective is a crucial development: on the one hand, it broadens the ethical basis of Goytisolo's exploration of the articulation of dissidence beyond a single narrative voice (frequently identifiable as his own); on the other, it places the reader of his novel within an explicitly mentioned community rather than in isolation, and thus highlights a public aspect to the reading process.

In the *Pájaro solitario*, the division between 'me' and 'them' evident in *Señas de identidad* and *Don Julián* has become one of 'us' and 'them'. The first-person plural pronoun includes a wide range of persecuted figures, and is thus the site of a dialogue between the first-person narrator and the voices of those with whom she/he identifies (she, in that feminine pronouns are frequently used in the text in echo of the use of the female 'alma' for the mystic's soul in San Juan's 'Cántico espiritual'; he, in that the themes of homosexuality and AIDS that the novel tackles are presented from a male perspective, and the dissident heroes to whom the narrator appeals are almost exclusively male).[21] As a supplement to the oppositional structure of earlier novels, predicated upon a singular marginal, or excluded, voice – the 'yo' for which the protagonist-narrator strived in *Señas*, *Don Julián* and so on – Goytisolo now develops a collective voice, if ultimately a male one, which becomes the site of the articulation of a plural, dissident identity.

As regards the use of pronominal shifts to articulate dissidence, the most obvious identification in the *Pájaro solitario* is that of the narrator with San Juan de la Cruz. This is not merely suggested as a form of psychological empathy, but is presented in the third part of the novel as a literal transforma-

---

20 Ricoeur, *Oneself as Another*, pp. 16, 18.

21 Perhaps the most notable example of this is the figure of Ben Sida, who, surprisingly, is not a creature of Goytisolo's imagination. In interview with Miguel Riera ('Regreso al origen', *Quimera*, 73 [1988], 36–40 [40]) Goytisolo explained: 'Se trata de un escritor árabe de la época clásica. [. . .] Yo lo implico como el retorno de lo reprimido. El personaje no quiere mencionar la enfermedad que tiene y lo hace indirectamente dando ese nombre a un profesor árabe.' Manuel Ruiz Lagos suggests that this writer may be Ibn Sida, el Ciego, from Murcia. See 'Pájaros en vuelo a Simorgh: Transferencias y metamorfosis textual en un relato de Juan Goytisolo, *Las virtudes del pájaro solitario*', in *Escritos sobre Juan Goytisolo*, pp. 171–228 (p. 214). The one enduring female literary presence in Goytisolo's work is Francisco Delicado's heroine, the Lozana andaluza, who is mentioned in the 'reconocimientos' at the end of the *Pájaro solitario* and plays an important role in other works, especially *Carajicomedia*.

tion: 'si se trataba tan sólo de un proceso de transferencia e identificación sicopática con el autor de la obra de tantos amores y penas', the narrator asks (p. 91), 'por qué me mantenían encerrado en aquel húmedo y cruel calabozo?' So, when he/she then refers to 'la fusión íntima de conocimiento y amor' (p. 92), the reference is polysemic, designating the mystical goal of union with the Divine; the intertextual union of works by San Juan, the Sufis, Goytisolo, and others listed in the 'reconocimientos' at the end of the novel; and the union of marginal figures in a collective discourse of dissidence.

There are instances when the singular, first-/second-person dialogic self of *Don Julián* does break through in this text. Just prior to the above literal identification with San Juan, for instance, we read:

> el silencio!, por qué este silencio?
> (eres tú quien ha hablado, transformando la pregunta en una especie de grito?) (p. 89)

Yet, such use of the second person is less insistent than in Goytioslo's earlier writing. The fluctuation between first and third persons is more frequent, as in the first part of the novel when the narrator asks:

> pero era ello o yo?
> pues me veo, la veo, desde dentro y fuera   (p. 26)

On another occasion at the end of the third part of the novel the narrator, having totally identified with the San Juan, then pulls back, remarking of the mystic, 'después de un largo encierro paulatinamente ensombrecido y sin esperanzas, tomó la resolución de huir, evadirse de aquella mazmorra en donde se pudría la vida' (p. 101). Of course, this distancing may be due to the fact that San Juan's escape from imprisonment is not mirrored in Goytisolo's text, since its narrator and his/her companions remain trapped in 'aquel espacio acotado, la ficción de un jardín de reposo' (pp. 19–20). There is also the following apparently illogical statement in which a first-person pronoun gives way to a third-person without the referent seemingly changing:

> pero vuelvo a lo *mío*
> a aquella decisión sin duda temeraria de dejar *su* escondrijo a fin de saber algo de las demás, averiguar el destino y vicisitudes de la comunidad
> (my italics, p. 25)

Such pronominal shifts are evidence both of Goytisolo's emphasis on social solidarity, and of the convergence of apparently fluid identities around a core of dissidence. In the *Pájaro solitario*, identity is both ever-shifting, in that it unites various figures under a single sign, and, at the same time, fixed, in that the sign of dissidence remains a constant. Another example of radical pronominal shifts that achieve a similar sense of simultaneous connection and disjunction occurs in the fourth part of the novel, where we read:

> se ha mirado y *te* has reconocido sin posible duda
> con *tu* arrugado traje blanco de verano y anticuado sombrero de paja, la estampa sepia y romántica *del* joven señor mayor   (my italics, p. 106)

One metaphor that aptly describes this is the idea of the 'ejido', or piece of common land, exploited by Goytisolo as the shared territory in which a variety of divergent experiences may come together. He speaks in the *Pájaro solitario* of 'un ejido común a experiencias distintas' (p. 87), referring specifically to the possible textual connections between San Juan and the Sufis, but the phrase might also allude more generally to a sense of community in which, through pronominal shifts, solidarity is achieved but pluralism is not lost through an imposed homogeneity or sense of sameness. This is evident, for example, in the sympathetic treatment of the figure of the 'dama de derechas' (p. 146), who might normally have been included in Goytisolo's group of oppressors, but who, because she is persecuted by her own kind, is subsumed into the community of the marginalized in this novel.[22]

If there are a variety of persecuted figures subsumed under the plural pronoun, 'us', and deemed to constitute a kind of solidarity in plurality, then, as in Goytisolo's earlier works, their persecutors are equally subsumed under a common grammatical category, 'they', although there is no attempt to explore diversity within this category. In the *Pájaro solitario* we find references to Francoism and National Catholicism (pp. 65–7, 93–4), to Fidel Castro (pp. 29–32, 94),[23] the Calced Carmelites (pp. 79–80), and the Inquisition, both direct (pp. 151–2) and indirect, through allusion to the case of Francisco Ortiz (pp. 83–4).[24] There are also scattered general references to racial and ethnic cleansing, which recall the Holocaust (for instance, gas chambers in the phrases 'cámara oscura', p. 79, and 'cámara negra', pp. 95, 117, 130, 154), and the expusion of Jews and Moors from the Iberian penin-

---

[22] This point is discussed by Colin Thompson, 'La presencia de San Juan de la Cruz en la literatura del siglo XX: España e Inglaterra', in *El sol a medianoche: la experiencia mística: tradición y actualidad*, ed. Luce López-Baralt and Lorenzo Piera (Madrid: Trotta, 1996), pp. 189–203.

[23] The reference is to his persecution of homosexuals, and it draws upon material in the documentary, *Conducta impropia*, by Néstor Almendros and Orlando Jiménez-Leal. Fidel Castro herded homosexuals into a sports stadium before transferring them to labour camps. For further discussion, see Linda Gould Levine, 'El papel paradójico del "Sida" en *Las virtudes del pájaro solitario*', in Manuel Ruiz Lagos (ed.), *Escritos sobre Juan Goytisolo: Actas del Segundo Seminario Internacional sobre la obra de Juan Goytisolo: 'Las virtudes del pájaro solitario'* (Almería: Instituto de Estudios Almerienses, 1990), pp. 225–36.

[24] This case is documented in Angela Selke, *El santo oficio de la Inquisición* (Madrid: Guadarrama, 1968), which is listed by Goytisolo in the 'reconocimientos' at the end of the novel.

sula in the sixteenth and seventeenth centuries ('mancha indelible en el buen nombre de la familia', p. 138; 'certificado de sangre limpia', p. 146). However, the lack of an attempt to discriminate among these figures, institutions, and historical events is a significant limitation to Goytisolo's work. They are presented under the deceptively homogeneous image of forces of persecution, and factors of historical context are not considered. It is not quite the same to equate an estimated six million Jewish deaths in the Holocaust with anti-Semitic expulsions in Golden Age Spain, nor is San Juan's imprisonment at the hands of fellow Carmelites akin to Castro's treatment of homosexuals in Cuba. So, although the opposition of 'I' and 'them' that emerged in *Señas de identidad* has become one of 'us' and 'them', thus broadening the reference beyond a single narrative voice, the elements designated by the impersonal 'they' have not become any more contextualized. This drives to the heart of Goytisolo's ethical concerns, and is even perhaps a result of them, for, despite seeking to open his narrative to pluralism through an awareness of multiplicity within dissidence, his particular preoccupations limit him to a singular view of the orthodox or official voice – a different type of other, but nonetheless an other – which seeks to repress pluralism.

Ethical Concerns, Linguistic Ambiguity, and the Visual Qualities of the Pájaro solitario

The association of mystical discourse with such ethical concerns might, at first, seem unusual, given that mysticism deals with highly individualized religious experiences, the communication of which to others is only of secondary concern. Nevertheless, as Thompson stresses at length in his recent book on San Juan, the Spaniard's mysticism, as reflected in his writings as a whole, was not merely a 'cult of spiritual possessiveness or of self-gratification', but was concerned to teach the value of a search for 'the true measure of the self'. Indeed, acutely aware of the Saint's resonance in our modern world, Thompson notes the liberatory intention behind his writing. 'His analysis', he remarks, 'of the way human attachments and desires lead to possessiveness and ultimately vitiate freedom seems to me worth spelling out in an age devoted to acquisition.'[25] The Christian life, of course, has an implicit ethical goal of serving God through good deeds, and while there may be debate about the meaning of 'good', Goytisolo and San Juan do share a general moral commitment to their fellow man. San Juan's rejection of material goods, for instance, recalls Goytisolo's own assault on Western capitalism in *Makbara* and *Paisajes después de la batalla*, and his concern for others is reflected in the *Pájaro solitario* in Goytisolo's call to solidarity with the oppressed, persecuted, and disadvantaged in society.

[25] Thompson, *St John of the Cross*, p. 18.

This is an enduring preoccupation in Goytisolo's writing, and, as we have frequently noted, he is often criticized for failing to create a truly liberatory discourse that evades the trap of inverse oppression through the simple reversal of the ethical hierarchies of Western value-systems. In *Don Julián* he failed to develop fully an incipient contextualized view of the issues presented, something that might have salvaged his argument there. In *Juan sin Tierra*, satire and irony replace a productive moral vision with negativity. Nevertheless, in the *Pájaro solitario*, Goytisolo does at last find an idiom that circumvents the sterile navel-gazing of post-structuralist narrative by investing language with new and unexpected depths of meaning. These derive, first, from his use of linguistic ambiguity as a positive contribution, rather than an impediment, to communication; and, second, from an exploration of the visual qualities of language that extend its communicative ability beyond mere textuality.

As I argue in 'Mystical Paradoxes and Moorish Resonances', Goytisolo uses linguistic ambiguity to positive ethical effect in the *Pájaro solitario*, though I did not draw there, as I shall below, on Ricoeur's work. Returning to Ricoeur's principle, outlined above (pp. 110–11), that language carries meaningful reference only when it is used, and, embracing his discussion of the working of metaphor as a tension within utterance in *Interpretation Theory*, I show how Goytisolo turns the creation of a surplus of textual meaning from a negative obstacle – post-structuralism's play of signifiers detached from external reference – to positive advantage in the articulation of a discourse of dissidence.

In discussing San Juan's use of language, López-Baralt, as we noted earlier, concludes that the mystic stretched reference to such a point that words, overflowing with possible sense, ultimately became emptied of meaning. In a more nuanced reading of San Juan's language as 'inflamed', rather than as overflowing with meaning, Thompson argues that, while 'language as overflow and language as inflamation are both images of excess' (p. 233), there is a difference between them. In a strongly contextualized reading of the poet's use of metaphor, he stresses that San Juan's inflamed language is not intended as an openness to multiple readings, but rather that it points beyond the limits of language to open 'doors of perception which more ordered discourse closes' (p. 279).[26]

Thus, an excess of meaning need not lead to a lack of meaning, a lesson that is also evident in the *Pájaro solitario*, and is spelt out in Ricoeur's discussion of the functioning of metaphor in *Interpretation Theory*. There, in arguing that literature is the 'positive and productive use of ambiguity' (p. 47), Ricoeur suggests that metaphor is not a derivation from an established

---

[26] The importance of context is stressed throughout Thompson's analysis of San Juan's use of metaphors, particularly those that might be construed as having a sexual meaning. See, for instance, his discussion of the 'llama', *St John of the Cross*, pp. 254–5.

meaning, but a tension between two interpretations of an utterance. This emphasis on a tension between interpretations, rather than the substitution of one sense for another, allows us to retain the idea of linguistic excess without concluding that meaning, communication, or reference are impossible. This is crucial for a text like the *Pájaro solitario*, in which ethical concerns are conveyed in a polysemic and paradoxical discourse that holds together a variety of horizons of reference, from the joys of Christian and Islamic mysticism, to the negativity of persecution, and the hope of redemption, if only in death.

The key metaphors of Goytisolo's novel are taken from López-Baralt's analysis of the mystical overlap between San Juan and the Sufis, and include the image of the solitary bird, that of wine or drunkenness, the dark night of the soul, and the flame of living love. In using these images, Goytisolo seeks to maintain an unresolved tension between a variety of possible meanings without the exclusion of any one of them. So, the 'pájaro solitario' designates not only the mystical image of the soul in search of God, but it also, through a secondary, Caribbean meaning of the word, refers to homosexuals. Throughout the *Pájaro solitario* there are references to nubile young men engaged in physical sports. These figures are eventually removed to a rather sinister 'estadio deportivo' where they are burnt at the stake as dissidents. The persecuted are dressed up as birds and taken to the stadium in cages: 'habíamos sido simbólicamente adornadas con picos, crestas, alas y plumas, pájaros abigarrados y exóticos' (p. 98). Just as San Juan attributes multiple, and often contradictory, meanings to images in his poetry, Goytisolo develops paradoxical meanings for the symbols he employs, and the positive mystical idea of the solitary bird co-exists with the negative sense of marginalized and persecuted dissidents.

This technique of maintaining unresolved tensions between opposites through the use of single, polysemic images is characteristic of Goytisolo's treatment of the mystical images of wine and attendant notions of drunkenness, and in the symbol of the dark night of the soul, representing both suffering and a necessary stage leading to mystical union. The second of these is an image which, in Goytisolo's novel, becomes laden with connotations of persecution and, more specifically, with allusions to the Holocaust. The hospital room-cum-prison cell where the narrator of the novel is imprisoned is described as a 'cámara negra' in which he sinks into 'los abismos de deleites del santo, noche interior de apertura y tinieblas, cámara negra de nuestros ruegos y derretimientos extáticos' (p. 130). However, given Goytisolo's preoccupation with persecution, the reader cannot but recall the gas chambers, or 'cámaras de gas', used during the Nazi Holocaust. Again, Goytisolo uses the paradoxes of the mystical idiom to unite positive qualities – the dark night of the soul as a necessary step in the mystic's progress towards union with God – with negative associations – in this instance, one of the most horrific cases of systematic persecution of modern times.

The 'cámara negra' can also be associated with the image of the flame, quoted earlier, which, in San Juan, both burns and rejuvenates. Goytisolo explores the potential of the dialogical symbolism implicit here by adopting San Juan's idea of the flame as positive and life-giving – 'llama que consume y no da pena' (*Vida y obras*, p. 407) – and yet also developing it in relation to the theme of burning at the stake. He combines the mystical sense of the *llama* with a reference to Golden Age *autos da fé*, and then extends this to include references to images of wine and, finally, the AIDS virus:

> nuestra vida era una ruleta rusa [. . .], cada visita al reino de tinieblas que apaga los enojos con llama que consume y no da pena se convertía en una ordalía, el amado de cuya bodega bebíamos y abandonábamos ahítos de su sabrosa ciencia, no sería el instrumento elegido por el destino para aniquilarnos, el disfraz seductor del sayón por el que la maldita de las dos sílabas procedía a ejecutar su sentencia?   (p. 157)

Alongside his positive approach to the question of lingustic ambiguity, Goytisolo also explores the intersection between the visual and the written aspects of language. In a similar manner to the way in which San Juan uses linguistic dislocations to communicate an experience that is beyond the scope of ordered discourse, so Goytisolo seeks to extend the range of his own refer-ence through the use of visual elements that create an emotive identification with dissident figures. Allusions to the visual and dramatic arts, an emphasis on colour and visual description, and the play of light and dark in the mystical idiom itself, all contribute to this broadening of communication beyond mere signs on a white page. Of course, the visual aspect of Goytisolo's fiction has been an important factor since *Señas de identidad*, where the move from more conventional discourse to experimentation was signalled in the arrange-ment of the words on the page, and *Don Julián*, where the labyrinthine nature of the text was paralleled in the unending stream of words with unorthodox punctuation. However, in the *Pájaro solitario*, the visual tendency evident in the novels that we discussed in chapter 5 is developed in a new direction.

In an interesting demonstration of the importance of what, in his study *Paratexts*, Genette calls the liminal, or transtextual, aspects of a book – that is to say, those elements that are neither inside the actual text nor truly outside it but which act as 'an influence on the public [for] a better reception for the text and a more pertinent reading of it'[27] – Goytisolo draws inspira-tion in the *Pájaro solitario* from the cover illustration of one of his earlier novels, thus becoming a reader of his own work in an unexpected sense. On the front of the Seix Barral edition of *Makbara* is Félicien Rops' *La mort qui sème la zizanie*, a hellish depiction of death embodied in the figure of an

---

27 Gérard Genette, *Paratexts: Thresholds of Interpretation*, trans. Jane E. Lewin, fore-word Richard Macksey (Cambridge: Cambridge University Press, 1997), p. 2.

'espantapájaros' dressed in a 'capa o mortaja de amplio vuelo, bolso arracimado de muñecos, greñas trenzadas y sombrías, ojos emboscados en la espesura, sombrero tutelar cuyas alas parecían convocar imperiosamente el vuelo de una bandada de cuervos' (*Pájaro solitario*, p. 11).[28] The appearance of this figure in the *Pájaro solitario* initiates, in the words of the text, 'el mecanismo devastador de nuestras vidas' (p. 13), and, by personifying AIDS, Goytisolo conveys a vivid sense of the impending apocalypse brought about by its advent in the world.

He also stresses visual qualities in the depiciton of the Second Empire room in which the vicitms of this horrific vision of death find themselves. He includes references to works of art, fusing them, at the end of the following quotation, with the mystical image of the flame:

> sus movimientos eran viciosamente lánguidos, tal vez bajo el velo o las greñas (el velo discontinuo y espeso formado por sus greñas), abarcaba ya el salón de descanso, los asientos laterales de gastado hule rojo, farolas Segundo Imperio, frescos murales de paisajes orientales, colinas verdes, jinetes, siluetas con albornoces y haiquies, algún espidado alminar de mezquita, una media luna nevada, cuadro ambiental, nostálgicamente familiar a nuestros esforzados galanes de un día, elaborado, según la Doña, por una gran artista, una discreta asidua de aquellos aposentos consagrados a la beatitud y limpieza del cuerpo   (p. 10)

The depiction of the 'vasta terraza marítima de balustre musgoso y macetones de hortensias' (p. 19), where the dissidents take the sun is, likewise, emphatically visual and theatrical. We are presented with 'un grupo de nobles damas', dressed 'con la elegancia sonámbula que exigía la escena, sombreros arborescentes, boas, plumas iguales a los de la mansión desvanecida y lejana', silhouetted against a sunset, of which the colours are 'la apoteosis de tonos rosa pastel', and which provides a backdrop to 'el cuadro que representábamos' (p. 19). An echo of the voyeuristic concerns we explored earlier even enters when these ladies are described as having to 'atalayar desde [allí], con simulado interés, el mar inmóvil, irreal, figurado' (p. 21).[29]

The description of the dissidents as birds is also highly visual in its stress on colours. In the 'Asamblea de los Pájaros' in the concluding section of the novel, the narrator is described as absorbed in 'la contemplación y aprendizaje de los lenguajes visuales' of which the dissidents make use in their attire. Before him he sees 'vuelos y adornos ostentativos, despliegue de colores vistosos y excentricidades de plumaje'. And he continues:

[28] Rops (1833–98), a friend of the French poet Charles Baudelaire, is best known for his etchings, which have a grotesque quality comparable to the Flemish painter Breugel.

[29] Another echo occurs later when the narrator observes 'con prismáticos', 'media docena de jayanes de cuerpo oleosos y rudo' engaged in 'sus viriles juegos' (p. 44).

mientras algunas aves se revestían de gris amarillo con designios humildes de camuflaje otras optaban por colas y airones extravagantes, las variedades cromáticas del atavío se extendían desde el cobre intenso y rojo anaranjado a los colores pastel delicados y suaves   (p. 168)

Colour and light are, of course, inherent features of the mystical imagery that Goytisolo borrows from San Juan and the Sufis. One of the qualities of the solitary bird is that is is colourless, yet it exudes all the colours of the spectrum, and the metaphors of the dark night of the soul and the flame of living love rely upon a contrast between light and dark in their portrayal of the mystic's search for, and experience of, union with God. Goytisolo conveys aptly their paradoxical relation in writing of 'el ígneo fulgor de la noche oscura, la antesala de la opacidad auroral, el suave umbral de la embriguez extática' (p. 58). In this he reverses the conventional positive and negative qualities of light and dark in order to turn them into spaces of suffering and redemption. He also plays upon a semantic tension, since 'umbral', meaning doorway, also echoes 'umbra', or shadow.

Similar linguistic play is evident in the description of a butterfly transfixed by the intense light of the day, a clear echo of the image of the moth circling a candle flame included by Goytisolo in other texts. In the *Pájaro solitario*, he refers to 'una falena pillada en el círculo de una intensa luz veraniega, obsesa, cegada, crepuscular, resignada con incaica majestad a un destino escrupulosamente fatal' (pp. 11–12). That Goytisolo should use the word 'falena', which is of Greek derivation, rather than the more common 'mariposa', is not insignificant, since the butterfly is an ancient metaphor for the human soul.[30] The image, as we saw earlier, has metafictional resonances in Goytisolo's work. It is used to describe his approach to textual unity through fragmentation in *Juan sin Tierra*, and in his 'Presentación crítica' to the work of Blanco White it refers to the association of disparate literary figures under the banner of marginality. In the *Pájaro solitario* it retains both these senses, since the structure of the novel, in emulation of Genet's *Captif amoureux*, is stellar, and the work seeks to unite a series of dissident figures through a web of mystical imagery. Indeed, the image is all the more apt in this context, since the metaphor of a flame, or at the very least an intense light source, is itself mystical. The novel thus brings to a climax the two senses of this pervasive image in Goytisolo's work.

However, the use of mystical images to portray the suffering of AIDS vicitms in the *Pájaro solitario* is not unproblematic. Towards the end of the novel, Goytisolo hints that the virus might be seen as a 'don sagrado' (p. 163).

---

[30] The entry for 'butterfly' in *The Oxford Companion to Christian Art and Architecture* (ed. Peter and Linda Murray [Oxford: Oxford University Press, 1996], p. 69) notes that in art its symbolism had pre-Christian origins associated with the myth of Cupid and Psyche (the Greek for butterfly). It originally symbolized the Resurrection, the chrysalis being death and the butterfly new life.

While the mystical idiom allows him to use one image, in a manner similar to San Juan, to encompass a wide range of possible themes without the mutual exclusion of any of them, the suggestion that AIDS might be welcomed is, at the very least, an escapist illusion, and at worst, a perversion. Furthermore, although the dissidents initially coralled into the football stadium are described as having been dressed up as birds against their will (p. 98), by the end of the novel they seem to accept their fate as marginals destined to suffer at the hands of society. The climactic 'Asamblea de los Pájaros' in the final part of the novel is thus a dubious vindication of dissidence and, in practical terms, it offers little solace to those afflicted with the AIDS virus.[31] The sense of solidarity that Goytisolo ultimately depicts in this novel is that of a stoical acceptance of shared persecution, rather than a call for the alleviation of suffering. Despite the success of the author's use of linguistic ambiguity to break down binary categories, and his emphasis on the existence of marginality inside the canon, through the use of an established literary figure as an exemplar of dissidence, the ethical import of this novel is ultimately questionable in humanitarian terms.

Mysticism and the 1991 Gulf War in La cuarentena

In *La cuarentena* Goytisolo continues his use of a mystical idiom in an ethical context, weaving together references to the Spanish quietist mystic, Miguel de Molinos, and the Sufi poet, Ibn Arabí. These are also linked to Dante, whose *Divine Comedy* Goytisolo takes as an iconic Christian representation of Heaven and Hell. Finally, they are fused with scenes depicting the 1991 Gulf War. Such an idiosyncratic range of reference is, of course, typical of Goytisolo's work, and it continues the *Pájaro solitario*'s connection between mysticism and a moral commitment to exposing the ills of contemporary society. Indeed, the connections between that novel and *La cuarentena* are considerable, and move beyond broad ethical principles to include specific shared imagery and a common interest in the importance of visual culture today. Indeed, this latter aspect rejoins the visual concerns in *La saga de los Marx* and *El sitio de los sitios*, thus uniting the mystical and voyeuristic aspects of Goytisolo's writing in the 1990s.[32]

It is significant that the image of the moth circling a flame should occur

---

[31] Paul Julian Smith objects to Goytisolo's use of mysticism in relation to AIDS in *Representing the Other: 'Race', Text and Gender in Spanish and Spanish American Narrative* (Oxford: Clarendon Press, 1992), p. 212.

[32] I cannot agree with Linda Gould Levine when she states, in an otherwise perceptive article entitled 'La escritura infecciosa de Juan Goytisolo: contaminación y cuarentena' (*Revista de Estudios Hispánicos*, 28 [1994], 95–110 [107]), that in the development of Goytisolo's work 'cada texto carece orgánicamente de las semillas de la obra anterior'.

early in *La cuarentena*, bringing with it earlier resonances from Goytisolo's writing that are given a new slant. In chapter 3, the novel's narrator, whose identity is, as Stanley Black notes, rather uncertain,[33] is depicted driving through a landscape of destruction and death in which people run towards the headlights of his (or her, for the gender of the narrator varies) car 'como polillas al ardor y consunción de la llama' (p. 16). The context is one of conflict, and, contrary to earlier instances of its use, the lure of the light for the moths would seem to symbolize here the horrible inevitability of man's self-destructive desire to wage war. But those previous senses of mystical love and of textual structure that were attached to the image in the *Pájaro solitario* cannot be excluded, for in his essay, 'Los derviches giróvagos', from *Aproximaciones a Gaudí en Capadocia* (something of a companion volume to *La cuarentena*), Goytisolo develops both, as well as providing a source for his latest wording of the image. It is taken from the poetry of the Sufi Mehmet Chelebi, who wrote in his *Tratado de la sesión meulevi*:

> Polilla amorosa de su luz,
> día y noche, oh loco, me consumo.[34]

In his essay Goytisolo also considers the importance of circularity as a metaphor for the Sufi life and understanding of the Divine. Discussing the *sama*, or whirling dance of the Dervishes, he writes, 'la danza circular constituye [. . .] el eje simbólico de su doctrina. La divina ebriedad [. . .] es un espejo del orden universal, del movimiento giratorio del mundo y planetas. Vida, tiempo, astros, rotan en danza perpetua: comulgar con ellos es unirse a la *sama*' (p. 38). The dance is not just a reflection of religious sentiment for Goytisolo, however, as it is also evokes the writing process. 'La *sama* de los derviches de Konya', he notes (p. 43), 'suscita en el ánimo la plenitud creadora, una impresión sólo comparable a ese poder efímero de la escritura cuando inesperadamente accede a la gracia: ronda vertiginosa, danza beoda, levedad esencial.' Indeed, when Goytisolo describes the dance as a 'vórtice, inmersión, sumidero' which 'aniquila la existencia ilusoria, alegoriza las etapas del ascenso a la desposesión' (p. 43), the reader of *La cuarentena* might see a parallel with the narrator's own entry into the realm of the *barzakh* to accompany a recently deceased friend through the forty days of quarantine that precede the soul's entry into paradise.[35]

---

[33] In 'Mysticism, Postmodernism and Transgression in *La cuarentena* by Juan Goytisolo' (*Bulletin of Spanish Studies*, 78 [2001], 241–57), Black writes (p. 252): 'we have, on the one hand, the narrator who descends into the barzakh, and, on the other, the author who composes the text. The former is an essentially passive receptor of visions, images and dreams. The latter is the active producer of the text. The distinction is not a stable one.'

[34] 'Los derviches giróvagos', in *Aproximaciones a Gaudí en Capadocia* (Barcelona: Mondadori, 1990), pp. 25–45 (p. 38).

[35] This basic premise is outlined in the opening, italicized chapter of the novel, which

The image of the moth circling the flame thus draws together the mystical idiom of Sufism with self-conscious allusions to the creative process and to the specific context of the 1991 Gulf War, to which Goytisolo was strongly opposed.[36] By connecting these three aspects of his writing – language, form, and content – Goytisolo weaves his novel into an organic whole in which apparent contradictions between his mystical search for quietude, symbolized by the Sufi poet Ibn Arabí and the Christian mystic Miguel de Molinos,[37] and his socio-political concerns over East–West international relations, are effectively resolved.[38] The polyvalency of the image achieves that union of form and content that was perceived by many to be lacking in novels such as *Don Julián* and *Juan sin Tierra*, and which was achieved so successfully in the *Pájaro solitario*. Another example of such semantic multiplicity is to be found in the very title of *La cuarentena*, for the term quarantine carries several,

---

Goytisolo dedicates to his lost friend. She is identified by Miguel Dalmau as Joelle Auerbach in *Los Goytisolo* (Barcelona: Anagrama, 1999), p. 549. The *barzakh* in Islamic thought is an intermediate realm outside the rational parameters of time and space. Lasting forty days, it is the hiatus, or isthmus, between life and the afterlife, in which the corporeal becomes spiritual and the spiritual corporeal. Goytisolo makes use of it to create, in López-Baralt's words, an 'intrigante españolización del espacio mortuorio musulmán', which becomes a metaphor for the writing of his novel itself. See 'Narrar después de morir: *La cuarentena* de Juan Goytisolo', *Nueva Revista de Filología Hispánica*, 43 (1995), 59–124 (62), in which she comprehensively explores the Islamic sources of the work. The relationship between the forty days of the *barzakh* and the forty chapters of Goytisolo's novel is obvious; what is less stressed by critics is that the number forty also has Christian resonances, representing, for instance, the number of days that Christ spent in the wilderness.

[36] His views were expressed in three newspaper articles later collected in the volume, *Pájaro que ensucia su propio nido* (Barcelona: Círculo de Lectores, 2001) in the section entitled 'La guerra del Golfo (pp. 167–88): 'No a la petrocruzada', *El País*, 29 November 1990; 'Exégesis de una victoria heroica', *El País*, 16 March 1991; and '¿Nuevo orden o caja de Pandora?', *El País*, 26 April 1991. Launching the English translation of the second volume of his autobiography in London on the eve of the outbreak of the Gulf War, Goytisolo argued that it was 'una cruzada para mantener el nivel de vida de los norteamericanos' (R. M. de Rituerto, 'Goytisolo censura a Sadam Husein, Kuwait y la "cruzada occidental" ', *El País*, 7 November 1991).

[37] I do not intend to discuss the intertextual links that Goytisolo weaves with the usual plethora of literary predecessors in *La cuarentena*. The reader is referred to López-Baralt, who declares Ibn Arabí to play the same tutelary role as San Juan de la Cruz in the *Pájaro solitario*, and Escudero Rodríguez, who considers the importance of Dante in the novel, pp. 124–42.

[38] Black explores this apparent dichotomy, suggesting that what he terms the 'metafictional materialism' ('Mysticism, Postmodernism and Transgression', p. 242) of Goytisolo's text may be at odds with the urge for mystical transcendence, and that this mysticism may, in turn, be at odds with social commitment. Nevertheless, as he puts it, 'the real activity of the narrative is textual' (p. 255), and in this sense the novel acts as a 'secular version of [Molinos'] mystical guide' indended to lead the reader to 'a superior awareness' (pp. 255–6). Quietism and revolution are thus united in this novel's ethical and emancipatory purpose.

contradictory meanings. It represents not only the Islamic *barzakh*, but also a medical form of disease control, and a powerful diagnostic tool, which, rather like the eye of the voyeur, Goytisolo turns upon contemporary society.

The nature of *La cuarentena* as a written text is compared, in chapter 28 of the novel, to the experience of quarantine in three ways: the quarantine of the writer during the creative stage; that of the reader when engrossed in a book; and that of the work itself, detached from the circumstances in which it was initially composed. In each case Goytisolo highlights the paradoxical nature of his notion of quarantine, which, rather than protecting from disease, facilitates its dissemination – his quarantine is a kind of incubation preventing the premature spread of disease before it has reached full potency. He also declares the aim of his novel to be the destabilization of the mind of the reader and its contamination with the 'acción energética, transformativa de la palabra escrita' (p. 86). Quite how this is to be achieved is not directly stated, although it is implicit in the text's multiple self-conscious references to the writing process,[39] and in its treatment of visual images of the 1991 Gulf War, to which we now turn.

Goytisolo's depiction of the Gulf War, and, indeed, his attitude towards it, are evident in the apocalyptic scenes of death and destruction that pervade his novel, as well as in the ironic reconstruction of scenes from the conflict and use of a satirical intertext as a narrative context for these images. Together these combine to offer a compelling voice of opposition to a campaign that he regarded as driven by commercial interests rather than humanitarian concerns or a preoccupation with international justice. The 1991 war is the historical backdrop to *La cuarentena* in the sense that it lasted just over forty days and coincided with the death of the friend whom the narrator of the novel accompanies in the *barzakh*. Images from it appear in the text via the narrator's recurrent viewing of television coverage of the conflict, and through what seems to be direct experience of it. In chapter 20, he/she watches a video of 'imágenes de devastación, y de ruina, vehículos atascados en ignición, fumigación letal de aviones en vuelo rasante, cuerpos carbonizados, helicópteros que vomitan llamas, [. . .] fuego, más fuego, apocalipsis, horror, vasta incineración colectiva' (p. 66). This viewing, placed amid a satire of Western consumerism and advertising, is sabotaged as someone changes the tape that the narrator watches. As Black notes, such 'technical hitches' are deliberately intended to subvert the media protrayal of the war, not through direct condemnation, but by manipulating the potential of the medium against itself.[40]

---

[39] For specific instances, see *La cuarentena*, chapters 1, 6, 11, 24, 26, 28, 33, 39, 40.

[40] He suggests that the contamination of the reader's mind at which the novel aims is the result of a subversive textual process that both 'assumes a Baudrillardian diagnostic of social reality (or hyperreality)' and 'seeks a way of contesting it on its own terms' ('Mysticism, Postmodernism and Transgression', p. 252).

A more interesting subversion of visual representation occurs, however, in other instances of the war's intrusion into the novel that appear to be directly witnessed by the narrator. The war's first appearance, in chapter 3, contrasts powerfully with the initial depiction of entry into the *barzakh*, with its 'delicada esterofonía que parecía emanar de los confines indecisos de aquel espacio onírico, neblinoso, irreal' (p. 11). Suddenly, the narrator is driving through a landscape peopled with the fugitives who are attracted, like moths, to his car lights. He/she now sees a vision of destruction that seems to bring together various aspects of war in a single picture: 'emigraciones masivas, cadáveres desenterrados con saña, estatuas grandiosas derribadas de sus pedestales y destruidas a martillazos, tratados doctinales y abecedarios políticos arrojados al fuego, quemas de huesos, calles y plazas desbautizadas, cuerpos agarrotadas y reducidos a cenizas, viviendas arrasadas con padrón de ignominia, figuras mortecinas, mustias y desmedradas' (p. 16). Yet he/she wonders if these are 'meras fantasías y mentiras' (p. 16).

On the one hand, this refers, of course, to the problem of the accuracy of reporting of the war, as well as to Jean Baudrillard's controversial suggestion that our media-age is such that the conflict was little more that a 'virtual war', or a simulacrum.[41] On the other, however, the description contrasts with one of the striking features of the coverage of the war on Western television, which was precisely the absence of scenes of carnage, partly because of a degree of Allied censoring but also due to the considerable time-delay in the transmission of images and the fact that some were judged too horrific to be placed in the public domain.[42] Goytisolo's depiction of the war is thus a rather complex matter. It is not simply a self-conscious collage of plausible images from the war. Rather, it is presented as a quasi-direct testimony of scenes that were not generally broadcast in the Western world, but perhaps should have been. In this sense, *La cuarentena* seeks to contaminate the mind of the Western reader who, as was the case with *El sitio de los sitios*, may have preferred to ignore the reality of conflict by using the excuse of media deception. As Philip Taylor notes (pp. 276–7), 'there is considerable evidence to suggest that viewers would not have wanted to see the "reality" of war anyway so long as the war was going well for the coalition. [. . .] War is a nasty business and television viewers know it.'

The context in which Goytisolo presents his testimony of carnage – with an intertextual reference to Luis Vélez de Guevara's Golden Age work, *El*

[41] 'The Gulf War: Is It Really Taking Place?', in *The Gulf War Did Not Take Place*, trans. and intro. Paul Patton (Bloomington: Indiana University Press, 1995), pp. 25–59 (p. 41).

[42] In *War and the Media: Propaganda and Persuasion in the Gulf War* (Manchester: Manchester University Press, 1992), Philip Taylor notes the general absence of scenes of destruction in Western reporting, and the consequent impact of the few, relating to battles at Amiriya and Mutlah Gap, which did gain currency (p. 276).

diablo cojuelo, as well as recourse to the voyeuristic issues outlined in the previous chapter – serves to expose the constructed nature of his narrative of war and to connect it to more personal issues that suggest a connection between the narrator and Goytisolo himself.[43] Chapter 4 of the novel begins with direct reference to Vélez de Guevara's 1641 work, a satirical depiction of seventeenth-century Spain revealed to a student, Don Cleofás Leandro Pérez Zambullo, when he releases from imprisonment a lame devil who acompanies him in a flight over Madrid and other peninsular cities. *El diablo cojuelo* is, for Goytisolo's purposes, suitably subtitled 'Verdades soñadas y novelas de la otra vida, traducidas a esta por Luis Vélez de Guevara'. It thus forms part of the long tradition of self-consciousness in Spanish fiction into which our author inserts his own writing.[44] Just as Cleofás' elevated perspective situates him as an onlooker viewing the ills of his society, so Goytisolo's narrator is presented as a voyeur in the use of verbs such as 'atalayar' (p. 19), 'contemplar' (p. 27), and 'divisar' (p. 32), and in his description as a 'mirón' (p. 31) who uses 'prismáticos' (p. 32), or positions himself in an 'atalaya' where 'gemelos' are not necessary (p. 33). The motif of flight as revelation, or a form of visionary experience, is, however, double-edged. It refers both to social satire aimed at the moral improvement of the reader – a form of contamination – and to the mystical sense of personal improvement through a journey towards union with the Divine. So the narrator's flight 'como un diablo cojuelo' is also that of an 'ave, sorprendida de tu propia agilidad y ligereza' experiencing 'la ingravidez rauda y embriaguez extática' (p. 19). Thus, an unexpected union of the self-conscious, satirical tradition in Spanish literature and the mystical one is achieved, allowing Goytisolo to unite apparently contradictory, or divergent, perspectives in an organic manner. In a sense this is appropriate in a novel that draws heavily upon the work of the Murcian Sufi poet, Ibn Arabí, since his work celebrates a union of opposites and expresses it as the fusion of the self with the other: 'unión [. . .], prueba de que el yo y lo ajeno se funden en uno' (*La cuarentena*, p. 59).

43 In interview with Javier Escudero Rodríguez, 'Muerte, erotismo y espiritualidad: entrevista con Juan Goytisolo' (*Revista de Estudios Hispánicos*, 27 [1991], 123–39) Goytisolo remarked (p. 128): 'tampoco soy exactamente el narrador, pero, en fin, digamos hay una afinidad entre el narrador y yo'. In 'Textuality Transcendent: Juan Goytisolo's *La cuarentena* and the Politics of Eschatology', *Journal of Hispanic Research*, 2 (1993–4), 307–24, Ryan Prout identifies the narrator with Goytisolo himself, and, like me, he stresses the union of form and content in this novel, arguing that it represents their binding 'round a common principle to a greater extent than any of Goytisolo's preceding works' (p. 309).

44 *El diablo cojuelo*, anthologized in *Biblioteca de autores españoles desde la formación del lenguaje hasta nuestros días: novelistas posteriores a Cervantes*, ed. Eustaquio Fernández de Navarrete (Madrid: Real Academia Española, 1950), pp. 21–50. This work brings to mind an earlier, more vicious satire of the seventeenth century, which also self-consciously makes use of the motif of two worlds, namely Quevedo's *Sueños y discursos*, first published in 1627.

López-Baralt explores the extensive echoes of Ibn Arabí's writing in *La cuarentena*, drawing a particular connection between his unorthodox works and Goytisolo's own search for a dissident literary tradition.[45] In particular, the emphasis that both place on the writer as a visionary, seeking a superior truth through the 'mind's eye', or 'ojo de la imaginación' (*La cuarentena*, p. 74), is striking. In Sufism, the *barzakh* is, according to López-Baralt, an 'imaginal' world in which 'el visionario auténtico "imagina" y proyecta sobre este plano fluido simultáneamente material e inmaterial toda una constelación privada de imágenes significativas que extrae de lo más recóndito – y de lo más auténtico de su propio ser' (p. 71). She thus interprets Goytisolo's analogy between this intermediate world and the realm of textual creativity as a search for a (literary) identity through the use of a 'pluma visionaria' (p. 78). Indeed, it is tempting to connect the writer's pen – 'pluma' – with the mystical birds of both the *Pájaro solitario* and *La cuarentena*. At the end of the former work, the search of the birds for the mystical Simorgh revealed that they, in together constituiting the Simorgh, were the goal of their own quest; in the latter novel, as we shall shortly see, there is a stong element of self-analysis channelled through intertextual references to previous works by Goytisolo.

Symbolism relating to the eyes pervades *La cuarentena*, uniting two ideas evident, but previously unconnected, in Goytisolo's work: the issue of the onlooker or voyeur, and the Sartrean exchange of glances as an expression of the self–other relationship. Chapter 24, especially, foregrounds the question of gazing, and being gazed at. In it, the narrator's friend describes her fear at a pair of emerald-green eyes, which scrutinize her every move like a 'virus maligno' (p. 74). López-Baralt persuasively argues (pp. 106–7) that these eyes, reminiscent of Goytisolo's own green eyes, symbolize the creative process in which characters are observed, initially by the writer, and later by the reader. However, the gaze need not be aggressive, in the Sartrean mode, as (still in chapter 24) it fades away through the power of the imagination to leave a vision of 'lo que ha sucedido, lo que sucede y lo que sucederá'. One may thus appreciate 'todo el universo [. . .] en la matriz privilegiada de un libro' (p. 75). The threatening gaze is replaced by one of mutual support, which recalls the philosophies of both Merleau-Ponty and Ricoeur, and is expressed memorably by Goytisolo in his citation of Mawlana at the end of his essay, 'Los derviches giróvagos' (p. 45): 'el que ve y el que es visto forman uno en ti mismo'.

Aside this view of self–other relations as mutually supportive, Goytisolo develops a second inflection in the narrative gaze – or 'vigilia de la imaginación' (pp. 79–80) – in *La cuarentena*, by turning it on himself. This is

---

[45] According to López-Baralt, 'Ibn Arabí es el Blanco White o el Miguel de Molinos del sufismo islámico' ('Narrar después de morir', p. 69).

a tendency that we have seen throughout Goytisolo's career, but it becomes most insistent in his last novels, as if, now at the end of his career, he were engaging in a retrospective review of his work. In *La cuarentena*, Goytisolo blurs the division between author and narrator, first, by referring to the *desdoblamiento* that characterized *Señas de identidad* and *Don Julián*, and, then, by alluding to aspects of earlier works. '¿Cómo dialogar', the narrator ponders (p. 20), 'con el cónclave de fantasmas de tu niñez y familia?' Reference is made to his 'doble o doblado' (p. 20) and possible access, through video tapes, to 'escenas de tu pasado' (p. 18). These scenes could be said to appear in the form of allusions to Xemaá-el-Fná, the focal point of *Makbara*, and in the recurrence of the image of a woman killed in an air-raid, which recalls the death of Goytisolo's mother described in *Coto vedado* and recuperated in *El sitio de los sitios*.[46] The narrator of *La cuarentena* wonders if 'las imágenes reproducidas en el telediario, ¿correspondían a lo acaecido después de cuarenta días de infierno aéreo o exhumaban recuerdos sepultos en su memoria de la sombría guerra civil?' (p. 108) *La cuarentena* also acts as a bridge – echoing the symbolic isthmus of the *barzakh* – between the *Pájaro solitario* and *Las semanas del jardín*, the next novel to occupy our attention, through its use of the literary topos of Paradise represented as a garden or, in the words of San Juan in the 'Cántico espiritual', an 'ameno huerto deseado' (*Vida y obras*, p. 405). The garden in *La cuarentena*, like the *barzakh*, is double-edged. It recalls, in its allusions to 'las balaustradas musgosas y macetas de hortensias' (p. 18), the sinister spa-resort where the persecuted figures of the *Pájaro solitario* are confined; but it also celebrates mystical union and looks forward to *Semanas* in representing the 'jardín de la bienaventuranza', which contains 'la fuente que refleja los Ojos alegóricos del Amado, el árbol que crece en el interior del alma contemplativa' (p. 66). The allusion to the lover's eyes is, of course, to San Juan's 'Cántico espiritual', but the reference to a tree also recalls the dissident literary tree that Goytisolo creates through his practice of intertextuality, an activity that makes his writing intensely introspective at the turn of the third millennium.

---

46 The echoes of *Makbara* are discussed by López-Baralt in 'Narrar después de morrir', pp. 85–6. Further parallels might be drawn between the supposed 'Medical Examination of Applicants' in *Juan sin Tierra* (pp. 237–8) and the planned interrogation by Naquir and Muncar in *La cuarentena* (chapter 18); and between the televised critique of Vosk's writing style (pp. 226–9) in the former novel, and the imaginary televised debate in chapter 27 of the latter. There is, however, a marked difference between the use of Arabic in each work. At the end of *Juan sin Tierra*, it both signals and, when translated, explicitly emphasizes, a break in communication; in *La cuarentena* it ironically draws attention to a lack of understanding of the Arab world on the part of the West. For translations of the Arabic see, respectively, Ugarte, *Trilogy of Treason*, p. 147, and López-Baralt, 'Narrar después de morrir', p. 111.

PART IV

AUTHORSHIP AND DISSIDENCE REVISITED

7

THE AUTHOR AS INTERTEXTUAL CRITIC:
LAS SEMANAS DEL JARDÍN, CARAJICOMEDIA
AND *TELÓN DE BOCA*

Nada es nunca seguro del todo, pero he escrito ya mucho,
he perpetrado demasiadas novelas para añadir más.
Me arrepiento de muchas páginas.
Pero escribir es lo único que sé hacer.
Juan Goytisolo[1]

Sunset on a Fictional Career?

In 2003, with the publication of *Telón de boca*, Goytisolo rather dramatically announced an end to his fifty-year career as a writer of fiction.[2] Whether or not this turns out to be the case, the last three novels of Goytisolo's career to date constitute a review of the main preoccupations of his writing since *Señas de identidad*. In this sense, they bring us full circle, for each novel tackles anew the themes of authorship, identity, and dissidence with which this book has been concerned. But these novels are not just a review or summary of past works. They also offer a critique of Goytisolo's dissident textual practice, both in terms of his approach to novel-writing and his thematic preoccupations over the course of almost five decades.[3] The picture of authorship that emerges from *Las semanas del jardín* (1997), *Carajicomedia* (2000), and *Telón de boca* (2003) is radically intertextual, in that it consists of a dialogue between a series of texts, and also paratextual, in that it incorporates elements conventionally regarded as on the margins of the literary text. Thus we find Goytisolo toying with his authorial signature in *Semanas*; critically reassessing his treatment of sexuality in *Carajicomedia*;

---

1   Quoted in Miguel Mora, 'El sábado, España dejó de ser un país de súbditos', *El País*, 18 February 2003.
2   Mora's report on the launch of *Telón de boca* draws a fortuitous parallel between the publication of the novel and Goytisolo's professed reconciliation with his mother country following national protests in Spain at the government's support for the 2004 American and British-led campaign against Saddam Hussein in Iraq.
3   Rafael Conte agrees, in 'Cambio de decorado', *El País*, 15 February 2003, when he writes of the 'proceso de corrección a que está sometiendo [Goytisolo] a su obra anterior en las nuevas aparaciones'.

and exploring the fracture line between fiction and autobiography in *Telón de boca*. This has significant implications for our present argument, since Goytisolo now deliberately flaunts his practice of simultaneously erasing and reinscribing the authorial presence in his works, and he also subjects that authorial identity to scrutiny as he reviews his fictional and non-fictional output. As if to defy Derrida's notion of thanatography – or the inscription of the authorial signature as fixity and so a form of death[4] – Goytisolo asserts authorial control as a means of correcting the past and reasserting, yet again, his identity as a dissident.

The Creation of the Author: Las semanas del jardín

Las semanas de jardín demonstrates well the interconnected nature of Goytisolo's late novels. In its title, first epigraph, and overall construction, it echoes that Cervantine trend that has broadly characterized the author's fiction since *Don Julián*; in the image of the 'culto y ameno jardín' with which it opens, it recalls the mystical novels discussed in the previous chapter; and in beginning with a reference to a heterodox poet named Eusebio, it quite literally picks up where *El sitio de los sitios* leaves off. The novel thus draws together the works discussed in chapters 5 and 6 above, and develops them through a quasi-Pirandellian search for a hero (rather than an author), which is presented as a collective writing process. With its 'círculo de lectores' who replace the traditional, univocal author, it dramatizes the active process of reading that lies at the heart of Goytisolo's view of the creative act.

Superficially, *Las semanas del jardín* would seem not so much to dethrone, as quite simply to ignore, the figure of the author. If we consider the paratextual aspects of the book – its external presentation through authorial attribution, the choice of title, and so on[5] – we note that the name Juan Goytisolo appears nowhere on the front cover or flaps of the novel, and it is only included in the copyright material with regard to the photograph of the author included in the cover illustration.[6] The standard layout of the title

---

[4] Jacques Derrida, *The Ear of the Other: Otobiography, Transference, Translation*, trans. Peggy Kamuf, ed. Christie McDonald (Lincoln: University of Nebraska Press, 1985), p. 6.

[5] Technically, in *Paratexts*, Genette distinguishes two types of paratextual element: the 'peritextual', with which I am specifically concerned here, and the 'epitextual' (more distanced relations, such as authorial interviews, private letters and other such commentaries). However, the distinction serves little purpose in the present context, and I have avoided unnecessarily confusing terminology.

[6] *Las semanas del jardín: un círculo de lectores* (Madrid: Alfaguara, 1997), p. 6. In fact there are two photographs of Goytisolo in the edition: one forming part of the cover illustration, the other on the inside front flap, where it is customary to give biographical

page and cover in Alfaguara literary editions is reversed: instead of the author's name appearing in large type and the work's title beneath it in smaller type, the title of *Semanas* replaces the authorial attribution and its supposed creators, 'un círculo de lectores', occupies the space normally given over to the title of the work.[7] In *Semanas*, the work itself can thus be said to usurp the position of the author.[8] As we shall see, though, the result of this rejection of conventional markers of authorship is not a Barthesian death of the author, but the simultaneous disappearance and reinscription of the figure of Juan Goytisolo as author. For as Gould Levine argues, Goytisolo's interest in the recuperation of memory in fiction extends to his own past in *Semanas*, and, as a consequence, 'por más que nosotros, los lectores, inventemos y textualicemos a Juan Goytisolo, el autor está siempre presente autorizando ciertas lecturas, satirizando otras o estableciendo los límites entre un tipo de literatura destinado a un público lector comerical y la escritura que cultiva él.'[9]

Las semanas del jardín does not reject the figure of the author, then, but dramatizes the complementary forces of centrifugal and centripetal movement which both dethrone him from his privileged position in the text and, paradoxically, reinscribe him as its focal point. In this sense, it recalls the attempted dethronement of the author in *Juan sin Tierra*, though the view is now more nuanced, offering not a textual *vagabundeo*, but an exploration of the mutual and complementary contribution of authors and readers in the creative process. This is evident in the Cervantine heritage upon which the book draws in its title and first epigraph. *Las semanas del jardín* is the title of a work announced by Cervantes in the prologue to *Los trabajos de Persiles y Segismunda* but never finished.[10] According to Daniel Eisenberg's edition of

and bibliographical details of the author of the work concerned. Instead of providing the latter, *Semanas* quotes the concluding section of the novel, which narrates the apparently arbitrary invention, by the circle of readers, of a certain Juan Goytisolo who might fulfil the conventional role of 'author' of the text.

7   This is evident from any Alfaguara edition, but all the more noticeable since Goytisolo's previous novel, *El sitio de los sitios*, also published by that Madrid house, followed the usual house style. The full title of Goytisolo's 1997 novel is conventionally given as *Las semanas del jardín: un círculo de lectores*, though this may in fact be inaccurate, given the play with authorship in which the work indulges.

8   Though the supposed circle of readers is arguably an allusion to the Círculo de Lectores, which has published editions of Goytisolo's works in recent years. In this case, the publisher would be usurping the place of the author.

9   Linda Gould Levine, 'En torno a Juan Goytisolo: un círculo de lectores', in *Un círculo de relectores: jornadas sobre Juan Goytisolo*, ed. Inger Enkvist (Almería: Instituto de Estudios Almerienses, 1999), pp. 125–34 (p. 127).

10 A more recent literary antecedent is Rafael Sánchez Ferlosio's *Las semanas del jardín* (1974). Beyond the titular similarity and a general looseness of structure, however, neither it nor Goytisolo's novel display any detailed engagement with Cervantes' work as we know it. On Sánchez Ferlosio, see Roberto Echavarren, ' "Las semanas del jardín" de

a brief and incomplete manuscript of the work, it consists of a dialogue between Selanio and Cilenia on a range of subjects, including the question of the pleasures and pitfalls of storytelling itself.[11] In this it echoes many of Cervantes' most famous works, including the *Quixote*, from which Goytisolo's novel takes its first epigraph concerning the discovery of the 'Novela de Rinconete y Cortadillo'.

The episode of the discovery of one of Cervantes' own works in the *Quixote* draws attention to the issue of literary pleasure in a variety of ways. It stresses the importance of the skill of the writer and high quality of his/her storytelling, the participation and judgements of readers in the oral delivery of a work, and the blurring of the boundaries between fiction and reality. Although it is tempting to see Cervantes' intertextual reference to one of his own short stories against the background of the game of mirrors that he plays in relation to the authorship of the *Quixote* – with its plethora of authors, editors, translators, and other such generally paratextual figures – the true impact of the allusion to what has become one of the most famous of the *Novelas ejemplares* is in fact to affirm his authorship. Indeed, given that the collection of stories in which 'Rinconete y Cortadillo' is now included was published in 1613, eight years after the first part of the *Quixote*, this reference might even be seen as a form of advance publicity.[12] The Cervantine epigraph therefore has a rather ambiguous function in Goytisolo's novel. On the one hand, it emphasizes the act of reading, both in reminding us that Goytisolo himself is a voracious reader, and in recalling the many contributions made by Cervantes' characters, acting as readers, to the picture that his work offers of the art of storytelling. On the other hand, it counters the concealment of the author that the paratextual material in *Semanas* appears to create, by reminding us of a moment in fiction when the mantle of authorial responsibility was flaunted by Cervantes. Although *Semanas* seems to point to the idea of literary creativity as an effect of reading, this epigraph undermines that by hinting that the author has a higher profile and a more active role than one might think. And Juan Goytisolo is, in fact, a very pervasive presence in *Semanas*, both through echoes of his earlier works and in the complex relationship that is woven between himself, as author, and Eusebio, the hero of the novel.

As I noted above, *Semanas* contains references to a plethora of Goytisolo's earlier works. The image of the garden and the quasi-mystical symbolism of

Sánchez Ferlosio: narratividad y sujeto', *Cuadernos Hispanoamericanos*, 384 (1982), 669–77; Squires, *Experience and Objectivity in the Writings of Rafael Sánchez Ferlosio.*

[11] *Las semanas del jardín de Miguel de Cervantes*, ed. Daniel Eisenberg (Salamanca: Diputación Provincial de Salamanca, 1988).

[12] The order of composition of the *Novelas ejemplares* is unclear, though in *Novel to Romance: A Study of Cervantes's 'Novelas ejemplares'* (Baltimore: Johns Hopkins University Press, 1974), Ruth El Saffar argues, on the basis of this reference in the *Quixote*, that a manuscript of 'Rinconete y Cortadillo' existed as early as 1604 (p. 30, n. 1).

the stork in search of happiness in the 'AÍN' section recall the *Pájaro solitario*; the early reference to the feminist scholar, Ms Lewin-Strauss, in 'ALIF' (p. 12) revives a character from *La saga de los Marx*;[13] and the discussion of approaches to writing in that same chapter echoes a similar debate in *Juan sin Tierra*. According to *Semanas*, there are two opposed narrative trends in the history of the novel (p. 13): 'una pretendía trazar en línea recta o zigzag la continuación de la historia y construir el personaje a bandazos; otra se inclinaba hacia un tipo de narración arborescente, con digresiones y alternativas que, desde un tronco central, engendraban relatos autónomos o engastados.' This is a reformulation of the contrast between 'aquellas novelas que [. . .] son reflejo veraz y sincero de las sociedades en que se crean, merced a la introducción de personajes vivos y auténticos, sometidos a las pasiones y achaques de los hombres de carne y hueso' (*Juan sin Tierra*, p. 211) and 'una escritura formal y abstracta, mera expresión enajenada, a menudo esquizofrénica, de obsesiones y complejos personales que, en lugar de ser reflejo objetivo del mundo, postulan tan sólo el intento de liberación, desesperado y parcial, de una mentalidad enferma' (*Juan sin Tierra*, p. 212). In the inverse symbolic scheme of *Juan sin Tierra*, of course, this sickly discourse is celebrated as a description of the novel itself. By the time of *Semanas*, Goytisolo's terminology may have changed, but his outline of the history of the novel genre has not, nor has his preference for the second approach. This novel is thus a 'jardín cervantino' and a Borgesian realm of 'senderos y bifurcaciones' (p. 13), a collection of chapters ordered by no more than chance selection 'por sorteo' (p. 13), and written by a series of figures from varying literary, political, social, and philosophical backgrounds.

Of course, the suggestion that the chapters are ordered by lottery raises the question of just who might have conducted the lottery in the first place,[14] and, indeed, transcribed the various contributions of the 'círculo de lectores'. We are told that there is an 'anónimo escribano' whose only role, with due deference to the ideas of Genette, was 'la estructuración de lo que algún crítico de vanguardia llamaría "hipertexto"' (p. 14).[15] So the work of the scribe who

---

13 Epps has suggested (*Significant Violence*, p. 439) that although this name is a parody of Claude Lévi-Strauss, it may also recall one of Goytisolo's foremost feminist critics, Linda Gould Levine. The latter is non-plussed by the comparison in 'En torno a Juan Goytisolo', p. 125, n. 3.

14 Genette notes the peremptory potential of paratextual elements that indicate in what order the elements of a book might be read (p. 11). Although Goytisolo's implicit instruction relates to the composition of *Semanas*, and is included within the actual text, it does point beyond it to that intermediate zone that Genette studies.

15 Goytisolo actually misuses Genette's term, since hypertext refers to the imposition of a later text on an earlier one, through its intertextual reworking – hence, Joyce's *Ulysses* is a hypertext imposed on Homer's *Odyssey*, which Genette terms the hypotext (see Macksey's foreword, *Paratexts*, p. xv).

intervened in the construction of *Semanas* apparently remained outside the main body of the text, and his role would seem to have consisted mainly in the concealment of the figure of the author through the removal of his name from the front cover of the book. Nevertheless, it is not so easy to separate the text from its external presentation, especially since the game of mirrors vis-à-vis authorial attribution that we considered above extends Goytisolo's usual metafictional practice beyond the bounds of the written text to include its presentation to the consumer public. In seeking, through the use of well-worn and readily recognizable strategies, to conceal himself behind the smoke-screen of a circle of authors and a neutral scribe, Goytisolo in fact uses paratextual elements to reinforce his own authorial responsibility for *Semanas*. And his presence is all the more evident in the metaphors chosen in the novel to describe his preferred form of narrative. If, in *Juan sin Tierra*, direct reference was made to an author drawing upon 'obsesiones y complejos personales', in *Semanas* the apparently more objective description of a 'narración arborescente', starting from and returning to 'un tronco central', is, in fact, highly personal to Goytisolo. It draws upon his standard image of literary inspiration, encapsulated in the title of the collection of essays, *El árbol de la literatura*, as arising out of personal readings of the branches of the Spanish literary tree, with special emphasis on a dissident central trunk.

Goytisolo's presence can also be detected behind the figure of Eusebio, the hero whose life the circle of readers attempt to uncover in the course of their twenty-eight interventions in *Semanas*. The difficulty of the circle of readers in fixing a clear identity for Eusebio would seem to echo a postmodern view of the subject as fluid, even performative. Eusebio recalls various other Goytisolan personages, including the persecuted poet in *El sitio de los sitios* and the mysterious narrator of the *Pájaro solitario* who suffers drug-induced hallucinations. His schizoid personality (p. 21) is reminiscent of the protagonist-narrator of *Señas de identidad* and *Don Julián*, as well as of the myticism of Ibn Arabí that informs *La cuarentena*. But the salient feature of Eusebio's character is the manner in which he adopts various guises throughout *Semanas*. He becomes Eugenio Asensio in the 'JA' section, and is then transformed into the early nineteenth-century Polish author Jan Potocki, author of *Le manuscrit trouvé a Saragosse*, in 'LAM' and 'MIM'.[16] Potocki is explicitly connected with Eugenio by the fact that the dates of the epitaph on his grave, 1903–72, coincide with Eugenio's and are not Potocki's at all (p. 155).

---

[16] Potocki's work was originally written in French. The first part was published in St Petersburg in 1804–5, and the second in Paris in 1813. There is an English edition, *The Manuscript Found in Saragossa*, trans. Ian Maclean (Harmondsworth: Penguin, 1996). A Spanish translation appeared in the same year, just one year before the publication of *Semanas*: Jan Potocki, *El manuscrito encontrado en Zaragoza*, ed. and preface Roger Caillois, trans. José Bianco (Barcelona: Minotauro, 1996).

Potocki, also known as Alphonse van Worden, even becomes Madame van Worden, disguised with 'maquillaje atroz, peluca rubia, traje de organdí de holgadas mangas' (p. 160), in a theatrical spectacle that recalls the fantastic figure of the 'doña' in the *Pájaro solitario*.

Identity as performance would seem, then, to lie behind the depiction of Eusebio, yet certain aspects of his presentation recall Goytisolo's discussion of personal identity in *Coto vedado*, and, in addition, bring to mind our author's identification with the poet Luis Cernuda, discussed in chapter 2 above. Eusebio's schizoid personality is explored in the 'ZA' section as a double identity, his 'true' nature as a homosexual concealed behind the reformed image he is forced to portray by his Nationalist mentors. 'Me veo obligado,' the hero remarks, 'a extremar las precauciones, controlar las menores palabras y gestos.' And he goes on,

> Constantemente me esfuerzo en observarme a mí mismo desde el punto de vista ajeno, el de los posibles confidentes que me acechan y aguardan un instante de descuido. [. . .] Este continuo ejercicio de fingir emociones que no siento y acallar las que me sacuden con la fuerza del deseo es a la larga corrosivo y agotador.   (p. 71)

Eusebio also recalls certain consoling lines from Cernuda 'leídos y releídos antes por mi *alter ego*'. 'Una chispa de aquellos placeres,' he notes (p. 75), 'podía destruir con su fulgor la opacidad del mundo.'

In several respects, this episode in *Semanas* is reminiscent of the 'guerra civil íntima de mi sexo y lengua' (*Coto vedado*, p. 38), which Goytisolo explores in his autobiography. First, although Eusebio's story is literally set against the backdrop of the 1936 uprising and is interwoven with references to Falangist discourse, duly acknowledged in the list of reading at the end of the novel, his life is the same metaphorical civil war between an authentic and inauthentic self that Goytisolo described as a feature of his own youth in *Coto vedado*. Second, the idea of censoring one's own actions in the face of others' opinions underpins Goytisolo's Jekyll-and-Hyde presentation of his first homosexual experience with his young friend Lucho, just as it characterizes Eusebio's actions in *Semanas*. Third, the allusion to an alter ego who finds delight in Cernuda's poetry recalls Goytisolo's own identification with the poet and his imitation of the *desdoblamiento* that is a feature of *La realidad y el deseo*. Thus, the seemingly absent author of *Semanas* reappears behind his novel's hero in a series of intertextual references that return us to the starting point of this study.

Goytisolo also enters his novel thanks to a paratextual interplay between the 'AÍN' section, which narrates the story of 'los hombres-cigüeña', and the collage of the front cover, where his photograph is juxtaposed with a picture of a stork. Text and paratext are thus linked more closely than might at first be suspected. The story of the stork-men is essentially an allegory representing the author's relationship to his fictional characters. If the quarantine of *La cuarentena* symbolized the author's withdrawal from society during a period of a literary creativity, then the 'transformista' (p. 116) of *Semanas* is a symbol of the author's ability to adopt various guises, imaginatively visit different locations, and speak through the personages he invents. Intriguingly, the 'transformista' is 'de aspecto similar al atribuido por mis colegas a Eusebio' (p. 117). The tale of the stork-men brings together the two aspects of literary creativity that Goytisolo weaves together in *Semanas*, namely reading and writing. The tale, we are told, may either be an invention of the 'transformista' or taken from folklore. It is presented in the storyteller's own words and recited only once, to a poet by the name of Eusebio who 'escribió palabra por palabra la misma historia que a usted le acabo de relatar' (p. 124). Thus Eusebio becomes the author of the story told by the stork-man, who is implictly linked to Goytisolo by the photomontage on the cover of *Semanas*. If Goytisolo is, in some instances, identified with Eusebio, and at others Eusebio is linked to Goytisolo, then the reader is left with the impression that, behind the shifting sands of Eusebio's shady identity lies the author whose presence has been superficially elided from his novel, only to be inserted in subtle ways through both intertextual and paratextual strategies. In the light of this, the invention of a certain Juan Goytisolo by the circle of readers at the conclusion of *Semanas*, and the insertion of his photo on the flap of the book, seems less a Foucaultian gesture, in which the author is simply reduced to a literary convention, than a last-minute reassertion of Goytisolo's authority over his work: his readers know that, despite the games he plays, he is the author of the book and, if nothing else, the owner of the copyright of his own picture on its cover.[17]

Intertextual Revision in Carajicomedia

The second novel that concerns us in this chapter, *Carajicomedia*, also relies upon an intertextual critique of Goytisolo's earlier works. As Juan Masoliver notes, the novel is an autobiographization of *Las virtudes del pájaro solitario* as well as a novelization of the second volume of Goytisolo's autobiography, *En los reinos de Taifa*.[18] It also contains imitations of several Golden Age works, thus continuing Goytisolo's interest in literary creativity

[17] Although, at the launch of *Semanas*, Goytisolo refused to answer questions in the name of its author, stating 'soy un autor inventado' (Miguel Vilena, 'Juan Goytisolo concibe la novela como una aventura, "y no como un trayecto en autobús"', *El País*, 6 November 1997), his desire to reject authorial responsibility reaches a limit with the need to protect his own identity through the copyright of his image. Furthermore, although beyond the bounds of his control, both the Biblioteca National de España and the Library of Congress have cataloged this novel under Goytisolo's authorship.

[18] Juan A. Masoliver Ródenas, 'El hipócrita y el escribidor', *La Vanguardia*, 11 February 2000. A more detailed discussion of *Carajicomedia* may be found in my article,

as a form of intertextuality. The most obvious of these references is to the original 'Carajicomedia', a burlesque poem, possibly written by a member of the clergy using the name Fray Bugeo Montesinos, which was included in the 1519 edition of the *Cancionero de obras de burlas provocantes a risa*. Itself a parody of another text, the medieval *Trescientas* by Juan de Mena, the sixteenth-century 'Carajicomedia' recounts in explicit language the sexual adventures of one Diego Fajardo, along with editorial comments from the 'author' on the merits of his story for contemplative souls.[19] Less obvious perhaps is the inclusion of the *Vida de don Gregorio Guadaña*, a pseudo-picaresque tale that formed part of a larger work, *El siglo pitagórico*, by Antonio Enríquez Gómez, first published in 1644. Enríquez employs metempsychosis, or the transmigration of souls through different ages, as a means to portray the customs of various eras. This is a gesture that Goytisolo imitates, in echo of Eusebio's fluid identity in *Semanas*, through the transmigrations of the figures of various gay 'priests' who recount their sexual adventures throughout Spanish history. Joyce-like, he will also imitate a variety of literary styles and allude to specific works that are identified by the inclusion of relevant citations at the end of *Carajicomedia*. The purpose of this, we are told rather didactically, is an invitation to future reading. What is shared by the texts Goytisolo chooses to feature in his 'Oxen of the Sun' episode is sexual frankness, a parodic tone, and a marked self-consciousness.

Against these intertexts is set the travesty of a modern religious work, *Camino*, by the founder of the Opus Dei movement, St Josémaría Escrivá de Balaguer. Through the apparently burlesque intertextualization of Escrivá's maxims, Goytisolo transforms the proselytizing zeal of Opus into an homosexualizing zeal in which a canon of saintly dissidents 'spreads the word' as they transmigrate through the centuries. The combination of sexuality, religion, and dissidence is thus completed through the intertextual play of various medieval and modern works. However, it is clear that the medieval intertexts that Goytisolo uses are regarded in a positive light – a kind of Bakhtinian parody that implies dialogue without condemnation – whereas *Camino* is mocked and ridiculed.

The technique that Goytisolo employs here relies on a simple reversal: the discourse of religion subverted by that of sexuality. Thus, the burlesque missionaries of *Carajicomedia* carry out their work in the 'temples' of the seedier public toilets of Paris districts such as Barbès and Rochechouart. The stated goal of the novel is 'una historia de la sexualidad a la luz de la doctrina católica por medio de un viaje por la lengua castellana desde la Edad Media

'The Mystical and the Burlesque: The Portrayal of Homosexuality in Juan Goytisolo's *Carajicomedia*', *Romance Studies*, 21 (2002), 105–14.

[19] See, for example, the authorial comment following copla XI. For the publication history of the *Cancionero de obras de burlas provocantes a risa*, see the introduction to Frank Domínguez's edition (Madrid: Albatros, 1978).

hasta hoy'.[20] Sexual intercourse becomes prayer and the partaking of communion; at other times, in a self-conscious mode that echoes *Juan sin Tierra*, it is (verbal) 'conjugation'.[21]

The travesty of Escrivá, however, works on another level, revealing what Goytisolo has termed the textual libido of *Camino*.[22] It, he suggests, contains a repressed admiration for virility that reveals a latent preoccupation with sexuality. Thus, he highlights self-mortification through whipping and the wearing of the 'cicilio' as masochistic activities. He also points to a maxim such as number 615, 'Viriliza tu voluntad: que sea, con la gracia de Dios, un espolón de acero', as containing a not-so-repressed sexual metaphor. In another example, he quotes the line 'una maza de acero poderosa, envuelta en una funda acolchada' (no. 397). Finally, he connects the following two maxims in order to highlight a potential sexual resonance: 'Sé instrumento . . . grande o chico, delicado o tosco: tu deber es ser instrumento' (no. 484) and 'Los instrumentos no pueden estar mohosos' (no. 486).[23]

Goytisolo's gay saints, then, do no more in *Carajicomedia* than follow to the letter the instructions of the author of *Camino*. One, Abdelkader, possesses a 'bastón de mando, generador y dador de placer y energías' and shows the narrator 'el látigo con el que disciplinaba a uno de sus fervorosos clientes, ávido de penitencia y mortificación' (pp. 51–3). Another, Abdalá, has a 'sagrario cuya mole, longitud y grosor he calibrado sólo cuatro o cinco veces en mi bienaventurada vida' (p. 42). A third, Kítir, drags the narrator 'casi a fuerza, a los lavabos del sótano' and submits him to 'una comunión ruda con la santa coacción y santa desvergüenza exhortadas por nuestro fundador' (p. 48). The saintly/sexual impudence of Goytisolo's saints is clear in these passages, but more significant is the emphasis upon clichéd notions of virility and sexual prowess. These gravitate around the idea of power, so that self-mortification becomes sado-masochistic pleasure, and the size and steel-like hardness of a partner's member is all important.

Goytisolo thus reveals a hidden sexual element within religious discourse. His descriptions of sex play upon the ambiguous relation between mystical and sexual satisfaction already evident in the *Pájaro solitario*, which is itself recuperated as an intertext in *Carajicomedia*. The term 'pájaro', for example,

---

[20] *Carajicomedia de Fray Bugeo Montesino y otros pájaros de vario plumaje y pluma* (Barcelona: Seix Barral, 2000), p. 20.

[21] See, for example, *Carajicomedia*, pp. 71, 48, and 28 respectively. In *Juan sin Tierra* the difficulty of sexual intercourse for the 'Parejita Reproductora' is signalled by an attempted conjugation of verbs, which lapses into the subjunctive mood as their failure becomes apparent (*Juan sin Tierra*, pp. 63–4).

[22] The phrase is from Goytisolo's speech at the launch of *Carajicomedia*, Círculo de Bellas Artes, Madrid, 24 February 2000, published as 'La libido textual de *Camino*', *El País*, 26 February 2000, and included in *Pájaro que ensucia su propio nido: artículos y ensayos* (Barcelona: Círculo de Lectores, 2001), pp. 132–6.

[23] These are all included in 'La libido textual de *Camino*'.

is retained in the full title of the new book – *Carajicomedia de Fray Bugeo Montesino y otros pájaros de vario plumaje y pluma* – and a number of important images are appropriated from the *Pájaro solitario*. Thus, we find references to the 'birds' as having both masculine and feminine gender. 'Pájaro' is, of course, grammatically masculine, but Goytisolo's use of the feminine deliberately imitates mysticism's designation of the poet as an 'alma' in search of God. In *Carajicomedia*, the gay saints not only prove their virility à la Escrivá, but are also at times the 'Hermanas del Perpetuo Socorro' (pp. 43, 71–2, 223). Gender, as an aspect of identity, thus becomes shifting and mutable. Furthermore, picking up on a very precise echo of the *Pájaro solitario* in a description of anal penetration as entry into the lover's 'bodega', Goytisolo creates a complex intertextual echo that retains the mystical idiom beneath a sexual metaphor. In the *Pájaro solitario*, the lines of two mystics, San Juan de la Cruz and Ibn al-Farid, were united as epigraphs: 'En la interior bodega de mi amado bebí [. . .] un vino que nos embriagó antes de la creación de la viña.'[24] The liquid metaphor of spiritual/literal drunkenness becomes an approximation to the experience of the mystic trance and, of course, a metaphor for sexual satisfaction. Slightly later in *Carajicomedia* another image from the *Pájaro solitario*, the divine 'bálsamo' of mystical satisfaction, reappears as the proselytizing zeal of one of the saints is described as a balsam and lubricant for his lovers.[25]

Along with these intertextual links to the *Pájaro solitario*, Goytisolo engages in a dialogue with his second autobiographical volume, *En los reinos de Taifa*, in what becomes a self-conscious meditation on his previous textual presentation of homosexuality. In that book Goytisolo recounted his first adult homosexual experience, with Mohamed, an Arab whom he met in a café – or 'temple'? – in Barbès. The attentive reader of Goytisolo will recognize echoes of that account of robust homosexual intercourse – described as 'goce viril' – in the characters of Abdelkader, Abdalá, and Kítir mentioned above.[26] To these might be added two further figures: Buselham, who is 'sujeto a ramalazos incontrolables de violencia' (p. 31), and Lajdar, with whom the narrator experiences 'visiones turbadoras de su miembro erguido, hieratismo facial, manos grandes y bastas, de inocente brutalidad' (p. 35). However, Mohamed himself also appears in *Carajicomedia*, making him a figure worthy of closer scrutiny.[27]

24 *Pájaro solitario*, p. 163; *Carajicomedia*, p. 61.
25 San Juan uses the phrase 'bálsamo divino' in the 'Cántico espiritual', p. 404. Goytisolo adapts it in the *Pájaro solitario* by giving it a sexual connotation, p. 165, and repeats this in *Carajicomedia*, p. 77.
26 The phrase 'goce viril' occurs in *En los reinos de Taifa*, p. 230.
27 We are explicitly told that he is the lover from *Reinos* in *Carajicomedia*, p. 27. Furthermore, the dates given there for the affair, beginning in April 1963, coincide with those mentioned in the autobiography (p. 223).

The description of the initial encounter with Mohamed, though only sketched in *Reinos*, reflects certain stereotypical notions of both the Arab world and of male virility. Mohamed has an earthy quality, with a 'mostacho montaraz y labios rotundos' (p. 225), and his frankness and sexual spontaneity are conveyed in the way in which he first casually invites Goytisolo to sleep with him after a few drinks and then jumps expectantly into bed as the author undresses. Mohamed exudes a magnetism that captivates Goytisolo. Thus begins his fascination with the Arab world, an 'acercamiento a un modelo físico y cultural de cuerpo cuyo fulgor e incandescencia me guiaban como un faro' (p. 225). The latent sexual imagery of the word 'faro' will be familiar to Goytisolo's readers,[28] as will his problematic idealization of Arab sexuality. As a result of this first, robust homosexual encounter, literature and desire mingle to offer Goytisolo a personal sexual and literary rebirth, for he realizes that 'conjugando de golpe sexualidad y escritura, podía forjar [. . .] un nuevo lenguaje alquitarado y decantado en la dura, pugnaz expression del deseo, largo, seminal proceso originado en el aleatorio encuentro inicial' (p. 226).

This association of homosexual intercourse and violent, innovative, rebellious writing – 'seminal' in both senses of the word – has, as we noted in chapter 1, been much criticized, as has the fact that Goytisolo deliberately embraces a sexually subservient role and then, through his activities as a letter-writer for his illiterate lovers, lords over them intellectually, reinforcing the master–slave relationship that structures the encounters. In Goytisolo's favour one might counter that he admits in *Reinos* to this sado-masochistic view of pleasure, noting that he instinctively sought 'la manera de contrapesar mi sumisión física con una dominación intelectual' (p. 228). More importantly, the parodic tone of *Carajicomedia* effects a retrospective questioning of the initial depiction of homosexual sex as violent and as an exchange between sexual and intellectual domination. In this sense, the different sets of intertexts – those from Goytisolo's own works and those written by other writers – are drawn into a dialogue in which each group influences the way in which the other is interpreted. Hence, the Arab lovers from *Reinos* are not simply reintroduced in *Carajicomedia*; the author's experience with them is actually refracted through his parody of repressed virility in *Camino*, so that the mockery of the textual libido of Escrivá's text also entails a parody of the presentation of homosexual intercourse in *Reinos*. If, in the autobiography, Mohamed's moustache, described as 'montaraz', symbolizes a wild, untamed sexuality that Goytisolo will later associate with the Arab world generally, then in *Carajicomedia* he is endowed with all the attributes of a virile 'saint'. He sports 'un espeso bigote negro del que se

---

[28] In *Juan sin Tierra* there is much word play associated with the terms 'faro' and 'falo', especially in the third section.

servía diestramente al besar', and is well-endowed: 'su mano de almirez enhestaba al menor roce su gloria como el viril de la custodia en manos del oficiante' (p. 27). The depiction of Mohamed, however, is not just part of Goytisolo's general parody of latent sexuality in *Camino*, for it also taps into the mystical idiom. 'Recuerdo algunas noches', the narrator recounts, 'de llama intensa cuando, después de las preces, escuchaba el ritmo pausado de su respiración y disponía a voluntad, con mi inmediatez corporal, de la instantánea rigidez de la columna central de su templo' (p. 27). Goytisolo thus uses humour against himself as well as Escrivá, uniting a burlesque discourse that reverses the terms of religion and sexuality – for example, 'la columna central de su templo' – with a mystical one – 'llama intensa', or, slightly later, 'el fervor de los rezos' and 'la unión transformante' (p. 28). The discursive instability thus established suggests that Goytisolo aims to move beyond an oppositional aesthetic, setting up an intertextual dialogue that hovers between the parodic and the ecstatic, the burlesque and the mystical, without either of them achieving total dominance.

To underline this mocking yet serious autobiographical reassessment in *Carajicomedia* Goytisolo inserts himself into the text in a standard meta-fictional manoeuvre. In the novel there features a copyist – presumably a reincarnation of the medieval scribe of the first 'Carajicomedia', but also an echo of the numerous scribes in Goytisolo's works from *Paisajes después de la batalla* onwards – by the name of Juan Goytisolo who has previously written novels and (apparently now) *fictive* autobiographies (p. 26). When a character from *Carajicomedia* queries the genre of the book, asking if it is an autobiography or a novel, he receives the following reply: 'Lo que nuestro común amigo pretende es disponer el oído a la escucha de las voces del pasado para apropiarse de ellas y convertirse en dueño y señor de su escritura' (p. 20). As we saw in chapter 2, this has been a constant of Goytisolo's writing throughout his career. And among the plethora of voices from the past in *Carajicomedia*, we discover Goytisolo's own, or rather, several of Goytisolo's past literary voices refracted through a corpus of texts that spans the medieval and modern eras. This intertextual play serves to problematize the author's earlier treatment of homosexuality, and, by means of a discursive flux which oscillates between the mystical and the burlesque, offers in *Carajicomedia* a new perspective on one of the constant themes of Goytioslo's writing.

The End of the Road: Telón de boca

The issue of the ambiguous overlap between autobiography and fiction, manifest in an exploration of the interconnectedness of life and death, is a central preoccupation of Goytisolo's literary swansong, the paradoxically named *Telón de boca*. Unrendered as yet into English, the title of this novel might be loosely translated as 'Curtains', since it designates the cloth concealing the stage from the audience prior to the beginning of a theatrical performance. As Black notes, the title echoes Beckett's *Waiting for Godot*,[29] though Goytisolo reverses the Irishman's understanding of the *theatrum mundi* motif, since his protagonist seeks to pass beyond the theatrical curtain in search of some more 'authentic' reality in the afterlife, whereas Beckett's characters, in a gesture that underlines the meaningless absurdity of life, seek to leave the stage via the backcloth. For Goytisolo, picking up, perhaps unconsciously, on Calderón's *El gran teatro del mundo* (though there is no direct reference in the novel to the Golden Age dramatist), life has been a mere prelude and the true performance is yet to begin.[30] Yet what that 'performance' may consist of is unclear, and therein, suggests Goytisolo, lies the real predicament of the human condition.

Telón de boca is, like *Carajicomedia*, a carthatic reassessment of the author's past life. Despite attempts by the narrator of the novel to take succour from 'la desmemoria [que] le ayudaría a salvar el bache' (p. 13), the past persistently returns in two parallel moments of personal tragedy, the death of 'ella', a haunting absence in the novel,[31] and 'la muerte materna escamoteada medio siglo atrás' (p. 14). As a result of a series of intertextual references, it becomes clear that these two female figures are direct echoes of Goytisolo's wife, Monique Lange, and his mother. 'Había un antes y un después', notes the narrator:

> El del niño privado súbitamente del calor materno y el del viejo que encajó la noticia y se sobrevivía a sí mismo en las ruinas del edificio construido por ella, sin admitir del todo que también él estaba muerto. (p. 19)

In the two sections of chapter 1 that follow, Goytisolo includes resonances of Lange's own literary works, alluding to her semi-autobiographical novel, *Las casetas de baño*, in which she narrates a solitary trip to the Normandy coast and laments the frequent absences of her husband (*Telón*, p. 69). Indeed, in its reference to the seemingly indeterminate, yet all pervasive, figure of 'ella', *Telón* pays homage to *Casetas*, where the narrator's husband is simply deignated by the third-person pronoun. Explaining her loneliness, and recalling Goytisolo's own travel writings, the narrator writes, 'Él se había

---

[29] 'Literary Swansong or Wild Goose Chase?: *Telón de boca* by Juan Goytisolo', unpublished paper, Annual Conference of the Association of Hispanists of Great Britain and Ireland, University of Cambridge, 28–31 March 2004.

[30] This is the import of Calderón's *auto sacramental*, in which the 'actors' are judged on their performance in life by the 'author', symbolizing God. *El gran teatro del mundo, El gran mercado del mundo*, ed. Eugenio Frutos Cortés (Madrid: Cátedra, 1989).

[31] A similarly vague strategy is used in *La cuarentena* to refer to the narrator's recently deceased friend. The connection between 'ella' and Monique Lange is evident in the time line of *Telón*'s writing, beginning in November 1996, the year of her death.

marchado a Carboneras, Murcia, Almería. Está camino de Marraquech o tal vez en Damasco, Tiznit, Estambul.'[32]

The absence, in *Telón*, of the narrator's mother from his life is more categorical. 'Nunca se veía a sí mismo en brazos maternos,' he writes (p. 25), 'sólo imágenes de la desaparecida sin relación directa con él.' Yet, paradoxically, his relationship with her was 'de entrega absoluta, de dicha efímera, pero total'. The most meaningful relationships in life are thus the most precarious, as the past is reduced to 'una colección de imágenes girsáceas, desesperadamente fijas' (p. 31). This emphasis on photos recalls their importance as visual memories in *Señas de identidad*. Instead of the search for meaning and coherence in life which that novel dramatized, however, *Telón* narrates the impossibly utopic nature of the search for an authentic identity. For Goytisolo's latest narrator (p. 31), 'su vida no tenía consistencia: actores y comparsas surgían y desaparecían en una incoherente sucesión de cuadros mudos'. And his mood at the end of the first chapter is somewhat sombre (p. 32): 'anochecía en torno a él y él mismo anochecía'.

There is, nevertheless, more to the novel than a pessimistic acceptance of death and oblivion.[33] While, in *Telón*, writing does not fulfil the conventional need to stave off mortality – the narrator notes that 'su escritura no sembraba pistas sino borraba huellas: él no era la suma de sus libros sino la resta de ellos' (p. 55) – the metaphor of the theatre of the world does add an element of humour that makes life tolerable. Thus we read, in echo of Beckett's black comedies, that 'la conciencia de ser mero actor o comparsa de acciones sin consecuencia le devolvía el buen humor' (p. 55). The parodic dialogue with the demiruge in chapter 4 also demonstrates a feisty refusal to accept both oblivion and easy, unquestioning beliefs in an afterlife. There, Goytisolo explores territory already covered by Unamuno in *Niebla*. His narrator is informed that he is no more than 'un ser de ficción', since 'el manuscrito es tu propia vida' (p. 82). The idea of life as a plotless narrative that must be given shape in retrospect recalls many of the issues surrounding the writing of autobiography with which we began this study. Hence, this comment by the demiurge could be taken as a comment on Goytisolo's own experience of five decades of writing in search of a dissident identity just as much as it articulates once again his consistent opposition to ideological closure (pp. 84–5): 'no hay persona, familia, linaje, nación, doctrina ni Estado que no funden sus pretensiones de legitimidad en una flagrante impostura. [. . .] El major enemigo de la mentira no es la verdad: es otra mentira.'

---

[32] *Las casetas de baño*, trans. José Martín Arancibia, intro. Juan Goytisolo, epilogue Manuel Ruiz Lagos (Barcelona: Círculo de Lectores, 1997), p. 19. Lange's novel was first published in French as *Les cabines de bain* in 1982, although I cite from the Spanish edition to which Goytisolo himself contributed.

[33] In interview with Valenzuela, 'La belleza del mundo es más duradera que el dolor humano', Goytisolo commented that the novel was not pessimistic, but 'pura lucidez'.

The matter arises, however, of the extent to which we identify Goytisolo directly with the narrator in *Telón*, and this problem goes right to the heart of the issues of authorship and authorial responsibility that we have considered throughout this study. On the one hand, it would, of course, be a mistake to make the link unquestioningly. On the other hand, certain intertextual features do break down the distance between the author and narrator in this work, as in so many others that we have analyzed. Some of these features we have already seen, in the clear citations from Lange's own semi-autobiographical works, and in the haunting loss of Goytisolo's mother at a young age, which increasingly appears as a motif in his late novels. But *Telón* also continues the intertextual critique of Goytisolo's works, begun in *Semanas* and developed in *Carajicomedia*, in two ways: through an explicit review of the author's mystical concerns in the late 1980s, and by means of a direct echo of the circular nature of *Don Julián*.

In the first chapter of *Telón*, the narrator recalls a period when, facing the spread of a new, devastating sexual disease and his own fear at having been infected, he immersed himself in 'la lectura impregnadora de los místicos', which, although initially consoling, ultimately 'acentuó aún su propensión al hermetismo y al alejamiento de toda vida social' (pp. 27–8). This, and his subsequent turn to 'la brutalidad de lo real', through travels to 'ciudades asediadas, países en guerra, [. . .] los paisajes caucasianos de barbarie y fiereza magistralmente pintados por Tolstói' (p. 28), is an accurate description of the development of Goytisolo's own writing, in essays, travelogues, and fiction, from the publication of the *Pájaro solitario*, through the *Cuaderno de Sarajevo*, *El sitio de los sitios*, to *Paisajes de guerra con Chechenia al fondo*. Indeed, these works culminate in the writing of *Telón* itself, where Tolstoy is a constant point of reference, and where the narrator rejects the escapist impulse of mysticism in a deliberate effort to 'rememorar lo pasado' (p. 28).

The importance of memory brings us right back to *Señas identidad* and *Don Julián*, the second of which is recalled in *Telón*'s closing lines. Imagining the attraction of the desert as a symbol of the unknown of the afterlife, the narrator remarks (p. 99): 'la cita sería para otro día: cuando se alzará el telón de boca y se enfrentase al vértigo del vacío.' The use of a theatrical metaphor and the notion of circularity both evoke the conclusion of *Don Julián*: 'mañana será otro día, la invasión recomenzará' (p. 304). The difference, though, marks a profound change in Goytisolo's attitude towards death and destruction, and consequently authorship and dissidence, across almost four decades of writing. Whereas the narrator of *Don Julián* was engaged in an imaginary, circular, and ultimately futile battle with his past, the narrator of *Telón* patiently and calmly awaits the future as a promise yet to be realized. So the motif of the *theatrum mundi*, far from expressing existential *angst* in the face of death, becomes optimistic acceptance of the fact that 'estaba todavía entre los espectadores en la platea del teatro' (p. 99). Or, as Goytisolo stated of himself in interview with Valenzuela: 'No soy nada pesimista. Vivo al día.' Goytisolo has written few more poetic, and more hauntingly personal, narratives than this, which implores his readers to look again at his long writing career. He thus defies the fixity of the authorial signature by writing not death, as Derrida would have it, but dramatizing a continual renewal through reading and re-reading, an activity that is not confined to the traditional reader, but becomes in Goytisolo's hands the preserve of the author as well.

WORKS CITED

WORKS BY JUAN GOYTISOLO

La resaca (Paris: Librarie Espagnole, 1958)
Campos de Níjar (Barcelona: Seix Barral, 1960)
La Chanca (Paris: Librarie Espagnole, 1962)
Libertad, libertad, libertad (Barcelona: Anagrama, 1978)
'De vuelta a Merimée', *El País*, 31 March 1981
El furgón de cola, 2nd edn (Barcelona: Seix Barral, 1982)
Paisajes después de la batalla (Barcelona: Montesinos, 1982)
Obra inglesa de José María Blanco White, 3rd edn (Barcelona: Seix Barral, 1982)
Contracorrientes (Barcelona: Montesinos, 1985)
Coto vedado, 8th edn (Barcelona: Seix Barral, 1985)
Reivindicación del Conde don Julián, ed. Linda Gould Levine (Madrid: Cátedra, 1985)
En los reinos de Taifa (Barcelona: Seix Barral, 1986)
Señas de identidad, 6th edn (Barcelona: Seix Barral, 1987)
Makbara, 4th edn (Barcelona: Seix Barral, 1988)
Crónicas sarracinas (Barcelona: Seix Barral, 1989)
Aproximaciones a Gaudí en Capadocia (Madrid: Mondadori, 1990)
Las virtudes del pájaro solitario, 3rd edn (Barcelona: Seix Barral, 1990)
'No a la petrocruzada', *El País*, 29 November 1990
Paisajes después de la batalla, ed. Andrés Sánchez Robayna (Madrid: Espasa-Calpe, 1990)
'Exégesis de una victoria heroica', *El País*, 16 March 1991
La cuarentena (Madrid: Mondadori, 1991)
'¿Nuevo orden o caja de Pandora?', *El País*, 26 April 1991
Disidencias (Madrid: Taurus, 1992)
Cuaderno de Sarajevo: anotaciones de un viaje a la barbarie (Madrid: El País/Aguilar, 1993)
La saga de los Marx (Barcelona: Mondadori, 1993)
Argelia en el vendaval (Madrid: El País/Aguilar, 1994)
Juan sin Tierra (Barcelona: Mondadori, 1994)
El bosque de las letras (Madrid: Alfaguara, 1995)
El sitio de los sitios (Madrid: Alfaguara, 1995)
Makbara, revised edn (Barcelona: Mondadori, 1995)
Paisajes de guerra con Chechenia al fondo (Madrid: El País/Aguilar, 1996)
Las semanas del jardín: un círculo de lectores (Madrid: Alfaguara, 1997)

Cogitus interruptus (Barcelona: Seix Barral, 1999)
Carajicomedia de Fray Bugeo Montesino y otros pájaros de vario plumaje y pluma (Barcelona: Seix Barral, 2000)
'España y sus Ejidos', *El País*, 20 March 2000
'La libido textual de *Camino*', *El País*, 26 February 2000
'Blanco White y la desmemoria española', *El País*, 5 June 2001
Paisajes de guerra: Sarajevo, Argelia, Palestina, Chechenia (Madrid: Aguilar, 2001)
Pájaro que ensucia su propio nido (Barcelona: Círculo de Lectores, 2001)
España y sus Ejidos (Madrid: Hijos de Muley-Rubio, 2003)
Telón de boca (Barcelona: El Aleph, 2003)

OTHER SOURCES

Actas de la Asamblea Cervantina de la Lengua Española (Madrid: Revista de Filología Española, 1948)
Adorno, Theodor, *Notes to Literature*, 2 vols, trans. S. Weber Nicholsen (New York: Columbia University Press, 1991)
Aguilar, Paloma, *Memory and Amnesia: The Role of the Spanish Civil War in the Transition to Democracy*, trans. Mark Oakley (New York: Berghahn Books, 2002)
Allinson, David B. (ed.), *The New Nietzsche: Contemporary Styles of Interpretation* (Cambridge, Mass.: MIT Press, 1985)
Anderson, Benedict, *Imagined Communities: Reflections on the Origin and Spread of Nationalism* (London: Verso, 1983)
Anderson, Reed, '*Señas de identidad*: Chronicle of Rebellion', *Journal of Spanish Studies: Twentieth Century*, 2 (1974), 3–19
Arriba, 15 March 1961, Goytisolo Archive, Diputación Provincial, Almería, 1195
Assmann, Jan, 'Collective Memory and Cultural Identity', *New German Critique*, 65 (1995), 125–33
Bakhtin, Mikhail, *The Dialogic Imagination: Four Essays*, trans. C. Emerson and M. Holquist (Austin: University of Texas Press, 1981)
——, *Rabelais and His World*, trans. Hélène Iswolsky (Bloomington: Indiana University Press, 1984)
Barthes, Roland, *Image–Music–Text*, ed. and trans. Stephen Heath (New York: Hill & Wang, 1977)
Baudrillard, Jean, *The Gulf War Did Not Take Place*, trans. and intro. Paul Patton (Bloomington: Indiana University Press, 1995)
Beneveniste, Émile, *Problems in General Linguistics* (Coral Gables, Florida: University of Miami Press, 1971)
Benson, Ciarán, *The Cultural Psychology of Self: Place, Morality and Art in Human Worlds* (London: Routledge, 2001)
Bhabha, Homi, *Nation and Narration* (London: Routledge, 1990)
Biriotti, Maurice and Nicola Miller (eds), *What Is An Author?* (Manchester: Manchester University Press, 1993)
Black, Stanley, 'Orality in *Makbara*: A Postmodern Paradox?', *Neophilologus*, 78 (1994), 585–98

————, *Juan Goytisolo: The Poetics of Contagion* (Liverpool: Liverpool University Press, 2001)

————, 'Mysticism, Postmodernism and Transgression in *La cuarentena* by Juan Goytisolo', *Bulletin of Spanish Studies*, 78 (2001), 241–57

————, 'Literary Swansong or Wild Goose Chase?: *Telón de boca* by Juan Goytisolo', unpublished paper, Annual Conference of the Association of Hispanists of Great Britain and Ireland, University of Cambridge, 28–31 March 2004

Blanco, María Luisa, 'En Marrakech puedo escribir y vivir', *Cambio16*, 20 April 1992, pp. 76–9

Blanco White, José María, *Antología de obras en español*, ed. and prologue Vicente Llorens (Barcelona: Labor, 1971)

Blanco White, Joseph, *The Life of the Rev. Joseph Blanco White, written by himself, with portions of his correspondence*, ed. John Hamilton Thom, 3 vols (London: Chapman, 1845)

Blasco, Francisco Javier, 'El palimpsesto urbano de *Paisajes después de la batalla*', *Anales de la Literatura Española Contemporánea*, 10 (1985), 11–30

Bloom, Harold *The Anxiety of Influence: A Theory of Poetry*, 2nd edn (New York: Oxford University Press, 1997)

Bogue, Ronald, *Deleuze and Guattari* (London: Routledge, 1989)

Booth, Wayne, *The Rhetoric of Fiction* (Chicago: University of Chicago Press, 1961)

Braun, Lucille V., 'Inside and Outside: Topology and Intertextuality in Juan Goytisolo's *Paisajes después de la batalla*', *Revista Canadiense de Estudios Hispánicos*, 14 (1989), 15–34

Brownlow, Jeanne P. and John W. Kronik (eds), *Intertextual Pursuits: Literary Mediations in Modern Spanish Narrative* (Lewisburg: Bucknell University Press, 1998)

Burke, Seán (ed.), *Authorship From Plato to the Postmodern: A Reader* (Edinburgh: Edinburgh University Press, 1995)

Byron, William, *Cervantes: A Biography* (London: Cassell, 1978)

Cabrera Infante, Guillermo, *Tres tristes tigres*, 7th edn (Barcelona: Seix Barral, 1998)

Calderón de la Barca, Pedro, *El gran teatro del mundo, El gran mercado del mundo*, ed. Eugenio Frutos Cortés (Madrid: Cátedra, 1989)

Camón Aznar, José, *Góngora en la teoría de los estilos* (Madrid: Dirección General de Archivos y Bibliotecas, 1962)

Castro, Américo, *La realidad histórica de España*, rev. edn (Madrid: Porrúa Turanzas, 1962)

Cave, Terence, *The Cornucopian Text: Problems of Writing in the French Renaissance* (Oxford: Clarendon Press, 1979)

Cernuda, Luis, *La realidad y el deseo*, 4th edn (Mexico City: Fundo de Cultura Ecónomica, 1964)

Chemris, Crystal, 'Self-Reference in Góngora's *Soledades*', *Hispanic Journal*, 12 (1991), 7–15

Christie, Ruth, Judith Drinkwater, and John Macklin, *The Scripted Self: Textual Identities in Contemporary Spanish Narrative* (Warminster: Aris & Phillips, 1995)

Close, Anthony, *The Romantic Approach to 'Don Quijote': A Critical History of the Romantic Tradition in 'Quijote' Criticism* (Cambridge: Cambridge University Press, 1977)

Coleman, Alexander, *Other Voices: A Study of the Poetry of Luis Cernuda* (Chapel Hill: University of North Carolina Press, 1969)

Conte, Rafael, 'Cambio de decorado', *El País*, 15 February 2003

Corbin, Harry, *L'Archange empourpré* (Paris: Fayard, 1976)

Crossley, Nick, *The Politics of Subjectivity: Between Foucault and Merleau-Ponty* (Aldershot: Avebury, 1994)

Dagenais, John, *The Ethics of Reading in Manuscript Culture: Glossing the 'Libro de buen amor'* (Princeton: Princeton University Press, 1994)

Dalmau, Miguel, *Los Goytisolo* (Barcelona: Anagrama, 1999)

Davis, Lisa E. and Isabel C. Tarán (eds), *The Analysis of Hispanic Texts: Current Trends in Methodology* (New York: Bilingual Press, 1976)

Davis, Stuart, 'Juan Goytisolo and the Institution of the Hispanic Canon', unpublished doctoral dissertation, University of Birmingham, 2003

de Man, Paul, *The Rhetoric of Romanticism* (New York: Columbia University Press, 1984)

——, *Blindness and Insight: Essays in the Rhetoric of Contemporary Criticism*, 2nd edn (London: Routledge, 1989)

de Rituerto, R. M., 'Goytisolo censura a Sadam Husein, Kuwait y la "cruzada occidental" ', *El País*, 7 November 1991

Deleuze, Gilles and Félix Guattari, *Anti-Oedipus: Capitalism and Schizophrenia*, trans. Robert Hurley, Mark Seem, and Helen R. Lane (New York: Viking Press, 1977)

——, *A Thousand Plateaus*, trans. and foreword Brian Massumi (London: Athlone, 1988)

Denzin, Norman, *The Cinematic Society: The Voyeur's Gaze* (London: Sage, 1995)

Derrida, Jacques, *The Ear of the Other: Otobiography, Transference, Translation*, trans. Peggy Kamuf, ed. Christie McDonald (Lincoln: University of Nebraska Press, 1985)

Doblado, Leucadio, *Letters from Spain* (London: Colburn, 1822)

Eakin, Paul John, *Fictions in Autobiography: Studies in the Art of Self-Invention* (Princeton: Princeton University Press, 1985)

Echavarren, Roberto, ' "Las semanas del jardín" de Sánchez Ferlosio: narratividad y sujeto', *Cuadernos Hispanoamericanos*, 384 (1982), 669–77

Eisenberg, Daniel, *Las semanas del jardín de Miguel de Cervantes* (Salamanca: Diputación Provincial de Salamanca, 1988)

El País [accessed 9 December 2003]

El Saffar, Ruth, *Novel to Romance: A Study of Cervantes's 'Novelas ejemplares'* (Baltimore: Johns Hopkins University Press, 1974)

Ellis, Robert Richmond, *The Hispanic Homograph: Gay Self-Representation in Contemporary Spanish Autobiography* (Urbana: University of Illinois Press, 1997)

Enkvist, Inger, *Un círculo de relectores: jornadas sobre Juan Goytisolo* (Almería: Instituto de Estudios Almerienses, 1999)

Epps, Brad, 'Thievish Subjectivity: Self-Writing in Jean Genet and Juan Goytisolo', *Revista de Estudios Hispánicos*, 26 (1992), 163–81

——, 'Estados de deseo: homosexualidad y nacionalidad (Juan Goytisolo y Reinaldo Arenas a vuelapluma)', *Revista Iberoamericana*, 62 (1996), 799–820

——, *Significant Violence: Oppression and Resistance in the Narratives of Juan Goytisolo, 1970–1990* (Oxford: Clarendon Press, 1996)

Escudero Rodríguez, Javier, 'Muerte, erotismo y espiritualidad: entrevista con Juan Goytisolo', *Revista de Estudios Hispánicos*, 27 (1991), 123–39

——, *Eros, mística y muerte en Juan Goytisolo (1982–1992)* (Almería: Instituto de Estudios Almerienses, 1994)

—— (ed.), *El epistolario: cartas de Américo Castro a Juan Goytisolo (1968–1972)* (Valencia: Pre-Textos, 1997)

Evans, Peter W. (ed.), *Conflicts of Discourse: Spanish Literature in the Golden Age* (Manchester: Manchester University Press, 1990)

Fernández, James, 'La novela familiar del autobiógrafo: Juan Goytisolo', *Anthropos*, 125 (1991), 54–60

Fernández de Navarrete, Eustaquio (ed.), *Biblioteca de autores españoles desde la formación del lenguaje hasta nuestros días: novelistas posteriores a Cervantes* (Madrid: Real Academia Española, 1950)

Ferry, Luc and Alain Renault, *French Philosophy of the Sixties: An Essay on Antihumanism*, trans. Mary Schnachenberg Cattani (Amherst: University of Massachusetts Press, 1990)

Foucault, Michel, *Discipline and Punish: The Birth of the Prison*, trans. Alan Sheridan (New York: Pantheon, 1977)

——, *History of Sexuality: The Will to Knowledge*, trans. Robert Hurley (Harmondsworth: Penguin, 1990)

——, *History of Sexuality: The Care of Self*, trans. Robert Hurley (Harmondsworth: Penguin, 1990)

Franco, Dolores, *España como problema* (Madrid: Alianza, 1988)

Freud, Sigmund, *On Metapsychology: The Theory of Psychoanalysis*, trans. J. Strachey (Harmondsworth: Penguin, 1987)

Fuery, Patrick, *New Developments in Film Theory* (Houndmills: Macmillan, 2000)

Fuss, Diana, *Essentially Speaking: Feminism, Nature and Difference* (New York: Routledge, 1989)

Gandelman, Claude, *Reading Pictures, Viewing Texts* (Bloomington: Indiana University Press, 1991)

Genette, Gérard, *Paratexts: Thresholds of Interpretation*, trans. Jane E. Lewin, foreword Richard Macksey (Cambridge: Cambridge University Press, 1997)

Gide, André, *Si le grain ne meurt* (Paris: Gallimard, 1955)

Gies, David T. (ed.), *The Cambridge Companion to Modern Spanish Culture* (Cambridge: Cambridge University Press, 1999)

Ginger, Andrew, *Political Revolution and Literary Experiment in the Spanish Romantic Period* (Lewiston: Mellen, 1999)

Goll, Ivan, *Jean sans terre*, ed. Francis B. Carmody (Berkeley: University of California Press, 1962)

Gould Levine, Linda, *Juan Goytisolo: la destrucción creadora* (Mexico City: Mortiz, 1976)

——, 'La escritura infecciosa de Juan Goytisolo: contaminación y cuarentena', *Revista de Estudios Hispánicos*, 28 (1994), 95–110

Greene, Thomas, *The Light in Troy: Imitation and Discovery in Renaissance Poetry* (New Haven: Yale University Press, 1982)

Gross, G., *Niños Santos* (Madrid: La Hormiga de Oro, n.d.)

Guillamon, Julià, 'Fellini por Goytisolo: *La saga de los Marx*', *Quimera*, 121 (1993), 46–53

Happold, F. C., *Mysticism: A Study and An Anthology* (Harmondsworth: Penguin, 1990)

Hernández, José A., 'Juan Goytisolo – 1975', *Modern Language Notes*, 91 (1976), 337–55

Herrera, Juan Carlos, 'La originalidad es volver a los orígenes', *La Nación*, 24 May 1992

Herzberger, David, 'Language and Referentiality in *Señas de identidad*', *Revista Canadiense de Estudios Hispánicos*, 11 (1987), 611–21

——, *Narrating the Past: Fiction and Historiography in Postwar Spain* (Durham: Duke University Press, 1995)

Huelbes, Elvira, 'Entrevista con Juan Goytisolo', *El Mundo*, 7 October 1990

Hutcheon, Linda, *A Theory of Parody* (New York: Methuen, 1985)

Irwin, Robert, *The Arabian Nights: A Companion* (Harmondsworth: Penguin, 1994)

Jameson, Fredric, *The Prison-House of Language: A Critical Account of Structuralism and Russian Formalism* (Princeton: Princeton University Press, 1972)

Javierre, José María, *Juan de la Cruz: un caso límite* (Salamanca: Sígueme, 1992)

Jay, Martin, *Downcast Eyes: The Denigration of Vision in Twentieth-Century French Thought* (Berkeley: University of California Press, 1994)

Jefferson, Ann and David Robey (eds), *Modern Literary Theory: A Comparative Introduction*, 2nd edn (London: Batsford, 1986)

Jesús, Crisógono de, *Vida y obras completas de San Juan de la Cruz*, 5th edn (Madrid: Biblioteca de Autores Cristianos, 1964)

Jesús, Crisógono de, Matías del Niño Jesús, and Lucinio Ruano, *Vida y obras de San Juan de la Cruz*, 9th edn (Madrid: Biblioteca de Autores Cristianos, 1975)

Juan sin Tierra, Espiral/Revista no. 2 (Madrid: Fundamentos, 1977)

Kearney, Richard, *Modern Movements in Philosophy: Phenomenology, Critical Theory, Structuralism*, 2nd edn (Manchester: Manchester University Press, 1994)

——, *Poetics of Imagining: Modern to Post-modern*, new edn (Edinburgh: Edinburgh University Press, 1998)

——, *On Stories* (London: Routledge, 2002)

Kennedy, Alison, 'Mystical Paradoxes and Moorish Resonances: A Solution to Juan Goytisolo's Problematic Aesthetic', *Journal of Iberian and Latin American Studies*, 4 (1998), 109–19

——, 'Juan Goytisolo, Miguel de Unamuno and Spanish Literary Criticism', *A*

Lifetime's Reading: Essays for Patrick Gallagher, ed. Don W. Cruickshank (Dublin: University College Dublin Press, 1999), pp. 135–52

Knuz, Marco, *La saga de los Marx: notas al texto* (Basel: Acta Romanica Basiliensia, 1997)

Kristeva, Julia, *Revolution in Poetic Language*, trans. Margaret Waller (New York: Columbia University Press, 1984)

Labanyi, Jo, 'The Ambiguous Implications of the Mythical References in Juan Goytisolo's *Duelo en El Paraíso*', *Modern Language Review*, 80 (1985), 845–57

——, *Myth and History in the Contemporary Spanish Novel* (Cambridge: Cambridge University Press, 1989)

——, 'The Construction/Destruction of the Self in the Autobiographies of Pablo Neruda and Juan Goytisolo', *Forum for Modern Language Studies*, 26 (1990), 212–21

——, *Gender and Modernization in the Nineteenth-Century Spanish Novel* (Oxford: Oxford University Press, 2000)

Lange, Monique, *Las casetas de baño*, trans. José Martín Arancibia, intro. Juan Goytisolo, epilogue Manuel Ruiz Lagos (Barcelona: Círculo de Lectores, 1997)

Lawrance, Jeremy, 'The Audience of the *Libro de buen amor*', *Comparative Literature*, 36 (1984), 220–37

Lecoy, Félix, *Recherches sur le 'Libro de buen amor' de Juan Ruiz*, ed. Alan Deyermond (Farnborough: Gregg International, 1974)

Ledesma Pedraz, Manuela (ed.), *Escritura autobiográfica y géneros literarios* (Jaén: Universidad de Jaén, 1999)

Ledford-Miller, Linda, 'History as Myth, Myth as History: Juan Goytisolo's *Count Julián*', *Revista Canadiense de Estudios Hispánicos*, 8 (1983), 21–30

Lee, Abigail E., '*La paradigmática historia de Caperucita y el lobo feroz*: Juan Goytisolo's Use of "Little Red Riding Hood" in *Reivindicación del Conde don Julián*', *Bulletin of Hispanic Studies*, 65 (1988), 141–51

——, 'Sterne's Legacy to Juan Goytisolo: A Shandyian Reading of *Juan sin Tierra*', *Modern Language Review*, 84 (1989), 351–7

Lee Six, Abigail, *Juan Goytisolo: The Case for Chaos* (New Haven: Yale University Press, 1990)

——, *Campos de Níjar* (London: Grant & Cutler, 1996)

Levine, Susan F., ' "Cuerpo" y "no-cuerpo" – una conjunción entre Juan Goytisolo y Octavio Paz', *Journal of Spanish Studies: Twentieth Century*, 15 (1977), 123–35

Lopate, Philip (ed.), *The Art of the Personal Essay: An Anthology from the Classical Era to the Present* (New York: Random House, 1995)

López-Baralt, Luce, *Huellas del Islam en la literatura española: de Juan Ruiz a Juan Goytisolo* (Madrid: Hiperión, 1985)

——, 'Juan Goytisolo aprende a reír: los contextos caribeños de *Makbara* y *Paisajes después de la batalla*', *Ínsula*, 468 (1985), 3–4

——, *San Juan de la Cruz y el Islam* (Mexico City: Colegio de México, 1985)

——, 'Narrar después de morrir: *La cuarentena* de Juan Goytisolo', *Nueva Revista de Filología Hispánica*, 43 (1995), 59–124

López-Baralt, Luce and Lorenzo Piera (eds), *El sol a medianoche: la experiencia mística: tradición y actualidad* (Madrid: Trotta, 1996)

Lukács, Georg, *Soul and Form*, trans. Anna Bostock (London: Merlin Press, 1974)

Machado, Manuel and Antonio Machado, *Obras completas*, ed. Heliodoro Carpintero (Madrid: Plenitud, 1967)

Martín Gaite, Carmen, *Agua pasada* (Barcelona: Anagrama, 1993)

——, *El cuarto de átras*, ed. Lluís Izquierdo (Barcelona: Destino, 1997)

Martín Morán, José Manuel, *Semiótica de una traición recuperada: génesis poética de 'Reivindicación del Conde don Julián'* (Barcelona: Anthropos, 1992)

Martín-Santos, Luis, *Tiempo de silencio*, 34th edn (Barcelona: Seix Barral, 1991)

Masoliver Ródenas, Juan A., 'El hipócrita y el escribidor', *La Vanguardia*, 11 February 2000

McHale, Brian, *Postmodernist Fiction* (London: Routledge, 1987)

Ménendez Pidal, Ramón, *Romancero hispánico (hispano-portugués, americano y sefardí)*, 2 vols (Madrid: Espasa-Calpe, 1953)

Mermall, Thomas, *The Rhetoric of Humanism: Spanish Culture After Ortega y Gasset* (New York: Bilingual Press, 1976)

Merleau-Ponty, Maurice, *Phenomenology of Perception*, trans. Colin Smith (London: Routledge, 1962)

——, *Signs*, trans. and intro. Richard C. McCleary (Evanston: Northwestern University Press, 1964)

Metz, Christian, *Psychoanalysis and Cinema: The Imaginary Signifier*, trans. Celia Britton, Annwyl Williams, Ben Brewster and Alfred Guzzetti (London: Macmillan, 1982)

Mitchell, W. J. T., *Picture Theory: Essays on Verbal and Visual Representation* (Chicago: University of Chicago Press, 1994)

Moi, Toril (ed.), *The Kristeva Reader* (Oxford: Blackwell, 1986)

Monaco, James, *How to Read a Film: Movies, Media, Multimedia*, 3rd edn (New York: Oxford University Press, 2000)

Montesinos, Fray Bugeo, *Cancionero de obras de burlas provocantes a risa*, ed. Frank Domínguez (Madrid: Albatros, 1978)

Mora, Miguel, 'El sábado, España dejó de ser un país de súbditos', *El País*, 18 February 2003

Moreiras-Menor, Cristina, 'Ficción y autobiografía en Juan Goytisolo: algunos apuntes', *Anthropos*, 125 (1991), 71–6

——, 'Juan Goytisolo, F.F.B. y la fundación fantasmal del proyecto autobiográfico contemporáneo español', *Modern Language Notes*, 111 (1996), 327–45

Morris, Brian, *Western Conceptions of the Individual* (Oxford: Berg, 1991)

Mulvey, Laura, *Visual and Other Pleasures* (Bloomington: Indiana University Press, 1989)

Murphy, Martin, *Blanco White: Self-Banished Spaniard* (New Haven: Yale University Press, 1989)

Murray, Peter and Linda Murray, *The Oxford Companion to Christian Art and Architecture* (Oxford: Oxford University Press, 1996)

Navajas, Gonzalo, *Teoría y práctica de la novela española posmoderna* (Barcelona: Mall, 1987)

———, 'Confession and Ethics in Juan Goytisolo's Fictive Autobiographies', *Letras Peninsulares*, 3 (1990), 259–78

Nesbit, Molly, 'What was an author?', *Yale French Studies*, 73 (1987), 229–57

Neutres, Jérôme, *Genet sur les routes du Sud* (Paris: Fayard, 2002)

O'Beirne, Emer, *Reading Nathalie Sarraute: Dialogue and Distance* (Oxford: Clarendon Press, 1999)

Olney, James, *Metaphors of Self: The Meaning of Autobiography* (Princeton: Princeton University Press, 1972)

———, *Memory and Narrative: The Weave of Life-Writing* (Chicago: University of Chicago Press, 1998)

Pereda, Rosa, 'Juan Goytisolo: Únicamente la ficción podía curarme de todo aquello', *El País*, 18 November 1995

Pérez, Genaro J., 'Form in Juan Goytisolo's *Juan sin Tierra*', *Journal of Spanish Studies: Twentieth Century*, 5 (1977), 137–59

Perrin, Annie, 'Pour une écriture–lecture–audition: *Makbara* ou la voix retrouvée', in *Cotextes*, 5 (1983), 41–57

———, '*Makbara*: The Space of Phantasm', *Review of Contemporary Fiction*, 4 (1984), 157–75

Persina, María Silvina, *Hacia una poética de la mirada: Mario Vargas Llosa, Juan Marsé, Elena Garro, Juan Goytisolo* (Buenos Aires: Corregidor, 1999)

Piras, Pina Rosa, 'El cervantismo de Juan Goytisolo', in *Cervantes*, 19 (1999), 167–79

Plaza, Sixto, '*Coto vedado*, ¿autobiografía o novela?', *Actas del IX Congreso de la Asociación Internacional de Hispanistas* (Frankfurt: Verlag, 1989), pp. 345–50

Pope, Randolph D., 'Theory and Contemporary Autobiographical Writing: The Case of Juan Goytisolo', *Siglo XX/20th Century*, 8 (1990–1), 87–101

———, 'El autoretrato postmoderno de Juan Goytisolo', *L'Autoportrait en Espagne: Littérature & Peinture* (Aix-en-Provence: L'Université de Provence, 1992), pp. 319–30

———, 'Juan Goytisolo y la tradición autobiográfica española', *Revista Chilena de Literatura*, 41 (1992), 25–32

———, *Understanding Juan Goytisolo* (Columbia: University of South Carolina Press, 1995)

Potocki, Jan, *The Manuscript Found in Saragossa*, trans. Ian Maclean (Harmondsworth: Penguin, 1996)

———, *El manuscrito encontrado en Zaragoza*, ed. and preface Roger Caillois, trans. José Bianco (Barcelona: Minotauro, 1996)

Prout, Ryan, 'Textuality Transcendent: Juan Goytisolo's *La cuarentena* and the Politics of Eschatology', *Journal of Hispanic Research*, 2 (1993–4), 307–24

———, *Fear and Gendering: Pedophobia, Effeminophobia, and Hypermasculine Desire in the Work of Juan Goytisolo* (New York: Lang, 2001)

Ribeiro de Meneses, Filipe, 'Popularising Africanism: The Career of Victor Ruiz Albeniz, El Tebib Arrumi', forthcoming in *Journal of Iberian and Latin American Studies*.

Ribeiro de Menezes, Alison, ' "En el principio de la literatura está el mito":

Reading Cervantes through Juan Goytisolo's *Reivindicación del Conde don Julián* and *Juan sin Tierra*', *Bulletin of Hispanic Studies* (Liverpool), 77 (2000), 587–603

———, 'Reciting/Re-siting the *Libro de buen amor* in the *zoco*: Irony, Orality and the Islamic in Juan Goytisolo's *Makbara*', *Modern Language Notes*, 117 (2002), 406–31

———, 'The Mystical and the Burlesque: The Portrayal of Homosexuality in Juan Goytisolo's *Carajicomedia*', *Romance Studies*, 21 (2002), 105–14

———, 'Language, Meaning, and Rebellion in Goytisolo's *Don Julián*: The Gongorine Intertexts', *Bulletin of Spanish Studies*, 80 (2003), 47–68

———, 'Juan Goytisolo's *Cuaderno de Sarajevo*: The Dilemmas of a Committed War Journalist', *Journal of Iberian and Latin American Studies* (forthcoming, summer 2005)

Ricoeur, Paul, *Interpretation Theory: Discourse and the Surplus of Meaning* (Fort Worth: The Texas Christian University Press, 1976)

———, *Oneself as Another*, trans. Kathleen Blamey (Chicago: University of Chicago Press, 1992)

Riera, Miguel, 'Regreso al origen', *Quimera*, 71 (1988), 36–40

Riley, Edward C., *Cervantes's Theory of the Novel* (Oxford: Clarendon Press, 1962)

Rodríguez Monegal, Emir, *El arte de narrar: diálogos*, 2nd edn (Caracas: Monte Avila, 1968)

Rorty, Richard, *The Linguistic Turn: Recent Essays in Philosophical Method* (Chicago: University of Chicago Press, 1967)

Rosales, Luis, 'La figuración y la voluntad de morir en la poesía española', *Cruz y Raya*, 33 (1936), 65–101

Rosen, Philip (ed.), *Narrative, Apparatus, Ideology: A Film Theory Reader* (New York: Columbia University Press, 1986)

Ruiz Lagos, Manuel (ed.), *Escritos sobre Juan Goytisolo: coloquio en torno a la obra de Juan Goytisolo, Almería, 1987* (Almería: Instituto de Estudios Almerienses, 1988)

——— (ed.), *Escritos sobre Juan Goytisolo: Actas del Segundo Seminario Internacional sobre la obra de Juan Goytisolo: 'Las virtudes del pájaro solitario'* (Almería: Instituto de Estudios Almerienses, 1990)

Said, Edward, *Orientalism*, reprinted with a new Afterword (Harmondsworth: Penguin, 1995)

Sánchez, Alberto, *La obra de Góngora* (Madrid: s.n., 1960)

Sánchez Albornoz, Claudio, *España: un enigma histórico*, 2 vols (Buenos Aires: Sudamericana, 1956)

Sánchez Ferlosio, Rafael, *Las semanas del jardín* (Madrid: Nostromo, 1974)

Saramago, José, *História do cerco de Lisboa* (Lisboa: Caminho, 1989)

Sartre, Jean-Paul, *Qu'est-ce que la littérature?* (Paris: Gallimard, 1948)

———, *Being and Nothingness*, trans. Hazel E. Barnes (London: Routledge, 1989)

Schaefer-Rodríguez, Claudia, *Juan Goytisolo: del 'realismo crítico' a la utopía* (Madrid: Porrúa Turanzas, 1984)

Schmidt, James, *Merleau-Ponty: Between Phenomenology and Structuralism* (Houndmills: Macmillan, 1985)

Schwartz, Kessel, 'Juan Goytisolo, *Juan sin Tierra* and the Anal Aesthetic', *Hispania*, 62 (1979), 9–19

——, 'Themes, Écriture, and Authorship in *Paisajes después de la batalla*', *Hispanic Review*, 52 (1984), 477–90

Searle, John, *Expression and Meaning: Studies in the Theory of Speech Acts* (Cambridge: Cambridge University Press, 1979)

Selke, Angela, *El santo oficio de la Inquisición* (Madrid: Guadarrama, 1968)

Smith, Colin (ed.), *Spanish Ballads* (Oxford: Pergamon Press, 1964)

Smith, Douglas, *Transvaluations: Nietzsche in France 1872–1972* (Oxford: Oxford University Press, 1996)

Smith, Paul, *Discerning the Subject* (Minneapolis: University of Minnesota Press, 1988)

Smith, Paul Julian, *The Body Hispanic: Gender and Sexuality in Spanish and Spanish American Literature* (Oxford: Clarendon Press, 1989)

——, *Laws of Desire: Questions of Homosexuality in Spanish Writing and Film* (Oxford: Clarendon Press, 1992)

——, *Representing the Other: 'Race', Text and Gender in Spanish and Spanish American Narrative* (Oxford: Clarendon Press, 1992)

Spires, Robert, 'Latrines, Whirlpools, and Voids: the Metafictional Mode of *Juan sin Tierra*', *Hispanic Review*, 48 (1980), 151–69

——, *Narrating the Past: Fiction and Historiography in Postwar Spain* (Durham: Duke University Press, 1995)

Squires, Jeremy, *Experience and Objectivity in the Writings of Rafael Sánchez Ferlosio* (Lewiston: Mellen, 1998)

Stace, W. T., *Mysticism and Philosophy* (Philadelphia: Lippincott, 1960)

Steiner, George, *Language and Silence: Essays 1958–1966* (London: Faber & Faber, 1985)

——, *After Babel: Aspects of Language and Translation*, 2nd edn (Oxford: Oxford University Press, 1992)

Taylor, Charles, *Sources of the Self: The Making of the Modern Identity* (Cambridge: Cambridge University Press, 1989)

Taylor, Philip, *War and the Media: Propaganda and Persuasion in the Gulf War* (Manchester: Manchester University Press, 1992)

Terry, Arthur, *Seventeenth-Century Spanish Poetry: The Power of Artifice* (Cambridge: Cambridge University Press, 1993)

Thompson, Colin, *The Poet and the Mystic: A Study of the 'Cántico espiritual' of San Juan de la Cruz* (Oxford: Oxford University Press, 1977)

——, *St John of the Cross: Songs in the Night* (Washington: Catholic University of America Press, 2003)

Tremkin, Ann, 'Barnett Newman on Exhibition', *Barnett Newman* (Philadelphia: Philadelphia Museum of Art, 2002)

Ugarte, Michael, 'Juan Goytisolo: Unruly Disciple of Américo Castro', *Journal of Spanish Studies: Twentieth Century*, 7 (1979), 353–64

——, *Trilogy of Treason: An Intertextual Study of Juan Goytisolo* (Columbia: University of Missouri Press, 1982)

——, *Literatura española en el exilio: un estudio comparativo* (Madrid: Siglo XXI, 1999)

Valenzuela, Javier, 'La belleza del mundo es más duradera que el dolor humano', *El País*, 15 February 2003

Varela, José Luis, 'Con la soledad y en las *Soledades* de Góngora', *Cuadernos de Literatura*, 1 (1947), 41–53

Vilaseca, David, 'Juan Goytisolo's Queer (Be)hindsight: Homosexuality, Epistemology, and the "Extimacy" of the Subject in *Coto vedado* and *En los reinos de Taifa*', *Modern Language Review*, 94 (1999), 426–37

Vilena, Miguel, 'Juan Goytisolo concibe la novela como una aventura, "y no como un trayecto en autobús" ', *El País*, 6 November 1997

Weintraub, Karl Joachim, *The Value of the Individual: Self and Circumstance in Autobiography* (Chicago: University of Chicago Press, 1978)

Whorton, Michael and Judith Still (eds), *Intertextuality: Theories and Practices*, (Manchester: Manchester University Press, 1990)

Williamson, Edwin (ed.), *Cervantes and the Modernists: The Question of Influence* (London: Tamesis, 1994)

Zaehner, R. C., *Mysticism: Sacred and Profane: An Inquiry into some Varieties of Praeternatural Experience* (London: Oxford University Press, 1957)

INDEX

Note: particular works appear under the author's name, unless anonymous, in which case they are listed by title.